SELECTIONS
FROM THE GREEK PAPYRI

Oxyrhynchus Papyrus 744 (= No. 12)

Letter of Hilarion to Alis, written in Alexandria, 17 June B.C. 1.
Now in possession of the Egypt Exploration Fund and
facsimiled with their permission.

Original size 25 × 14·7 cm.

SELECTIONS
FROM THE GREEK PAPYRI

EDITED WITH TRANSLATIONS AND NOTES

BY

GEORGE MILLIGAN, D.D.

PROFESSOR OF DIVINITY AND BIBLICAL CRITICISM IN THE
UNIVERSITY OF GLASGOW

CAMBRIDGE:

at the University Press

1927

CAMBRIDGE
UNIVERSITY PRESS

University Printing House, Cambridge CB2 8BS, United Kingdom

Published in the United States of America by Cambridge University Press, New York

Cambridge University Press is part of the University of Cambridge.

It furthers the University's mission by disseminating knowledge in the pursuit of
education, learning and research at the highest international levels of excellence.

www.cambridge.org
Information on this title: www.cambridge.org/9781107697294

© Cambridge University Press 1910

First edition 1910
First published 1910
Reprinted 1912, 1927
First paperback edition 2014

A catalogue record for this publication is available from the British Library

ISBN 978-1-107-69729-4 Paperback

TO
M. C. M.

PREFACE

THE aim of this book is to bring within the reach of those who are interested in the recent discoveries of Greek Papyri in Egypt certain typical documents from the principal collections. These collections have now attained large dimensions, and are often very inaccessible to the ordinary reader. But it is hoped that the present *Selections* will at least serve to indicate the absorbing and varied character of their contents, and, more particularly, to illustrate their linguistic and historical importance for students of the Greek New Testament.

In this latter respect a special interest attaches to Bishop Lightfoot's striking prophecy, recorded on p. xx, which has now been so signally confirmed. The passage was communicated to Prof. J. H. Moulton (see *Prolegomena*[2 or 3], p. 242) by the Rev. J. Pulliblank from his notes of Bishop Lightfoot's lectures in 1863. It is also noteworthy to find Dr A. Peyron so far back as 1826 appealing in his Preface to the Turin Papyri (i p. 21) to the Septuagint and New Testament writers in connexion with the meaning of words found in the papyri (see p. 136 of this volume).

For permission to make use of the following documents, my hearty acknowledgments are due to the Trustees of the British Museum, the Committee of the Egypt Exploration Fund, the General Administration of the Royal Museums at Berlin, and the University Press of Chicago, as well as to the distinguished Editors of the various collections. Amongst these last I desire especially to mention Dr F. G. Kenyon,

Prof. B. P. Grenfell, Dr A. S. Hunt, Prof. J. P. Mahaffy, Prof. E. J. Goodspeed, Prof. G. Vitelli, Prof. A. Deissmann, and Dr W. Schubart, without whose ready co-operation and encouragement these *Selections* could hardly have been attempted at all.

To Prof. J. H. Moulton and Dr A. Souter I am also under deep obligations for their kind assistance in reading the proofs and offering many useful suggestions. Nor can I forget the courtesy of the Syndics of the University Press in undertaking the publication of this work, and the well-known skill and accuracy of their officials and workmen in passing it through the press.

G. M.

Caputh Manse, Perthshire,
November 30, 1909.

PREFACE TO SECOND EDITION

IT has not been found possible in this new edition to do more than insert a few additional notes and references and remove certain typographical and other *errata*. To friends and critics who have drawn attention to these last I tender my best thanks.

In order to facilitate reference, the numbers of the documents in the present collection have been inserted at the tops of the pages.

G. M.

University of Glasgow,
July 5, 1911.

CONTENTS

"Papyri natura dicetur, cum chartae usu maxime humanitas vitae constet, certe memoria."

PLINY, *N. H.* xiii. 11.

PRINCIPAL COLLECTIONS OF GREEK PAPYRI
WITH ABBREVIATIONS

P. Amh. = *The Amherst Papyri*, ed. B. P. Grenfell and A. S. Hunt. 2 vols. London, 1900–01.

B. G. U. = *Aegyptische Urkunden aus den Koeniglichen Museen zu Berlin: Griechische Urkunden*. Vols. I—IV (in progress). Berlin, 1895—

P. Brit. Mus. = *Greek Papyri in the British Museum*. Vols. I, II, ed. F. G. Kenyon; Vol. III, ed. F. G. Kenyon and H. I. Bell. London, 1893—1907.

C. P. Herm. = *Corpus Papyrorum Hermopolitanorum*. Part I, ed. C. Wessely. Leipzig, 1905.

C. P. R. = *Corpus Papyrorum Raineri*. Vol. I, *Griechische Texte*, ed. C. Wessely. Vienna, 1895.

P. Fay. = *Fayûm Towns and their Papyri*, ed. B. P. Grenfell, A. S. Hunt, and D. G. Hogarth. London, 1900.

P. Flor. = *Papiri Fiorentini*, ed. G. Vitelli and D. Comparetti. Vols. I, II— . Milan, 1906— .

P. Gen. = *Les Papyrus de Genève*, ed. J. Nicole. Parts I, II. Genève, 1896—1900.

P. Giss. = *Griechische Papyri* from the *Museum des Oberhessischen Geschichtsvereins zu Giessen*, ed. O. Eger, E. Kornemann and P. M. Meyer. Vol. I— . Leipzig, 1910— .

P. Goodspeed = *Greek Papyri from the Cairo Museum*, ed. E. J. Goodspeed. Chicago, 1902.

P. Grenf. I = *An Alexandrian Erotic Fragment, and other Greek Papyri, chiefly Ptolemaic*, ed. B. P. Grenfell. Oxford, 1896.

P. Grenf. II = *New Classical Fragments, and other Greek and Latin Papyri*, ed. B. P. Grenfell and A. S. Hunt. Oxford, 1897.

P. Hamb. = *Griechische Papyrusurkunden der Hamburger Stadt-bibliothek*, ed. P. M. Meyer. Vol. I— . Leipzig, 1911— .

P. Heid. = *Heidelberger Papyrus-Sammlung.* Vol. I, *Die Septua-ginta Papyri und andere altchristliche Texte*, ed. A. Deissmann. Heidelberg, 1905.

P. Hib. = *The Hibeh Papyri.* Vol. I, ed. B. P. Grenfell and A. S. Hunt. London, 1906.

P. Leid. = *Papyri graeci Musei antiquarii publici Lugduni-Batavi*, ed. C. Leemans. 2 vols. 1843, 1885.

P. Leip. = *Griechische Urkunden der Papyrussammlung zu Leipzig.* Vol. I, ed. L. Mitteis. Leipzig, 1906.

P. Lille = *Papyrus Grecs* from the *Institut Papyrologique de l'Université de Lille*, ed. P. Jouguet. Vol. I, Parts 1, 2. Paris, 1907-08.

P. Magd. = Papyri from Magdola, ed. Lefebvre in *Bulletin de correspondance hellénique*, 1902 ff.

P. Oxy. = *The Oxyrhynchus Papyri*, ed. B. P. Grenfell and A. S. Hunt. Vols. I—VIII. London, 1898—1911.

P. Par. = Paris Papyri in *Notices et Extraits* XVIII, ii, ed. Brunet de Presle. Paris, 1865.

P. Petr. = *The Flinders Petrie Papyri*, in the *Proceedings of the Royal Irish Academy—"Cunningham Memoirs,"* Nos. viii, ix, xi. Parts I, II, ed. J. P. Mahaffy; Part III, ed. J. P. Mahaffy and J. G. Smyly. Dublin, 1891—1905.

P. Reinach = *Papyrus Grecs et Démotiques*, ed. Th. Reinach. Paris, 1905.

P. Rylands = *Catalogue of the Greek Papyri in the John Rylands Library Manchester*, ed. A. S. Hunt. Vol. I. Manchester, 1911.

P. Strass. = *Griechische Papyrus der Kaiserlichen Universitäts- und Landesbibliothek zu Strassburg.* Parts I, II, ed. F. Preisigke. Strassburg, 1906-07.

P. Tebt. = *The Tebtunis Papyri.* Vol. I, ed. B. P. Grenfell, A. S. Hunt, and J. G. Smyly; Vol. II, ed. B. P. Grenell, A. S. Hunt, and E. J. Goodspeed. London, 1902-07.

P. Tor. = *Papyri graeci regii Taurinensis Musei Aegyptii*, ed. A. Peyron. 2 vols. Turin, 1826, 1827.

TABLE OF PAPYRI PUBLISHED IN THIS VOLUME

AUTHORITIES QUOTED AND RECOMMENDED

Archiv = *Archiv für Papyrusforschung*, ed. U. Wilcken. Leipzig, 1901—.

Blass, F. *Grammar of New Testament Greek*. Eng. Tr. by H. St John Thackeray. 2nd Edit. London, 1905.

Crönert, W. *Memoria Graeca Herculanensis*. Leipzig, 1903. See p. xxiv.

Deissmann, A. *Bible Studies* (= *BS.*). Eng. Edition by A. Grieve Edinburgh, 1901.

Deissmann, A. *Licht vom Osten* (= *LO.*²). 2ᵗᵉ Aufl. Tübingen, 1909. An English translation of this work has appeared under the title *Light from the Ancient East.*

Dittenberger *Syll.* = *Sylloge Inscriptionum Graecarum*, ed. W. Dittenberger. 2nd Edit. 2 vols. and Index. Leipzig, 1888—1901.

Erman and Krebs = *Aus den Papyrus der Königlichen Museen*, by A. Erman and F. Krebs. Berlin, 1899. One of the handbooks to the Royal Museums at Berlin, containing German translations of a number of Greek and other Papyri, with an interesting Introduction.

Exp. = *The Expositor.* London, 1875— . Cited by series, volume and page.

Gerhard, G. A. *Untersuchungen zur Geschichte des griechischen Briefes.* Heft i. *Die Anfangsformel.* Diss. Heidelb. Tübingen, 1903.

Gradenwitz, O. *Einführung in die Papyruskunde.* Heft i. Leipzig, 1900.

Hatzidakis, G. N. *Einleitung in die Neugriechische Grammatik.* Leipzig, 1892.

Herwerden, H. van. *Lexicon Graecum suppletorium et dialecticum.* Editio altera. Lugd. Batav., 1910.

Hohlwein, N. *La Papyrologie Grecque.* Louvain, 1905. A classified bibliography of all papyrological publications, including reviews and magazine articles, up to Jan. 1, 1905.

Jannaris, A. N. *An Historical Greek Grammar.* London, 1897.

Kennedy, H. A. A. *Sources of New Testament Greek, or the*

Influence of the Septuagint on the Vocabulary of the New Testament. Edinburgh, 1895.

Kenyon, F. G. *The Palaeography of Greek Papyri.* Oxford, 1899.

Kuhring, G. *De Praepositionum Graecarum in Chartis Aegyptiis Usu.* Diss. Bonn. Bonn, 1906.

Laqueur, R. *Quaestiones Epigraphicae et Papyrologicae Selectae.* Strassburg, 1904.

Lex. *Notes = Lexical Notes from the Papyri,* by J. H. Moulton and G. Milligan, in the *Expositor,* VII, v— (in progress). See p. xxx.

Lietzmann, H. *Greek Papyri.* Cambridge, 1905. Eleven Texts with Notes, published by Deighton Bell & Co., Cambridge, as No. 14 of *Materials for Theological Lecturers and Students.*

Mayser, E. *Grammatik der Griechischen Papyri aus der Ptolemäerzeit: Laut- und Wortlehre.* Leipzig, 1906.

Meisterhans, K. *Grammatik der Attischen Inschriften,* by K. Meisterhans. 3rd Edit. by E. Schwyzer. Berlin, 1900.

Mélanges Nicole. Geneva, 1905. A collection of studies in classical philology and in archaeology, dedicated to Prof. J. Nicole.

Moulton, J. H. *A Grammar of New Testament Greek.* Vol. I, *Prolegomena.* 3rd Edit. Edinburgh, 1908. See p. xxx.

Moulton, J. H. *New Testament Greek in the light of modern discovery* in *Cambridge Biblical Essays,* pp. 461—505.´ London, 1909.

Nägeli, Th. *Der Wortschatz des Apostels Paulus.* Göttingen, 1905. A study of the Pauline vocabulary (in so far as it falls under the first five letters of the alphabet), more particularly in its relation to the Κοινή.

O. G. I. S. = Orientis Graeci Inscriptiones Selectae, ed. W. Dittenberger 2 vols. Leipzig, 1903–05.

Otto, W. *Priester und Tempel im Hellenistischen Ägypten.* 2 vols. Leipzig and Berlin, 1905, 1908.

Preisigke, F. *Familienbriefe aus alter Zeit,* in the *Preussische Jahrbücher* 108 (1902), pp. 88—111.

Reitzenstein, R. *Poimandres: Studien zur Griechisch-Ägyptischen und Frühchristlichen Literatur.* Leipzig, 1904.

Rossberg, C. *De Praepositionum Graecarum in Chartis Aegyptiis Ptolemaeorum Aetatis Usu.* Diss. Ien. Jena, 1909.

Rutherford, W. G. *The New Phrynichus.* London, 1881.

Schubart, W. *Das Buch bei den Griechen und Römern.* Berlin, 1907.

Sophocles, E. A. *Greek Lexicon of the Roman and Byzantine Periods.* New York, 1887.

Thackeray, H. St John. *A Grammar of the Old Testament in Greek according to the Septuagint.* Vol. I, *Introduction, Orthography and Accidence.* Cambridge, 1909.

Thess. = The writer's edition of *St Paul's Epistles to the Thessalonians.* (London, Macmillan, 1908.) The notes in this edition are cited as 1 Thess. i 1 (note).

Thumb, A. *Die Griechische Sprache im Zeitalter des Hellenismus. Beiträge zur Geschichte und Beurteilung der* Κοινή. Strassburg, 1901.

Völker, F. *Papyrorum Graecarum Syntaxis Specimen: de accusativo.* Diss. Bonn. Bonn, 1900.

Völker, F. *Syntax der griechischen Papyri.* I. Der Artikel. Münster i. W. 1903.

Wessely, C. *Les plus anciens Monuments du Christianisme écrits sur papyrus* (being *Patrologia Orientalis* IV, 2). Paris [1907]. See p. xxix.

WH. or WH. *Notes*[2] = *The New Testament in the original Greek*, by B. F. Westcott and F. J. A. Hort. Vol. I, *Text;* Vol. II, *Introduction and Appendix* containing *Notes on Select Readings, etc.* Revised Editions. London, 1898 and 1896.

Wilamowitz-Moellendorf, U. von. *Griechisches Lesebuch.* Four half-volumes. Berlin, 1902.

Wilcken, U. *Die griechischen Papyrusurkunden.* Berlin, 1897.

Wilcken, U. *Griechische Ostraka.* 2 vols. Leipzig, 1899.

Witkowski, S. *Epistulae Privatae Graecae quae in papyris aetatis Lagidarum servantur.* Leipzig, 1906.

Witkowski, S. *Prodromus grammaticae papyrorum graecarum aetatis Lagidarum.* Cracow, 1897.

WM. = *A Treatise on the Grammar of New Testament Greek*, by G. B. Winer, tr. and enlarged by W. F. Moulton. 8th Eng. Edit. Edinburgh, 1877.

W. Schm. = *Grammatik des neutestamentlichen Sprachidioms*, by G. B. Winer. 8th Edit. newly revised by P. W. Schmiedel (in progress). Göttingen, 1894—.

Z. N. T. W. = *Zeitschrift für die neutestamentliche Wissenschaft.* Giessen, 1900—.

2

TABLE OF MONTHS

Egyptian	Macedonian	Honorific Roman	Corresponding in an ordinary year to our
Θώθ	Δῖος	{Σεβαστός {Γερμανικός	Aug. 29—Sept. 27
Φαῶφι	Ἀπελλαῖος	Δομιτιανός	Sept. 28—Oct. 27
Ἀθύρ	Αὐδυναῖος	Νέος Σεβαστός	Oct. 28—Nov. 26
Χοιάκ	Περίτιος	{Νερώνειος {Νερώνειος Σεβαστός {Ἀδριανός	Nov. 27—Dec. 26
Τῦβι	Δύστρος		Dec. 27—Jan. 25
Μεχείρ	Ξανδικός		Jan. 26—Feb. 24
Φαμενώθ	Ἀρτεμίσιος		Feb. 25—March 26
Φαρμοῦθι	Δαίσιος		March 27—April 25
Παχών	Πάνημος	Γερμανίκειος	April 26—May 25
Παῦνι	Λώιος	Σωτήριος	May 26—June 24
Ἐπείφ	Γορπιαῖος		June 25—July 24
Μεσορή	Ὑπερβερεταῖος	Καισάρειος	July 25—Aug. 23

Ἐπαγόμεναι ἡμέραι=Aug 24—28, with a sixth ἐπαγομένη ἡμέρα (=Aug. 29) were inserted once in four years. In such intercalary years (A.D. 3/4, 7/8 &c.) the English equivalents have to be put one day on till our Feb. 29, after which the old correspondence is restored: that is, in an intercalary year Thoth 1 is Aug. 30 and so on, Phamenoth 4 equalling Feb. 29.

The Macedonian Calendar was equated to the Egyptian towards the end of ii/B.C.

GENERAL INTRODUCTION

M.

"You are not to suppose that the word [some New Testament word which had its only classical authority in Herodotus] had fallen out of use in the interval, only that it had not been used in the books which remain to us: probably it had been part of the common speech all along. I will go further, and say that if we could only recover letters that ordinary people wrote to each other without any thought of being literary, we should have the greatest possible help for the understanding of the language of the New Testament generally."

BISHOP LIGHTFOOT in 1863.

1. Amongst recent discoveries in Egypt few have awakened

Interest of
Papyrus-
discoveries.
a more widespread interest than the countless papyrus documents that have been brought to light. Some of these have been found amongst the ruins of ancient temples and houses; others have formed part of the cartonnage in which crocodile-mummies were enveloped; but far the largest number have come from the rubbish heaps (Arab. Kôm) on the outskirts of the towns or villages, to which they had been consigned as waste-paper, instead of being burnt as amongst ourselves.

Of these Greek papyri, for it is with Greek papyri alone that we are concerned, the earliest dated document is a marriage-contract of the year B.C. 311–10 (No. 1), and from that date they extend throughout the Ptolemaic and Roman periods far down into Byzantine times. Their special interest, however, for our present purpose may be said to stop with the close of the fourth century after Christ, though it will be necessary to add a few documents that fall still later, owing to their importance for the student of religion. Meanwhile, before passing to notice certain general characteristics of these documents, and their significance in various departments of learning, it may be well to describe briefly the material of which they are composed, and the history of their discovery.

2. That material was papyrus, so called from the papyrus-

Manu-
facture of
Papyrus.
plant (*Cyperus papyrus* L.), from which it was derived by a process of which the elder Pliny has left a classical account[1]. The pith (βύβλος) of the stem was cut into long strips, which were laid down

---

[1] *N. H.* xiii 11–13. Cf. the careful *Mémoire sur le Papyrus et* *la Fabrication du Papier chez les Anciens* by M. Dureau de la Malle

vertically to form a lower or outer layer. Over this a second layer was then placed, the strips this time running horizontally. And then the two layers were fastened together and pressed to form a single web or sheet (κόλλημα), the process being assisted by a preparation of glue moistened, where possible, with the turbid water of the Nile, which was supposed to add strength to it. After being dried in the sun, the surface was carefully rubbed down with ivory or a smooth shell, and was then ready for writing.

The side preferred for this purpose was as a rule the side on which the fibres lay horizontally, or the *recto*, as it is technically called, but this did not prevent a frequent subsequent use of the *verso* or back[1]. Official documents in particular which were no longer required were frequently utilized for other purposes, the original writing being either crossed or washed out[2], as when we find a private letter (B. G. U. 594) written over an effaced notice of a death (B. G. U. 582), or as when the *verso* of an old taxing-list serves a schoolmaster and his pupil for a writing-lesson (see introd. to No. 35).

---

in the *Mémoires de l'Académie des Inscriptions et Belles-Lettres* (Institut de France), XIX 1 (1851), pp. 140—183, where this passage of Pliny is fully discussed, and see the other authorities quoted in the Excursus on 'St Paul as a Letter-Writer' in my *Commentary on the Epp. to the Thessalonians*, p. 121 ff.

[1] The distinction between *recto* and *verso*, which is of great value in the dating of documents, the document on the *recto* being in accordance with the above rule the earlier, was first laid down by Wilcken in *Hermes* XXII (1887), p. 487 ff.: cf. *Archiv* I, p. 355 f. It should be noted however that it is only generally applicable between B.C. 250 and A.D. 400, the preference for the *recto* disappearing in

Byzantine times with the deterioration of papyrus manufacture, and the introduction of a new style of writing: see Schubart *Das Buch bei den Griechen und Römern* (Berlin, 1907), p. 9 f., and *Archiv* V, p. 191 ff.

[2] The technical term for crossing out was χιάζομαι. Hence a decree that was annulled was said χιασθῆναι, cf. P. Flor. 61. 65 (A.D. 86—88), and see further Deissmann *LO.*[2] p. 249 ff. In B.G.U. 717. 22 ff. (A.D. 149) we hear of a χειρόγρα-[φον]...χωρὶς ἀλίφατος καὶ ἐπιγραφῆς 'a decree neither washed out nor written over': cf. Col. ii 14 ἐξαλεί-ψας τὸ καθ' ἡμῶν χειρόγραφον. On the process of washing out, which seems to have been comparatively easy, see Erman *Mélanges Nicole*, p. 119 ff.

The size and character of these papyrus-sheets naturally varied considerably with the quality of the papyrus, of which they were formed, but for non-literary documents a very common size was from 5 to 5½ inches in width, and 9 to 11 inches in height[1]. When more space was required, this was easily obtained by joining a number of sheets together to form a roll. A roll of twenty sheets, which could be cut up or divided at will, was apparently a common size for selling purposes. This was, however, a mere matter of convenience, and smaller quantities would be easily procurable on demand[2].

The price paid was of course determined by the size and nature of the paper provided, and in view of our ignorance on these points the few figures that are available do not give much guidance[3]. But it is clear that papyrus was by no means a cheap commodity, and this helps to explain the frequent use of the *verso* already referred to, and the difficulty which the poor often experienced in procuring the necessary material for writing[4].

In itself papyrus is a very durable material, when not exposed to much handling, or to the action of damp, and it is consequently, thanks to their sandburial and to the singularly dry climate of Egypt, that so many documents and

---

[1] See Kenyon *Palaeography of Greek Papyri* (Oxford, 1899), p. 16 ff.

[2] An extra sheet seems to have been known as ἐπιχάρτη (P. Oxy. 34. 15, A.D. 127). For other writing-materials see P. Grenf. II 38 (B.C. 81), where directions are given for the purchase of pens (κάλαμοι γραφικοί, cf. 3 Macc. iv 20) and ink (μέλας, cf. 2 Jo. 12). In P. Oxy. 326 (c. A.D. 45) we hear of τὸ βροχίον τοῦ μέλανος ('the inkpot') and τὸ σμηλίο[ν] [ὅ]πως γακήσῃ τοὺς καλάμους.

[3] Thompson (*Greek and Latin Palaeography*, p. 28) refers to an inscription relating to the expenses of the rebuilding of the Erechtheum at Athens in B.C. 407, from which it appears that two sheets (χαρταὶ δύο) cost at the rate of a drachma and two obols each, or a little over a shilling of our money: see also Schubart *op. cit.* p. 12 f.

[4] In P. Gen. 52, a letter written on the *verso* of a business document, the writer explains—χάρτιον (Wilcken *Archiv* III, p. 399) καθαρὸν μὴ εὑρὼν πρὸς τὴν ὥραν εἰς τοῦ[τ]ον ἔγραψα: cf. B.G.U. 822 (iii/A.D.) *verso* πέμψον μοι ἄγραφον χάρτην, ἵνα εὕρο[με]ν ἐπιστολ[ὴν] γράψαι.

letters have been preserved there, while they have almost wholly disappeared elsewhere[1].

3. The earliest discoveries took place in 1778 at Gizeh, where the fellaheen produced a chest containing about fifty papyri. As however no purchasers were forthcoming, all these, except one now in the Museum at Naples (the *Charta Borgiana*), were destroyed for the sake, so it is said, of the aromatic smell which they gave forth in burning[2].

History of Papyrus-discoveries.

No further discoveries are reported for about twenty years, after which we hear of various sporadic finds, more particularly at Saqqârah, the ancient Memphis, about a half of the documents recovered there relating to its Serapeum, or great temple in honour of Serapis (see Nos. 4, 5, 6). In view of the novelty and intrinsic interest of these documents, it is astonishing that they did not attract more notice at the time. But, as a matter of fact, it was not until 1877, when several thousand papyri of widely different characters and dates were found amongst the ruins of Crocodilopolis, or Arsinoe, the old capital of the Fayûm district[3], that public attention was fully awakened to the far-reaching importance of the new discoveries.

[1] The principal exception is Herculaneum, where as a matter of fact the first Greek papyri were brought to light in the course of the excavations in 1752 and the following years. From the calcined nature of the rolls, the work of decipherment was unusually difficult, but eventually it was found that the greater part were occupied with philosophical writings of the Epicurean school. A few fragments of Epicurus himself were also recovered, including a charming letter to a child (No. 2). The evidence of the Herculaneum papyri on questions of accidence and grammar is fully stated in W. Crönert's great work *Memoria Graeca Herculanensis* (Leipzig, 1903).

[2] See Wilcken *Die griechischen Papyrusurkunden* (Berlin, 1897), p. 10. The result of an experiment, conducted along with Prof. E. J. Goodspeed on some papyrus-fragments, leads the present writer rather to doubt the 'aromatic' part of the story.

[3] The great bulk of these now form the Rainer collection at Vienna, which was still further enriched in 1896, and their contents are gradually being made available through the labours of Dr C. Wessely and others. To the collections mentioned on p. xi f. add in this connexion Wessely's monographs on *Karanis und Socnopaei Nesos* and *Die Stadt Arsinoe* (Vienna, 1902).

From that time the work of exploration has gone steadily on, a foremost place in it being occupied by our own Oxford scholars, Prof. B. P. Grenfell and Dr A. S. Hunt, to whose remarkable labours in this field, whether as discoverers or as interpreters, almost every page of the following *Selections* will bear witness.

4. The collections that have thus been formed are named **Papyrus Collections.** either from the locality where the texts were first discovered, as e.g. the *Oxyrhynchus Papyri* or the *Hibeh Papyri*, or from the place where they are now preserved, as the *British Museum* or *Chicago Papyri*, or the *Berliner Griechische Urkunden*, or in a few instances from their owners, as the *Amherst Papyri* or the *Reinach Papyri*. And through the patient labours of many scholars, both in this country and abroad, these collections are yearly being added to[1].

5. Of the papyri now available a comparatively small **Literary Papyri.** number, about 600 in all, are literary, one fourth of these supplying us with texts not previously known. Amongst these is what can claim to be the oldest Greek literary MS. in existence, a poem of Timotheus of Miletus, dating from the fourth century before Christ, while fragments of Homeric and other texts, belonging to the succeeding century, are still some thirteen hundred years older than the generality of Greek MSS. Other new texts embrace fragments of Sappho and the *Paeans* of Pindar, the *Odes* of Bacchylides, the *Comedies* of Menander, the *Constitution of Athens* by Aristotle, and the *Mimes* of Herodas. And as proof that surprises in this direction are by no means

[1] For a list which comprises the titles of most of the existing collections see p. xi f.; but how much still remains to be done before even the existing materials can be made available for general use is shown by Prof. Grenfell's statement (as reported in the *Athenaeum*, Aug. 22, 1908, p. 210) that of the Papyri from Oxyrhynchus alone, only about one-sixth have as yet been deciphered.

exhausted, the last two volumes of the *Oxyrhynchus Papyri*
(v, vi, both 1908) contain respectively a new history of B.C.
396—5, variously ascribed to Theopompus or Cratippus[1], and
large fragments of the *Hypsipyle* of Euripides, from a papyrus
of the second or early third century[2].

6. The number of non-literary texts that have been
Non-literary similarly recovered cannot be stated with any
Papyri. degree of exactness, but they may certainly be
reckoned by tens, if not hundreds, of thousands. And their
variety is as remarkable as their number.

The larger proportion consist of official or semi-official
documents—such as the reports of judicial proceedings,
petitions, census and property returns, wills, contracts and
so forth.

But there are in addition a large number of private
letters which, like all true letters, are often of the most
self-revealing character, and throw the clearest light upon
the whole domestic and social relationships of the people.
Not, perhaps, that their actual contents are often of any
special interest. Their authors, whether they write with their
own hands, or, owing to their illiteracy, avail themselves of
the services of professional scribes (cf. note on No. **20.** 43),
are as a rule content to state the matter in hand as briefly and
baldly as possible, while the lengthy introductions and closing
greetings with their constantly-recurring formal and stereotyped
phrases, produce a general effect of monotony[3]. At the same

[1] The attribution to the latter is
cogently argued by Prof. Bury in
his recent Harvard lectures on *The
Ancient Greek Historians* (Macmillan, 1909).
[2] For these and other facts regarding the literary papyri see a
useful article by Dr F. G. Kenyon
on the 'Greek Papyri' in the
Quarterly Review, April 1908,
pp. 333—55, and Dr R. Y. Tyrrell's
Essays on Greek Literature (Lond.

1909) 'The Recently-Discovered
Papyri,' p. 85 ff.
[3] In B.G.U. 601 (ii/A.D.) the
closing greetings, which are conveyed from a number of persons,
occupy no less than 13 out of the
31 lines, of which the letter consists, and similarly in one of
the letters addressed to Abinnaeus (see the introd. to No. **51**),
the writer takes up nearly one-
half of his short communication

time it is impossible not to feel the arresting charm of these frail papyrus messages, written with no thought of any other public than those to whom they were originally addressed, and on that very account calling up before our minds, as more elaborate documents could never have done, the persons alike of their senders and recipients.

Most of these letters are single detached communications upon some point of purely personal interest, whose interpretation is often a matter of extreme difficulty owing to our ignorance of the special circumstances that called them forth[1]. But occasionally we find ourselves in possession of a whole family budget as in the case of that keen agriculturist and shrewd old man Gemellus (No. 24), or of the official letters that have survived from the bureau of the military Prefect Abinnaeus (No. 51): while in other cases it is possible to piece together from separate documents various facts in some domestic story (see e.g. the introd. to No. 20).

7. The significance of the papyri, however, as veritable *documents humains*, is very far from being exhausted by their merely personal interest. And their value, both direct and indirect, in many and varied fields of learning is being increasingly realized[2].

Significance of the Papyri.

To the palaeographer, for example, they offer a continuous chain of documents, extending over a period of about a thousand years, very many of them exactly dated by year and month and day[3], and the rest usually easily assignable within comparatively narrow limits, by means of which many old errors can be

---

with personal greetings to his 'lord and patron' and the members of his household—'almost as generous a scale as in a Pauline epistle' (Kenyon, *Brit. Mus. Papyri* II, p. 305).

[1] See e.g. the curious and illiterate letter of Apollonius (No. 7) and from a later period the letter of Psenosiris (No. 49), which has been so variously interpreted.

[2] See especially Wilcken's valuable lecture, already cited, *Die griech. Papyrusurkunden*, p. 29 ff.

[3] Official documents are as a rule so dated up till the end of the first century after Christ, after that only by month and day. Cf. the Table of Months on p. xviii, which Dr A. S. Hunt has kindly revised for me.

corrected, and the whole history of book production before the adoption of vellum put in a new and striking light. Thus, to refer only to a single point, the New Testament student can no longer have any possible doubt that the books of the New Testament were written originally on papyrus, and that in such a letter as is reproduced in facsimile as a frontispiece to this volume he can see the prototype, so far as outward appearance is concerned, of an original Pauline Epistle[1].

To the historian again their value is no less remarkable. If it be the case, as we recently have been assured, that it was the want of adequate 'records' that prevented the Greeks themselves from being the founders of scientific history, that is certainly no longer the fate of any one who seeks to reconstruct the internal condition of Greco-Roman Egypt. Contemporary documents, whose genuineness is incontestable, now lie before him in such abundance, that their very number constitutes one of his greatest difficulties. And it will need much careful sifting and comparison before their results can be fully appreciated or stated[2]. But confining ourselves again to their relation to Christian history, it is impossible not to recognize the importance of having the 'enrolment' of Luke ii 1, 2 illustrated by the recovery of a large number of similar enrolments or census-returns, known by the same name (ἀπογραφαί, cf. No. 17), and even the method of the enumeration by the return of each man to his own city (ver. 3) confirmed by the discovery of an exactly analogous order (No. 28). When too we find a Prefect releasing a prisoner in deference to the wishes of the multitude (see note on No. 55. 28), or the summary of a trial with the speech of the prosecuting counsel (No. 18), we are at once

[1] See further Kenyon *Palaeography*, p. 92 ff., and *Handbook to the Textual Criticism of the New Testament* (Macmillan, 1901), Chap. II 'The Autographs of the New Testament.'

[2] The student will find much valuable information in the vols. on *The Ptolemaic Dynasty* by Prof. Mahaffy and on *Under Roman Rule* by Mr J. S. Milne in Methuen's *History of Egypt*, Vols. IV, V (1898).

reminded of what took place in the case of our Lord (Mk xv 15) and of St Paul (Ac. xxiv 2 ff.). Or, to pass to a later period in the history of the Church, while the persecution of the Christians under Decius, and the consequent demand for *libelli*, or certificates of conformity to the state-religion, were previously well known, it is surely a great gain to be able to look upon actual specimens of these *libelli*, attested by the signatures of the *libellatici* themselves, and counter-signed by the official commission that had been appointed to examine them (No. 48).

The value of the papyri, however, for the Biblical student is very far from being exhausted in ways such as these. They have added directly to his materials not only a certain number of Biblical texts[1], but also several highly important fragments of extra-canonical writings, including the so-called *Logia* of Jesus, which have attracted such widespread attention[2]. Nor is this all, but the indirect aid which they constantly afford for the interpretation of our Greek Bible is perhaps even more striking. It will be one of the principal objects of the commentary that accompanies the following selections to illustrate this in detail, but it may be convenient to recapitulate here that this aid is to be looked for principally in three directions.

(1) In the matter of *language*, we have now abundant proof that the so-called 'peculiarities' of Biblical Greek are due simply to the fact that the writers of the New Testament

---

[1] These include some third and fourth century fragments of the LXX, a third century MS. of Mt. i (P. Oxy. 2), and about one-third of the Ep. to the Hebrews from the early part of the fourth century (P. Oxy. 657). So far as they go, the N.T. texts confirm on the whole the evidence of the great uncials אB, or what we know as the Westcott and Hort text. A list of the principal Biblical papyri is given by Deissmann *Enc. Biblica*, col. 3559 f.

[2] The original *Logia* (P. Oxy. 1), the *New Sayings of Jesus* (P. Oxy. 654) and the *Fragment of an Un-canonical Gospel* (P. Oxy. 840) have all been published separately in convenient forms (Frowde, 1897, 1904 and 1908): see also Swete's edition of *Two New Gospel Fragments* (Deighton, Bell & Co., 1908). In *Les plus anciens Monuments du Christianisme* (*Patrologia Orientalis* IV 2 [1907]) Wessely has edited the most important early Christian documents written on papyrus, with translations and commentaries.

for the most part made use of the ordinary colloquial Greek, the Κοινή of their day.

This is not to say that we are to disregard altogether the influence of translation Greek, and the consequent presence of undoubted Hebraisms, both in language and grammar[1]. Nor again must we lose sight of the fact that the sacred writers, especially in the case of the New Testament, deepened and enriched the significance of many everyday words, and employed them in altogether new connotations. At the same time the best way to get at these new connotations is surely to start from the old, and to trace, as we are now enabled to do, the steps by which words and phrases were raised from their original popular and secular usage to the deeper and more spiritual sense, with which the New Testament writings have made us familiar[2]. It is sufficient by way of illustration to point to the notes that follow on such words as ἀδελφός (No. 7. 2), αἰώνιος (No. 45. 27), βαπτίζω (No. 7. 13), κύριος (No. 18. 6), λειτουργέω (No. 5. 2), παρουσία (No. 5. 18), πρεσβεύω (No. 40. 14), πρεσβύτερος (Nos. 10. 17, 29. 11), προγράφω (No. 27. 11), σωτήρ (No. 19. 18), σωτηρία (No. 36. 13), and χρηματίζω (No. 25. 2)[3].

---

[1] An over-tendency to minimize these last is probably the most pertinent criticism that can be directed against Dr J. H. Moulton's *Prolegomena* to his *Grammar of New Testament Greek*, a book that is as useful to the papyrologist as it is indispensable to the student of the Greek New Testament. See further the valuable sections (§§ 3, 4) on 'The κοινή—the Basis of Septuagint Greek,' and 'The Semitic Element in LXX Greek' in Thackeray's *Grammar of the Old Testament in Greek* I, p. 16 ff.

[2] The denial of a distinctive 'Biblical' or 'New Testament Greek' is often too unqualified today owing to the recoil from the old position of treating it as essentially an isolated language, and the whole question of how far the Greek of the New Testament deviates from the Κοινή requires a fuller discussion and statement than it has yet received. Some good remarks on the 'eigenartig' character of the New Testament writings, notwithstanding the linguistic and stylistic parallels that have been discovered, will be found in Heinrici's monograph *Der litterarische Charakter der neutestamentlichen Schriften* (Leipzig, 1908).

[3] For many more examples of the influence of the Κοινή on N.T. Greek than are possible in the limits of the present volume reference may perhaps be allowed to the 'Lexical Notes from the Papyri' which Dr

(2) The *form*, again, which the New Testament writers so frequently adopted for the conveyance of religious truth is reflected in the clearest manner in the private letters that have been rescued from the sands of Egypt. It may seem strange at first sight to those who have had no previous acquaintance with the subject, that those simple and artless communications, the mere flotsam and jetsam of a long past civilization, should for a moment be put in evidence alongside the Epistles of St Paul. But even if they do nothing else, they prove how 'popular' rather than 'literary' in origin these Epistles really are[1], and how frequently the Apostle adapts the current epistolary phrases of his time to his own purposes[2].

(3) Once more, the papyri are of the utmost value in enabling us to picture the *general environment*, social and religious, of the earliest followers of Christianity. These followers

J. H. Moulton and the present writer are contributing to the *Expositor* VII v, p. 51 ff. &c.

[1] The distinction holds good, even if we cannot go all the way with Deissmann (*BS*. p. 3 ff.) in pronouncing all the Pauline writings 'letters' rather than 'Epistles.' This may be true of the short Epistle to Philemon, which is little more than a private note, but surely the Epistle to the Romans stands in a different category, and, if only by the character of its contents, is to be widely differentiated from the unstudied expression of personal feeling, that we associate with the idea of a true 'letter.'

[2] The first recognition I have come across in this country of the value of the papyri for N.T. study occurs in Dean Farrar's *The Messages of the Books*, first published in 1884, where in a note to his chapter on the 'Form of the New Testament Epistles' the writer remarks—'It is an interesting subject of inquiry to what extent there was at this period

an ordinary form of correspondence which (as amongst ourselves) was to some extent fixed. In the papyrus rolls of the British Museum (edited for the trustees by J. Forshall [in 1839]) there are forms and phrases which constantly remind us of St Paul' (p. 151). But he does not seem to have followed up the hint, and it was left to Prof. A. Deissmann, following independently on lines already hinted at by A. Peyron in his introduction to the Turin Papyri (*Papyri graeci regii Taurinensis Musei Aegyptii*, Turin, 1826), to show in detail in *Bibelstudien* (1895) and *Neue Bibelstudien* (1897) (together translated into English as *Bible Studies* (1901)), and more recently in *Licht vom Osten* (1 Aufl. 1908, 2 u. 3 Aufl. 1909), the wealth of material they contain in this and other respects. Mention should also be made of Dean Armitage Robinson's interesting Excursus 'On some current epistolary phrases' in his *Commentary on Ephesians*, p. 275 ff.

belonged for the most part, though by no means exclusively[1], to the humbler and poorer classes of the population, whom the ordinary historian of the period did not think it worth his while to notice[2]. But now by means of their own autographic letters and documents we can see them in all the varied relationships of everyday life and thought. Notices of Birth (No. 32) and of Death (No. 35) are intermingled with Marriage-Contracts (Nos. 1, 34) and Deeds of Divorce (No. 16): the oppressed appeal to the ruling powers for protection (Nos. 10, 29), and the village 'elders' arrange for dancing-girls to enliven an approaching festival (No. 45): the youth who has wasted all his substance with 'riotous living' (No. 27), and the poor prodigal with his humble confession of sin (No. 37), stand before us in the flesh: while the mourners 'sorrowing as those who have no hope' (No. 38), and the perplexed and diseased seeking help in dreams or oracles (Nos. 6, 25, cf. 54) and enchantments (Nos. 46, 47), prove how deep and real were the needs of those to whom the Gospel was first preached.

8. There may be a temptation perhaps at present, in view of the unusual and romantic character of the new discoveries, to exaggerate the significance of the papyri in these and similar directions. Much requires still to be done before their exact linguistic and historical value can be fully estimated. But there can be no doubt as to the richness of the field which they present to the student alike of religion and of life. And one main object of the present volume of *Selections* will have been fulfilled, if it succeeds in any measure in arousing a more wide-spread interest in the larger collections, and the notable work of their first editors and interpreters.

The Richness of the Field.

---

[1] Cf. Orr, *Neglected Factors in the Study of the Early Progress of Christianity* (London, 1899), p. 95 ff.

[2] Deissmann (*LO.*[2] p. 217 f.) strikingly recalls the *Prosopographia Imperii Romani* which catalogues 8,644 men and women of note during the first three centuries, but omits of set purpose 'hominum plebeiorum infinitam illam turbam' —Jesus and Paul among them ! See also the same writer's articles on 'Primitive Christianity and the Lower Classes' in *Exp.* VII vii, pp. 97 ff., 208 ff., 352 ff.

TEXTS, TRANSLATIONS
AND NOTES

τοῖς

βιβλίοις σου αὐτὸ μόνον πρόσεχ[ε] φιλολογῶν
εαὶ ἀπ' αὐτῶν ὄνησιν ἕξεις.

CORNELIUS to his son HIERAX

[P. OXY. 531. 10 ff. (ii/A.D.)]

For the convenience of the reader, the following Texts are given in modern form with accentuation and punctuation. Letters inserted within square brackets [ ] indicate the Editors' proposed restorations for lacunae in the original, and those in round brackets ( ) the resolutions of abbreviations or symbols. Angular brackets < > are used to denote words or phrases that have been accidentally omitted in the original, double square brackets ⟦ ⟧ letters that have been erased in the original and braces { } a superfluous letter or letters. Dots placed inside brackets [...] represent the approximate number of letters that have been lost or erased, and dots outside brackets mutilated or illegible letters. A dot under a letter, e.g. ạ, shows that the letter is uncertain.

As regards dating, i/B.C. = 1st century B.C., i/A.D. = 1st century A.D., and i/ii A.D. = a date falling about the end of the 1st or the beginning of the 2nd century A.D.

1. A MARRIAGE CONTRACT

P. ELEPH. 1.   B.C. 311–10.

Discovered at Elephantine, and edited by Rubensohn in the *Elephantine-Papyri*, p. 18 ff.

The following marriage contract from Elephantine is the oldest Greek specimen of its class that has hitherto been discovered (cf. P. Gen. 21 of ii/B.C., as completed by Wilcken, *Archiv* III, p. 387 ff., and P. Tebt. 104, B.C. 92), and also the earliest dated Greek papyrus document that we possess. Rubensohn in his commentary draws special attention to its pure Greek character, as proved by the nationality of the contracting parties, and the terms employed, e.g. the 'patriarchal' part played by the bride's father, and her own repeated designation as ἐλευθέρα (l. 4 f.). Noteworthy too are the stringent provisions regulating the married life of the pair (ll. 6, 8 ff.) which, with faint echoes in the Oxyrhynchus documents, disappear from the contracts of the Roman period, to be renewed later under Christian influences; cf. C. P. R. 30. 20 ff. (vi/A.D.) πρὸς τῷ καὶ αὐτὴν ἀγαπᾶν καὶ θάλπειν καὶ θεραπεύειν αὐτόν...ὑπακούειν δὲ αὐτῷ καθὰ τῷ νόμῳ καὶ τῇ ἀκολουθίᾳ συμβαίνει[ν] οἶδε, and see Wilcken, *Archiv* I, p. 490.

M.

Ἀλεξάνδρου τοῦ Ἀλεξάνδρου βασιλεύοντος ἔτει ἑβδόμωι
Πτολεμαίου σατραπεύοντος ἔτει τεσσαρε-
σκαιδεκάτωι μηνὸς Δίου. Συγγραφὴ συνοικισίας Ἡρακλείδου καὶ Δημητρίας. Λαμβάνει Ἡρακλείδης
Δημητρίαν Κώιαν γυναῖκα γνησίαν παρὰ τοῦ πατρὸς Λεπ-
τίνου Κωίου καὶ τῆς μητρὸς Φιλωτίδος ἐλεύθερος
ἐλευθέραν προσφερομένην εἱματισμὸν καὶ κόσμον(δραχμὰς)
͵α, παρεχέτω δὲ Ἡρακλείδης Δημητρίαι
ὅσα προσήκει γυναικὶ ἐλευθέραι πάντα, εἶναι δὲ ἡμᾶς κατὰ
ταὐτὸ ὅπου ἂν δοκῆι ἄριστον εἶναι βουλευομένοις
κοινῆι   5
βουλῆι Λεπτίνηι καὶ Ἡρακλείδηι. Εἰὰν δέ τι κακοτεχνοῦσα
ἀλίσκηται ἐπὶ αἰσχύνηι τοῦ ἀνδρὸς Ἡρακλείδου Δημητρία,

In the seventh year of the reign of Alexander the son of
Alexander, the fourteenth year of the satrapy of Ptolemaeus, the
month Dios.   Contract of marriage between Heraclides and
Demetria.

Heraclides takes Demetria of Cos as his lawful wife from her
father Leptines of Cos and her mother Philotis, both parties being
freeborn, and the bride bringing clothing and adornment of the
value of 1000 drachmas, and let Heraclides provide for Demetria
all things that are fitting for a freeborn woman, and that we should
live together wherever shall seem best to Leptines and Heraclides
in consultation together.   And if Demetria shall be detected doing
anything wrong to the shame of her husband Heraclides, let her

3. γνησίαν] 'lawful,' 'legally
wedded': cf. P. Amh. 86. 15
(A.D. 78) χωρὶς γνησίων δημοσίων,
'apart from the legal public charges.'
The same sense of 'true,' 'genuine,'
underlies the use of the word in
Phil. iv 3 γνήσιε σύνζυγε; for a
definite spiritual application see
1 Tim. i 2, Tit. i 4.
    5. εἶναι δὲ ἡμᾶς] an unexpected
change to the 1st pers., showing

perhaps that Heraclides drafted the
agreement.
    6. κακοτεχνοῦσα] Cf. 3 Macc.
vii 9 ἐάν τι κακοτεχνήσωμεν πονηρόν,
and for the corresponding adj. see
Sap. i 4, xv 4.
    ἐπὶ αἰσχύνηι] Cf. P. Gen. 21. 11
(see introd. above) μηδ' αἰ[σ]χύνειν
Μενεκράτην ὅσα φέρει ἀνδρὶ αἰσχύνην.

στερέσθω ὤμ προσηνέγκατο πάντων, ἐπιδειξάτω δὲ Ἡρακλείδης ὅ τι ἂν ἐγκαλῆι Δημητρίαι. ἐναντίον ἀνδρῶν
τριῶν,
οὓς ἂν δοκιμόζωσιν ἀμφότεροι. Μὴ ἐξέστω δὲ Ἡρακλείδηι
γυναῖκα ἄλλην ἐπεισάγεσθαι ἐφ' ὕβρει Δημητρίας μηδὲ
τεκνοποιεῖσθαι ἐξ ἄλλης γυναικὸς μηδὲ κακοτεχνεῖν μηδὲν
παρευρέσει μηδεμιᾶι Ἡρακλείδην εἰς Δημητρίαν·
εἰὰν δέ τι ποῶν τούτων ἀλίσκηται Ἡρακλείδης καὶ ἐπι-
δείξηι Δημητρία ἐναντίον ἀνδρῶν τριῶν, οὓς ἂν δοκι-
μάζωσιν   10
ἀμφότεροι, ἀποδότω Ἡρακλείδης Δημητρίαι τὴμ φερνὴν
ἣν προσηνέγκατο (δραχμὰς) ͵α, καὶ προσαποτεισάτω
ἀργυρί-
ου Ἀλεξανδρείου (δραχμὰς) ͵α. Ἡ δὲ πρᾶξις ἔστω καθάπερ
ἐγ δίκης κατὰ νόμον τέλος ἐχούσης Δημητρίαι καὶ τοῖς
μετὰ

be deprived of all that she has brought, and let Heraclides state
whatever charge he brings against Demetria in the presence of three
men, whom both shall approve. And let it not be allowed to
Heraclides to bring in another woman to the insult of Demetria, nor
to beget children by another woman, nor shall Heraclides do any
wrong to Demetria on any pretext. And if Heraclides shall be
detected doing any of these things, and Demetria shall prove it in
the presence of three men, whom both shall approve, let Heraclides
repay to Demetria the dowry which she brought to the value of
1000 drachmas, and let him pay in addition 1000 drachmas of
Alexander's coinage. And let the right of execution be as if a formal
decree of the court had been obtained to Demetria and to those

7. ἐπιοειξάτω] In Ac. xviii 28,
Heb. vi 17 the verb is used in the
same sense of 'prove,' 'demonstrate.'
ἐναντίον ἀνδρῶν τριῶν] With this
private separation before witnesses
contrast such a later 'deed of
divorce' as No. 16. For ἐναντίον,
frequent in this sense in the LXX,
cf. Lk. i 6 ἦσαν δὲ δίκαιοι ἀμφότεροι
ἐναντίον τοῦ θεοῦ.
8. δοκιμάζωσιν] 'approve,' as

generally in the N.T.: see 1 Thess.
ii 4 (note).
9. παρευρέσει μηδεμιᾶι] Cf. P.
Tebt. 5. 61 (B.C. 118), B.G.U. 241.
40 (ii/A.D.).
11. ἀργυρίου Ἀλεξανδρείου] 'perhaps the earliest documentary mention of Alexander's coinage, unless
Dittenberger *Syll.* 176 is about two
years older' (Rubensohn).

Δημητρίας πράσσουσιν ἔκ τε αὐτοῦ Ἡρακλείδου καὶ τῶν
  Ἡρακλείδου πάντων καὶ ἐγγαίων καὶ ναυτικῶν. Ἡ
  δὲ συγγραφὴ
ἥδε κυρία ἔστω πάντηι πάντως ὡς ἐκεῖ τοῦ συναλλάγματος
  γεγενημένου, ὅπου ἂν ἐπεγφέρηι Ἡρακλείδης κατὰ
Δημητρίας ἢ Δημητρία τε καὶ τοὶ μετὰ Δημητρίας πράσ-
  σοντες ἐπεγφέρωσιν κατὰ Ἡρακλείδου. Κύριοι δὲ
  ἔστωσαν Ἡρακλεί-   15
δης καὶ Δημητρία καὶ τὰς συγγραφὰς αὐτοὶ τὰς αὐτῶν
  φυλάσσοντες καὶ ἐπεγφέροντες κατ᾽ ἀλλήλων. Μάρ-
  τυρες
Κλέων Γελῴιος Ἀντικράτης Τημνίτης Λῦσις Τημνίτης
  Διονύσιος Τημνίτης Ἀριστόμαχος Κυρηναῖος Ἀρισ-
  τόδικος
Κῷος.

acting with Demetria or Heraclides himself and all Heraclides'
property both on land and sea. And let this contract be valid under
all circumstances, as if the agreement had been come to in that place
wheresoever Heraclides brings the charge against Demetria, or
Demetria and those acting with Demetria bring the charge against
Heraclides. And let Heraclides and Demetria enjoy equal legal
rights both in preserving their own contracts, and in bringing
charges against one another. Witnessed by Cleon of Gela,
Anticrates of Temnos, Lysis of Temnos, Dionysius of Temnos,
Aristomachus of Cyrene, and Aristodicus of Cos.

14. ὅπου κτλ.] a clause inserted in view of the fact that, according to strict Greek law, the contract was only binding in the place where it was entered into.

2. EPICURUS TO A CHILD

EX VOL. HERCUL. 176.   iii/B.C.

Discovered at Herculaneum and edited by Gomperz, *Hermes*, v,
p. 386 ff. See also H. Usener, *Epicurea*, p. 154, and Wilamowitz,
Gr. Les. I, p. 396; II, p. 260.

The following fragment of a letter to a child is interesting,
not only on account of the writer, the well-known philosopher,
Epicurus († B.C. 270), but also from its own artless and affec-
tionate character. According to Wilamowitz the child addressed
was one of the orphan children of a certain Metrodorus, of
whom Epicurus took charge.

> ...[ἀ]φείγμεθα εἰς Λάμψακον ὑ-
> γιαίνοντες ἐγὼ καὶ Πυθο-
> κλῆς κα[ὶ Ἕρμ]αρχος καὶ Κ[τή]-
> σιππος, καὶ ἐκεῖ κατειλήφα-
> μεν ὑγ[ι]αίνοντας Θεμίσ-   5
> ταν καὶ τοὺς λοιποὺς [φί]λο[υ]ς.
> εὖ δὲ ποιε[ῖ]ς καὶ σὺ ε[ἰ ὑ]γι-
> αίνεις καὶ ἡ μ[ά]μμη [σ]ου,

We have arrived in health at Lampsacus, myself and Pythocles
and Hermarchus and Ctesippus, and there we have found Themistas
and the rest of the friends in health. It is good if you also are in
health and your grandmother, and obey your grandfather and

1. Λάμψακον] in Mysia, an early
home of Epicurus, where he was
engaged for several years in teaching
philosophy. It was the native town

of Metrodorus.
8. μάμμη] 'grandmother,' as in
later Gk: cf. 2 Tim. i 5.

καὶ πάπαι καὶ Μάτρω[ν]ι πάν-
τα πε[ί]θη[ι, ὥσπ]ερ καὶ ἔ[μ]-   10
προσθεν. εὖ γὰρ ἴσθι, ἡ αἰτία,
ὅτι καὶ ἐγὼ καὶ ο[ἱ] λοιποὶ
πάντες σε μέγα φιλοῦμεν,
ὅτι τούτοις πείθῃ πάντα···.

Matron in all things, as you have done before. For be sure, the reason why both I and all the rest love you so much is that you obey these in all things....

9. πάπαι] Like μάμμη the word πάπας is of Asiatic origin, and was apparently first introduced as a term of endearment by Phrygian slaves into Athenian nurseries (Wilam.). For its later use as an ecclesiastical title see No. 51.

11. εὖ γὰρ ἴσθι] a common classical phrase, of which we have traces in the ἴστε (imper.) of Eph. v 5, Heb. xii 17, Jas. i 19.

3. POLYCRATES TO HIS FATHER

P. Petr. ii. xi (1).   iii/B.C.

First edited by Sayce in *Hermathena* XVII, and afterwards by Mahaffy in the *Flinders Petrie Papyri* II, p. [27]: cf. I, p. [80] and III, p. 112. See also Wilamowitz, *Gr. Les.* I, p. 396 f.; II, p. 261 f.; and *Reden und Vorträge*, p. 251; Witkowski, *Ep. Priv. Gr.* p. 5 ff.

This letter belongs to the correspondence of the architect Cleon, who acted as commissioner of public works in the Fayûm district, about the middle of the 3rd cent. B.C. It contains a request from his younger son Polycrates, who had apparently been borrowing from his brother Philonides, that Cleon will interest himself on his behalf with Ptolemy II, on the occasion of the King's visit to celebrate the Arsinoe festival. The text, in which there are no lacunae, is written 'in a beautifully clear and correct hand' (Mahaffy).

Πολυκράτης τῶι πατρὶ χαίρειν. καλῶς ποιεῖς εἰ ἔρρωσαι
καὶ τὰ λοιπά σοι κατὰ γνώμην ἐστίν, ἐρρώ-
μεθα δὲ καὶ ἡμεῖς. πολλάκις μὲν γέγραφά σοι παραγενέσθαι καὶ συστῆσαί με, ὅπως τῆς ἐπὶ τοῦ
παρόντος σχολῆς ἀπολυθῶ. καὶ νῦν δέ, εἰ δυνατόν ἐστιν
καὶ μηθέν σε τῶν ἔργων κωλύει,
πειράθητι ἐλθεῖν εἰς τὰ Ἀρσινόεια· ἐὰν γὰρ σὺ παρα-
γένηι, πέπεισμαι ῥαιδίως με τῶι βασιλεῖ
συσταθήσεσθαι. γίνωσκε δέ με ἔχοντα παρὰ Φιλωνίδου
(δραχμὰς) οʹ· ἀπὸ τούτου τὸ μὲν ἥμυσυ   5

Polycrates to his father, greeting. I am glad if you are in
good health, and everything else is to your mind. We ourselves
are in good health. I have often written to you to come and introduce me, in order that I may be relieved from my present occupation. And now if it is possible, and none of your work hinders
you, do try and come to the Arsinoe festival; for, if you come, I
am sure that I shall easily be introduced to the King. Know that
I have received 70 drachmas from Philonides. Half of this I have

---

1. καλῶς ποιεῖς] a common formula, cf. 1 Macc. xii 18, 22, Ac.
x 33, Phil. iv 14, 3 Jo. 6.
   εἰ ἔρρωσαι κτλ.] Mahaffy ʻ(P.
Petr. II, Appendix p. 10) has
pointed out that the occurrence of
this common Greek formula at this
early date establishes beyond dispute
that the corresponding Roman S.V.
B.E.E.Q.V. was derived from it,
and not *vice versa*, as Cobet
believed.
   2. παραγενέσθαι] The verb is
common in vernacular documents
where classical writers would more
naturally have used ἀφικνοῦμαι or
ἥκω. The literary complexion
therefore which Harnack gives to
it in certain passages in Luke (*Saying: of Jesus*, p. 86) cannot be
maintained: see Moulton *Exp.* vii,

vii, p. 413.
   συστῆσαι] 'bring together,' hence
'introduce,' 'recommend': see the
note on P. Oxy. 292. 5 f. (= No. 14).
In Gen. xl 4 καὶ συνέστησεν ὁ ἀρχι-
δεσμώτης τῷ Ἰωσὴφ αὐτούς, καὶ
παρέστη αὐτοῖς, the meaning is
somewhat different. 'put under the
charge of.'
   3. σχολῆς] 'studium' (Wilamowitz).
   4. εἰς τὰ Ἀρσινόεια] the festival
held in honour of the deceased
Queen Arsinoe, who had already
been raised to divine honours.
   5. ἥμυσυ] almost always so
written in the papyri of iii/B.C.:
in the two following centuries ἥμυσυ
and ἥμισυ occur with about equal
frequency, see Mayser *Gramm.*
p. 100 f.

εἰς τὰ δέοντα ὑπελιπόμην, τὸ δὲ λοιπὸν εἰς τὸ δάνειον
κατέβαλον. τοῦτο δὲ γίνεται
διὰ τὸ μὴ ἀθροῦν ἡμᾶς, ἀλλὰ κατὰ μικρὸν λαμβάνειν.
γράφε δ᾽ ἡμῖν καὶ σύ, ἵνα εἰδῶ-
μεν ἐν οἷς εἶ, καὶ μὴ ἀγωνιῶμεν. ἐπιμέλου δὲ καὶ σαυτοῦ,
ὅπως ὑγιαίνῃς καὶ πρὸς ἡ-
μᾶς ἐρρωμένος ἔλθῃς.   εὐτύχει.

kept by me for necessaries, but the rest I have paid as an instalment of interest. This happens because we do not get our money
in a slump sum, but in small instalments. Write to us yourself
that we may know how you are circumstanced, and not be anxious.
Take care of yourself that you may be well, and come to us in good
health. Farewell.

6. εἰς τὰ δέοντα] Cf. P. Par.
38. 25 ff. (ii/B.C.) ὅπως...ἔχω τὰ
δέοντα, καὶ μὴ διαλύωμαι τῷ λιμῷ.
εἰς τὸ δάνειον κατέβαλον] 'I have
paid as an instalment of interest'—
a rendering suggested by Wyse, and
adopted by Mahaffy (P. Petr. II,
App. p. 4) in place of his original
'I have put out to interest.'
8. ἀγωνιῶμεν] Cf. P. Petr. III,
53 (*l*) 15 f. οὐ γὰρ ὡς ἔτυχεν ἀγωνιῶμεν, 'for we are in a state of no

ordinary anxiety' (Edd.), and for
the corresponding subst., as in Lk.
xxii 44, cf. P. Tebt. 423. 13 f.
(early iii/A.D.) ὡς εἰς ἀγωνίαν με
γενέσθαι ἐν τῷ παρόντι.
9. εὐτύχει] the form of greeting
generally adopted when the person
addressed is of superior rank: in the
case of an inferior, ἔρρωσο is the
ordinary formula. For exceptions
see Wilcken *Archiv* I, p. 161.

4. ISIAS TO HEPHAESTION

P. BRIT. MUS. 42.   B.C. 168.

Discovered at Memphis, and edited by Kenyon in the *British
Museum Papyri* I, p. 29 ff. For various improved readings, which
have been followed here, see Wilcken, *G. G. A.*, 1894, p. 722, and
for the text with commentary see Wilamowitz, *Gr. Les.* I, p. 397 f.,
II, p. 262, and Witkowski, *Ep. Priv. Gr.*, p. 37 fi.

The following letter is addressed by a certain Isias to
Hephaestion, apparently her husband, who was 'in retreat'
in the Serapeum at Memphis, urging him to return home.

The exact position of the Serapeum recluses is still a matter
of discussion amongst scholars. By some they are regarded
as a kind of monkish community: by others, as persons who
in special sickness or trouble had sought the aid of the god,
and were for the time being 'possessed,' or under his influence
and protection. In any case this letter makes clear that,
whatever the nature of the vows they took upon them, these
were not binding for all time, but lasted only until the κάτοχοι
had attained the end they had in view (l. 26). On the whole
subject see Preuschen, *Mönchtum und Sarapiskult* (2ᵗᵉ Aufl.,
Giessen, 1903), where the latter of the above-mentioned views
is strongly supported, and cf. *Archiv* IV, p. 207. For further
particulars regarding the Serapeum see Nos. 5 and 6.

Ἰσιὰς Ἡφαιστίωνι τῶι ἀδελφῶ[ι χαί(ρειν).
εἰ ἐρρωμένωι τἄλλα κατὰ λόγον
ἀπαντᾶι, εἴηι ἂν ὡς τοῖς θεοῖς εὐχο-
μένη διατελῶ· καὶ αὐτὴ δ' ὑγίαινον
καὶ τὸ παιδίον καὶ οἱ ἐν οἴκωι πάντες   5
< σοῦ διαπαντὸς μνείαν ποιούμενοι >
κομισαμένη τὴν παρὰ σοῦ ἐπιστολὴν
παρ' Ὥρου, ἐν ἧι διεσάφεις εἶναι

Isias to Hephaestion her brother greeting. If you are well,
and things in general are going right, it would be as I am continually praying to the gods. I myself am in good health and
the child, and all at home, making mention of you continually.
When I got your letter from Horus, in which you explained

1. τῶι ἀδελφῶι] 'brother,' i.e.
'husband,' in accordance with a well-
established Egyptian usage, and in
keeping with the general tone of the
letter, and the references to τὸ παιδίον (l. 5) and ἡ μήτηρ σου (l. 28, not
ἡμῶν). (Wilam., Witk.)
    2. κατὰ λόγον] as in P. Par. 63.
i 5 (ii/B.C.) καὶ σὺ ὑγιαίνεις καὶ
τἄλλα σοι κατὰ λόγον ἐστίν.
    6. μν. ποιούμενοι] a common
epistolary phrase, cf. 1 Thess. i. 2

(note).
    7. κομισαμένη] Cf. P. Fay. 114.
3 f. (A.D. 100) κομισάμενός μου τὴν
ἐπιστολήν, 'on receipt of my letter.'
Other passages such as P. Hib. 54. 9
(iii/B.C.), P. Tebt. 45. 33 (ii/B.C.),
bear out the meaning 'receive *back*,'
which Hort (on 1 Pet. i 9) finds in
all the N.T. occurrences of the
word.
    8. διεσάφεις] Cf. Mt. xiii 36,
xviii 31.

ἐν κατοχῆι ἐν τῶι Σαραπιείωι τῶι
ἐν Μέμφει, ἐπὶ μὲν τῶι ἐρρῶσθα[ί] σε   10
εὐθέως τοῖς θεοῖς εὐχαρίστουν,
ἐπὶ δὲ τῶι μὴ παραγίνεσθαί σε [πάντω]ν
τῶν ἐκεῖ ἀπειλημμένων παραγεγο[νό]των
ἀηδίζομαι, ἔ[νε]κα τοῦ ἐκ τοῦ το[ιού]του
καιροῦ ἐμαυτή[ν] τε καὶ τὸ παιδί[ον σ]ου   15
διακεκυβερνηκυῖα καὶ εἰς πᾶν τι
ἐληλυθυῖα διὰ τὴν τοῦ σίτου τιμήν,
καὶ δο[κο]ῦσα ν[ῦ]γ [γ]ε σοῦ παραγενομένου
τεύξεσθαί τινος ἀναψυχῆς, σὲ δὲ
μηδ᾽ ἐντεθυμῆσθαι τοῦ παραγενέσθαι   20
μηδ᾽ ἐνβεβλοφέναι εἰς τὴν ἡμετέραν περί-
στασιν. ὡς ἔτ[ι] σοῦ παρ[όν]τος πάντων ἐπεδεόμην,
μὴ ὅτι γε τοσούτου χρόνου ἐπιγεγονότος

that you were in retreat in the Serapeum at Memphis, I immediately gave thanks to the gods that you were well; but that you
did not return when all those who were shut up with you
returned distresses me; for having piloted myself and your child
out of such a crisis, and having come to the last extremity
because of the high price of corn, and thinking that now at last on
your return I should obtain some relief, you have never even
thought of returning, nor spared a look for our helpless state.
While you were still at home, I went short altogether, not to
mention how long a time has passed since, and such disasters,

14. ἀηδίζομαι] The verb is not
found in the N.T., but for the vernacular ἀηδία, as Lk. xxiii 12 D, cf.
P. Par. 48. 7 ff. (ii/B.C.) τοῦ πρός σε
τὴν ἀήδειαν ποιήσαντος, 'who had
that disagreement with you.'

19. ἀναψυχῆς] The word, which
is classical, is found several times
in the LXX, along with the corresponding verb ἀναψύχω (cf. 2 Tim.
i 16). For the later form ἀνάψυξις
see Exod. viii 15, Ac. iii 19.

20. ἐντεθυμῆσθαι] For the gen.
constr. cf. P. Par. 63. vii. 9 (ii/B.C.)
ἐντεθυμῆσθαι τῶν ἐξηριθμημένων.

21. περίστασιν] The word is
frequent in a bad sense in Polybius,
e.g. iv. 45. 10 εἰς πᾶν περιστάσεως
ἐλθεῖν, cf. also 2 Macc. iv 16 περιέ-
σχεν αὐτοὺς χαλεπὴ περίστασις,
'sore calamity beset them.'

23. ἐπιγεγονότος] For ἐπιγίνομαι 'praeterlabor' Witkowski compares P. Par. 25. 8 f. (ii/B.C.) καθ᾽
ὃν καιρὸν τὸ πένθος τοῦ Ἄπιος ἐπε-
γένετο: see also P. Fay. 11. 19
(ii/B.C.) ἄλλων ἐπιγεγονότων πλεόνων
(sc. χρόνων), 'still further periods
having elapsed.'

καὶ τοιούτων καιρῶν < καὶ > μηθὲν σοῦ ἀπεσταλκότος.

ἔτι δὲ καὶ Ὥρου τοῦ τὴν ἐπιστολὴν παρακεκο-   25
μικό[το]ς ἀπηγγελκότος ὑπὲρ τοῦ ἀπολελύσθαι σε
ἐκ τῆς κατοχῆς παντελῶς ἀηδίζομαι.
οὐ μὴν ἀλλ᾽ ἐπεὶ καὶ ἡ μήτηρ σου τυγχάνει
βαρέως ἔχουσα, κα[λῶ]ς ποιήσεις καὶ διὰ ταύτην
καὶ δι᾽ ἡμᾶς παραγ[εν]όμενος εἰς τὴν πόλιν, εἴπερ μὴ   30
ἀναγκαιότερόν σ[ε] περισπᾷ. χαριεῖ δὲ καὶ τοῦ
σώματος ἐπιμε[λό]μενος, ἵν᾽ ὑγιαίνῃς.
            ἔρρωσο. (ἔτους) β᾽ Ἐπεὶφ λ᾽.

On the *verso*

            Ἡφαιστίωνι.

and you having sent nothing. And now that Horus who brought
the letter has told about your having been released from your
retreat, I am utterly distressed. Nor is this all, but since your
mother is in great trouble about it, I entreat you for her sake
and for ours to return to the city, unless indeed something most
pressing occupies you. Pray take care of yourself that you may
be in health.

            Good-bye.   Year 2 Epeiph 30.

(Addressed)

    To Hephaestion.

26. ὑπὲρ τοῦ ἀπολελύσθαι κτλ.]
'Ἀπολύομαι 'withdraw oneself from,'
'depart,' as frequently in Polybius,
e.g. vii 17. 2 τῶν μὲν φυλάκων
ἀπολυομένων ἀπὸ τοῦ τόπου τούτου:
cf. Exod. xxxiii 11 ἀπελύετο εἰς τὴν
παρεμβολήν, Ac. xxviii 25 ἀσύμ-
φωνοι δὲ ὄντες πρὸς ἀλλήλους ἀπε-
λύοντο.

31. περισπᾷ] For περισπάω 'occupy,' detain,' cf. P. Tebt. 37. 15 ff.
(i/B.C.) ἐγὼ οὖν περισπώμενος περὶ
ἀναγκαίων γέγραφά σοι ἵνα κ.τ.λ.
The metaphorical sense of ' worry,'

'distract,' as in Lk. x 40 (cf. 1 Cor.
vii 35), is also common in the vernacular, e.g. P. Brit. Mus. 24. 29
(=1, p. 33) (ii/B.C.) ὅπως καὶ αὐτὸς
τῆι Ταθήμει ἀποδοὺς μὴ περισπῶμαι,
'that I myself, having paid Tathemis,
may be no more worried,' P. Tebt.
43. 36 ff. (ii/B.C.) ὅπως μηθενὶ ἐπιτρέ-
πηι...παρενοχλεῖν ἡμᾶς μηδὲ περισπᾶν
κατὰ μηδεμίαν παρεύρεσιν, 'that no
one may be permitted to trouble
us or to worry us on any pretext
whatsoever.'

5. PETITION FROM THE SERAPEUM TWINS

P. PAR. 26.   B.C. 163-2.

Discovered at Memphis and edited by Brunet de Presle among the Paris Papyri, *Notices et Extraits* XVIII, 2, p. 274 ff. See also Witkowski, *Prodromus* p. 30, for various amended readings.

Of the Serapeum documents that have been recovered (cf. No. 6), the greater number refer to the grievances of two girls, twins, by name Thaues and Thaus or Taous. Their story has been graphically reconstructed by Kenyon (*British Museum Papyri* I, p. 2 ff.). Here we can only notice that the twins acted as attendants in the Serapeum, and were consequently entitled to a certain allowance of oil and bread. For some reason this allowance was withheld in B.C. 164-2, and accordingly we find them with the assistance of their friend Ptolemy, son of Glaucias, one of the Serapeum recluses, presenting various petitions for the restitution of their rights. Amongst these is the following document, in which, apparently for the third time, they addressed themselves directly to King Ptolemy Philometor and Queen Cleopatra, on the occasion of a royal visit to Memphis, with the result that, as later reports prove, the temple officers were at length stirred up to look into the matter, and the twins recovered most, if not all, of what was due to them.

COL. I.

Βασιλεῖ Πτολεμαίῳ καὶ Βασιλίσσῃ Κλεοπάτρᾳ τῇ
ἀδελφῇ,
θεοῖς Φιλομήτορσι, χαίρειν. Θαυὴς καὶ Ταοὺς
δίδυμαι, αἱ λειτουργοῦσαι
ἐν τῷ πρὸˢ Μέμφει μεγάλῳ Σαραπιείῳ, καὶ πρότερον
μὲν ὑμῖν
ἐπιδημήσα[σι]ν ἐν Μέμφει καὶ ἀναβᾶσιν εἰς τὸ
ἱερὸν θυσιάσαι
ἐνετύχομεν, καὶ ἐπεδώκαμεν ἔντευξιν, προφερόμεναι
μὴ κομίζεσθαι   5
τὴν καθήκουσαν ἡμῖν δίδοσθαι σύνταξιν τῶν δεόντων
ἔκ τε τοῦ

To King Ptolemy and Queen Cleopatra the sister, gods Philo-
metores, greeting. We, Thaues and Taous, the twin-sisters who
minister in the great Serapeum at Memphis, on a former occasion
when you were in residence at Memphis and had gone up to the
temple to sacrifice petitioned you, and gave in a petition, bringing
before you our plea that we are not receiving the contribution of
necessaries which it is fitting should be given to us both from the

2. λειτουργοῦσαι] For the ceremonial use of this verb, which prepares us for its religious significance
in the Gk Bible, see Deissmann
BS. p. 140 f.

4. ἐπιδημήσασιν] The regular
word for arrival and temporary
sojourn in a place as P. Oxy. 705.
ii. 36 f. ἐπιδημήσ[αν]τες τῷ ἔθνει of
Severus and Caracalla's visit to
Egypt in A.D. 202, and especially
P. Par. 69 (iii/A.D.) where the
arrivals and departures of a strategus are recorded in his day-book by
ἐπι- and ἀποδημέω respectively: see
Archiv IV, p. 374.   Cf. Ac. ii 10,
xvii 21.

5. ἔντευξιν] properly the act of
approaching the king, and thence
the petition addressed to him, his
answer being known as χρηματισμός
(cf. l. 21 χρηματιζόμενα).   In the
N.T. the word is found only in
1 Tim. ii 1, iv 5.
κομίζεσθαι] See the note on P.
Brit. Mus. 42. 7 (= No. 4).

6. σύνταξιν] the regular term for
a contribution from the royal treasury for religious purposes: see
Otto *Priester* I p. 366 ff.   Occasionally the word is used, almost in
the sense of φόρος, of payments to
the government, e.g. P. Fay. 15. 2
(with the Editors' note).

Σαραπιείου καὶ 'Ασκληπιείου. Μέχρι δὲ τοῦ νῦν
οὐ κεκομισμέναι
ἐκκ πλήρους ἠναγκάσμεθ' ὑπὸ τῆς ἀνάγκης ἐπειγό-
μεναι, ὡς ἂν
ὑπὸ τῆς λιμοῦ διαλυόμεναι, πάλιν ἐντυχεῖν ὑμῖν,
καὶ δι' ὀλίων
τὴν τῶν ἀδικούντων ἡμᾶς φιλαυτίαν ἐχθεῖναι. Ὑμῶν
γὰρ ἐκτιθέντων   10
ἔτι ἀπὸ τῶν ἔνπροσθεν χρόνων σύνταξιν τῷ τε
Σαραπιείῳ
καὶ τῷ 'Ασκληπιείῳ, καὶ ἐκ τούτων καὶ τῶν προτοῦ
γενηθεισῶν
δ[ι]δύμων κομισαμένων τὰ ἑαυτῶν καθ' ἡμέραν
δέοντα, καὶ ἡμῖν,
ὅταν ἔβημεν κατ' ἀρχὰς εἰς τὸ ἱερόν, παραχρῆμα
μὲν ὀλίας ἡμέρας,
ὑπέδειξαν ὡς ἂν εὐτακτηθησομένων ἡμῖν τῶν καθη-
κόντων,   15

Serapeum and the Asclepeum. And having failed to receive them
up to the present time in full, we have been compelled, under pressure
of necessity, wasting away as we are through starvation, to petition
you again, and in a few words to set before you the selfishness of
those who are injuring us. For although you already from former
times have proclaimed a contribution for the Serapeum and
Asclepeum, and in consequence of this the twins who were there
before us daily received what they required, to us also when we
first went up to the temple straightway for a few days the impression was conveyed as if everything fitting would be done for us in

---

9. *τῆς λιμοῦ*] Λιμός is masc. in
P. Par. 22. 21: cf. for a like incon-
sistency of gender Lk. iv 25 and
xv 14, and see Moulton *Proleg.*
p. 60.
   δι' ὀλίων]=δι' ὀλίγων, cf. 1 Pet.
v 12, and for the spelling see
Thackeray *Gramm.* I, p. 112.

10. *φιλαυτίαν*] For the corresponding adj. see 2 Tim. iii. 2.
14. *ὅταν ἔβημεν*] One of the
rare instances in the papyri of ὅταν
c. indic., as in Mk iii 11, &c.: see
further Moulton *Proleg.* pp. 168, 248.
15. *ὡς ἂν*] See Moulton *Proleg.*
p. 167.

τὸν δὲ λοιπὸν χρόνον οὐκ ἐξετίθεσαν. Διὸ καὶ πρὸς τοὺς
ἐπιμελητὰς ἐπέμπομεν τοὺς ἐντευξομένους,
καὶ ὑμῖν, καθ᾽ ἃς ἐποεῖσθ᾽ ἐν Μέμφει παρουσίας,
ἐνεφανίζομεν
ὑπὲρ τούτων. Τῶν δὲ πρὸς τοῖς χειρισμοῖς ἐν τῷ Σαραπιείῳ
καὶ Ἀσκληπιείῳ τεταγμένων κατατετολμηκότων καὶ τὰ   20
ὑφ᾽ ὑμῶν ἡμῖν χρηματιζόμενα ἐκφερομένων καὶ οὐδεμίαν
εὐλάβειαν προορωμένων· ἡμῶν δὲ τοῖς δέουσι θλιβομένων

good order, but for the remainder of the time this was not carried out. Wherefore we both sent repeatedly to the supervisors persons to petition on our behalf, and laid information on these matters before you, on the occasion of your visits to Memphis. And when those who had been appointed to the administration in the Serapeum and Asclepeum had insolently maltreated us, and were removing the privileges conferred on us by you, and were paying no regard to religious scruple, and when we were being crushed by our wants, we often made representations even to

18. παρουσίας] For the use of π. as a kind of *term. techn.* in the papyri to describe the official visit of a king or other great personage, cf. *Thess.* p. 145 f., where the corresponding light thrown on the N.T. usage of the word is discussed. See also Deissmann *LO.*² p. 278 ff.

ἐνεφανίζομεν] lit. 'laid information,' but frequently with the added thought of 'against' as in Ac. xxiv 1, xxv 2, 15; cf. P. Eleph. 8. 3 f. (iii/B.C.) ἐμφανίζω σοι Ὧρον Πασᾶτος, a report to the Praetor, and P. Tor. 1. 8. 12 ἐμφανιστοῦ καὶ κατηγόρου (with Peyron's note).

20. κατατετολμηκότων] a LXX

word, 2 Macc. iii 24, v 15 (κατετόλ-μησεν εἰς τὸ...ἱερὸν εἰσελθεῖν).

21. χρηματιζόμενα] See the note on l. 5 above.

22. εὐλάβειαν] The word has apparently the same religious connotation in Prov. xxviii 14: for a corresponding use of the adverb see P. Par. 12. 10 (B.C. 157) εὐλαβῶς μου σχόντος, 'when I was in a devout frame of mind,' and cf. 2 Macc. vi 11, Lk. ii. 25 (adj.).

προορωμένων] an interesting example of the rare Midd. use of π. = 'pay regard to,' 'set before one,' as in Ac. ii 25 (LXX).

καὶ 'Αχομάρρῃ μὲν τῷ ἐπιστάτῃ τοῦ ἱεροῦ πλεονάκι
    διεστάλμεθα
ἀποδιδόναι ἡμῖν· καὶ τῷ υἱῷ δὲ Ψινταέους τοῦ
    ἐπιστάτου τῶν
ἱερῶν, ἀναβάντι πρώην εἰς τὸ ἱερόν, προσήλθομεν,
    καὶ περὶ ἑκάστων   25
μετεδώκαμεν. Καὶ προσκαλεσάμενος τὸν 'Αχομάρρην
συνέταξεν ἀποδοῦναι ἡμῖν τὰ ὀφειλόμενα. Ὁ δέ,
    πάντων
ἀνθρώπων ἀγνωμονέστατος ὑπάρχων, ἡμῖν μὲν ὑπέσ-
    χετο
τὸ προκείμενον ἐπιτελέσειν· τοῦ δὲ τοῦ Ψινταέους
    υἱοῦ ἐκ τῆς

Col. II.

Μέμφεως χωρισθέντος, οὐκέτι   30
οὐδένα λόγον ἐποήσατο. Οὐ μόνον δ᾽ οὗτος
ἀλλὰ καὶ ἄλλοι τῶν ἐκ τοῦ Σαραπιείου

Achomarres the supervisor of the temple to give us (our rights).
And we approached the son of Psintaes the supervisor of
the sacrifices, when he went up to the temple the day before
yesterday, and gave him detailed information. And having called
Achomarres to him, he strictly commanded him to give what was
owing to us. And he, being by nature the most unfeeling of all
mankind, promised us that he would perform what he had been
directed to do, but no sooner had the son of Psintaes departed
from Memphis than he took no further account of the matter.
And not only this man, but also others connected with the

26. μετεδώκαμεν] a quasi-legal
term, suggesting that a certain
responsibility henceforth devolves
on the person to whom the information has been given: cf. P. Brit. Mus.
1231. 12 ff. (=III, p. 109) (A.D. 144)
ἀξιοῦμεν δὲ τοῦ διαστολικοῦ ἀντίγραφον αὐτῷ μεταδοθῆναι...ὅπως ἔχ[ω]ν
ἔγγραπτον παραγγελείαν πρόνοιαν
ποιήσηται τῆς γε[ώρ]γείας κτλ., and
see the introduction to P. Strass. 41.
31. οὐδ. λόγ. ἐπο(=οι)ήσατο] as
in Ac. xx 24.

καὶ ἔτεροι τῶν ἐκ τοῦ Ἀσκληπιείου
ὄντες πρὸς χειρισμοῖς, παρ᾽ ὧν ἔθος ἐστὶν
ἡμᾶς τὰ δέοντα κομίζεσθαι, ἀποστε-   35
ροῦσιν, ὧν τά τε ὀνόματα καὶ τὰ ὀφειλόμενα,
διὰ τὸ εἶναι πλείονα, οὐκ ἐκρίναμεν κατα-
χωρίσαι. Δεόμεθα οὖν ὑμῶν, μίαν
ἔχουσαι ἐλπίδα τὴν ὑφ᾽ ὑμῶν ἐσομέ-
νην ἀντίληψιν, ἀποστεῖλαι ἡμῶν   40
τὴν ἔντευξιν ἐπὶ Διονύσιον τῶν φίλων
καὶ στρατηγόν, ὅπως γράψῃ Ἀπολλωνίῳ
τῷ ἐπιμελητῇ, ἐπιλαβόντα παρ᾽ ἡμῶν
τὴν γραφὴν τῶν ὀφειλομένων ἡμῖν
δεόντων καὶ τίνα πρὸς τίνας χρόνους   45
προσωφείληται καὶ ὑπὸ τίνων,
ἐπαναγκάσῃ αὐτοὺς ἀποδοῦναι ἡμῖν,

Serapeum, and others connected with the Asclepeum in the administration, from whom it is usual for us to receive what we need,
are defrauding, whose names and obligations, because they are
numerous, we have decided not to record.

We beg you therefore, having as our one hope the assistance
that lies in your power, to send away our petition to Dionysius
Privy Councillor and strategus, that he may write to Apollonius the
supervisor to compel them to render to us (what is owing), when he
has received from us the written list of the necessaries owing to
us and what further debts are due us along with the periods for
which they have been owing and the persons who owe them, so

33. ἔτεροι] of the Asclepeum as
distinguished from the ἄλλοι (l. 32)
of the Serapeum. See further Moulton *Proleg.* pp. 79 f., 246.

35. ἀποστεροῦσιν] absol. as Mk
x 19, 1 Cor. vi 8.

38. δεόμεθα] the general term for
petitioning a king, as distinguished
from ἀξιῶ addressed to magistrates:
see Laqueur *Quaestiones* p. 7.

40. ἀντίληψιν] 'assistance,' 'help,'

a sense by no means limited to 'Bibl.
speech' (as Grimm), but frequent in
petitions to the Ptolemies and elsewhere: see Deissmann *BS.* pp. 92,
223.

41. τ. φίλων] partitive gen.: cf.
Ac. xxi 16.

43. ἐπιλαβόντα] accus. attracted
to Διονύσιον.

46. προσωφείληται] Cf. Philem.
19 σεαυτόν μοι προσοφείλεις.

M

ἵνα, πᾶν τὸ ἑξῆς ἔχουσαι, πολλῷ μᾶλλον
τὰ νομιζόμενα τῷ Σαράπει καὶ τῇ Ἴσει
ἐπιτελῶμεν ὑπέρ τε ὑμῶν καὶ τῶν   50
ὑμετέρων τέκνων. Ὑμῖν δὲ γίνοιτο
κρατεῖν πάσης ἧς ἂν αἱρῆσθε χώρας.

                                    Εὐτυχεῖτε.

that, when we have everything in order, we may be much better
able to perform our regular duties to Serapis and to Isis, both for
your own sakes and for the sake of your children.   May it be given
you to hold fast all the territory you desire.   Farewell.

48. τὸ ἑξῆς] Cf. P. Oxy. 282. 7 f.
(A.D. 30—35) ἐπεχορήγησα αὐτῇ τὰ
ἑξῆς καὶ ὑπὲρ δύναμιν.
52. αἱρῆσθε] 'desire,' 'choose';
cf. P. Oxy. 489. 4 (A.D. 117), a will
where the testator reserves the power

during his lifetime of disposing of his
property καθ᾽ ὃν ἐὰν αἱρῶμαι [τρόπον],
'in any manner I choose.'   The aor.
is used of the Divine election in
Deut. xxvi 18, 2 Thess. ii 13 (note).

6.   A DREAM FROM THE SERAPEUM

P. PAR. 51.   B.C. 160.

Discovered at Memphis and edited by Brunet de Presle among
the Paris Papyri, *Notices et Extraits* XVIII, 2 p. 323 f.   See also
Witkowski, *Prodromus*, p. 40, for various amended readings.

In Egypt, as in Assyria and Babylonia, the significance of
dreams was fully recognized, and visitors resorted to the
temple of Serapis at Memphis and other sacred spots in the
hope of receiving assistance in visions of the night regarding
their illnesses and other concerns.

With the following dream may be compared the similar
visions of Ptolemy and Tages recorded in P. Leid. C (Leemans'
Papyri graeci I, p. 117) and the well-known dream of
Nectonabus in P. Leid. U (*ibid.* p. 122), especially as re-
published with a revised text and commentary by Wilcken in
Mélanges Nicole p. 579 ff.

The Bible student hardly needs to be reminded of the dreams of Pharaoh (Gen. xli), or, from other localities, of the Divine messages granted, as they slept, to Jacob (Gen. xxviii 10 ff.) and to Solomon (1 Kings iii 5 ff.).

Πτολε[μαῖος
(ἔτους) κβ', Τῦβι ιβ'. εἰς τὴν ιγ'. Ὤμ[ην
βατίζειν με [ἀπ]ὸ λειβὸς ἕως ἀ[πηλι]ώτου,
καὶ ἀναπίπτομαι ἐπ' ἄχυρον· καὶ [ἄν]θρωπ[ος
ἀπὸ λιβός μου, ἐχόμενός μου· ἀναπίπτει   5
καὶ αὐτός, καὶ ὥσπερ κεκλειμ[ένοι] μου
ἦσαν οἱ ὀφθαλμοί μου, καὶ ἐξαί[φνης] ἀνύγω
τοὺς ὀφθαλμούς μου, καὶ ὁρῶ [τὰς] Διδύμας
ἐν τῷ διδασκαλήῳ τοῦ Τοθῆ[τος]. Ἐκάλεσαν, προσ-
έλεγον. Ὄμμα .. ψυχῆς θάρσ[ει] .. καμητην   10
τὴν ὁδὸν ἐπ' ἐμέ, ὅτι μεταβέβλ[ηκα] τὴν κοίτην
μου. Ἤκουσα Τοθῆς λέγων· Ἐπεύχομαι·

Ptolemy, in the 22nd year, Tubi 12 to 13. I dreamt that I was going from West to East, and sat down upon chaff. And West from me there was someone, who was near to me. He also sat down, and my eyes were as it were closed. Suddenly I open my eyes, and see the Twins in the school of Tothes. They called, I answered. Eye...of my soul, take courage...for I have changed my bed. I heard Tothes saying, I am praying. Why are you

2. ἔτους κτλ.] The date, which forms part of the heading, shows that Ptolemy had come to Memphis in the 22nd year of his reign, and that the dream was granted to him on·the night between Tubi 12 and 13, or Jan. 7—8, B.C. 160. With εἰς τ. ιγ' cf. Mt. xxviii 1.

3. βατ(=δ)ίζειν ἀπὸ λειβός] By a special usage λίψ could mean West to the Egyptians, as Libya lay directly west from them: hence, as Deissmann (BS. p. 141 f.) has pointed out, its occurrence in the LXX, 2 Chron. xxxii 30, xxxiii 14, Dan. viii 5 in this sense, though

elsewhere it is used accurately for South; cf. e.g. Gen. xiii 14, xx. 1, and from the N.T. Ac. xxvii 12.

4. ἐπ' ἄχυρον] Cf. Mt. iii 12, Lk. iii 17.

5. ἐχόμενός μου] For ἔχομαι of local contiguity cf. Mk i 38 (with Swete's note).

7. ἐξαίφνης] For the form ἐξαί-φνης, which is read by WH. only in Ac. xxii 6, see their Notes², p. 158.

8. τὰς Διδύμας] See the introd. to No. 5.

12. ἐπεύχομαι] Cf. Deut. x 8 ἐπεύχεσθαι ἐπὶ τῷ ὀνόματι αὐτοῦ.

τί ταῦτα λέγεις; Ἐγὼ καταστήσ[ας] Διδύμας
ἐπί σε· ὁρῶ σοι αὐτὸν καθιστῶντα
αὐτάς. Κλάγω ἔμπροσθεν αὐτῶν. Ἐπορευόμην   15
ἕως καταλάβω αὐτὰς καὶ ἔρχομαι εἰς τὴν ῥύβην
μετ' αὐτῶν. Ἔλεγον αὐτὰς αὐτ[.] ὅτι ἔτι βραχὺ
ἔχω ἐν τῷ ἄθρει καὶ πρωὶ ἔσται ὡς μὴ [προ]τοῦ.
Ἴδον
μίαν αὐτῶν ἐρχομένην πρὸς ...... σκοτινὸν
τόπον, καὶ καθιζάνει ὀ⟨ύ⟩ρούσα. Εἶδον εὐσ... αὐτῶν   20
ἀποκεκαθίσται. Εἶπα Ἁρμάει σπ[εῦσαι ἐλ]θῖν αὐτόν,
καὶ ἄλλα τινὰ εἶδον πολλά, καὶ πάλιν ἠξίωκα τὸν
Σάραπιν καὶ τὴν Ἴσιν λέγων· Ἐλθέ μοι, θεὰ θεῶν,
εἵλεως γινομένη, ἐπάκουσόν μου, ἐλέησον τὰς Διδύμας.

saying this? I have conducted the Twins to you. I see him
conducting them to you. I weep before them. I went on until
I had laid hold of them, and I came to the street along with them.
I said, 'I have still for a little while to gaze (in the temple), and it will
be early as not formerly.' I saw one of them going to a dark place,
and she sits down—. I saw...sat down. I told Hermais to hasten
to come himself, and many other things I saw, and again I asked
Serapis and Isis saying: Come to me, goddess of the gods, show
thyself merciful, hear me, have pity on the Twins. Thou hast con-

13. καταστήσ[ας]] 'conducted':
cf. Josh. vi 23, 2 Chron. xxviii 15,
and from the N.T. Ac. xvii 15 οἱ δὲ
καθιστάνοντες τὸν Παῦλον ἤγαγον
ἕως Ἀθηνῶν.

16. ῥύβ(=μ)ην] 'street' or 'lane,'
as generally in later Gk, a usage well
known from the four occurrences of
the word in the N.T. (Mt. vi 2,
Lk. xiv 21, Ac. ix 11, xii 10): cf.
Kennedy *Sources of N.T. Gk*, p. 15 f.

17. ὅτι] For ὅτι *recitativum* in
the N.T. cf. WM. p. 683 note 1,
Blass *Gramm.* pp. 233, 286.

22. ἠξίωκα] aor. perf.: see Moul-

ton *Proleg.* p. 143 ff. For the weakened sense of the verb cf. P. Par.
49. 10 f. (ii/B.C.) τοῦ δὲ ἀδελφοῦ σου
συμπεσόντος μοι...καὶ ἀξιώσαντός με.

23. ἐλθέ μοι, θεὰ θεῶν κτλ.] practically the same formula as in P.
Leid. U. ii, 17 ff., and evidently
belonging to the living Isis-cult
(Wilcken).

24. εἵλεως γινομένη] Cf. Mt.
xvi 22, Heb. viii 12.

ἐπάκουσόν μου] Cf. 2 Cor. vi 2
(LXX).

ἐλέησον κτλ.] Cf. Mt. ix 27, &c.

Σὺ κατεδίκας Διδύμας· ἐμὲ λέλυκας πολιὰς ἔχων·   25
ἀλλὰ οἶδα ὅτι ἐν .... χρώνῳ παύσομαι. Αὗται δὲ
γυναῖκές εἰσιν. 'Εὰν μιανθῶσιν, [οὐ μ]ὴ γένονται
καθαραὶ πώποτε.

demned the Twins. Me with my gray hairs hast thou absolved ;
but I know that in a...time I shall have rest. But these are women.
If they are defiled, they shall never at all be pure.

25. κατεδίκας] = κατεδίκασας, here construed with the acc. of the person, as in the LXX and N.T. In classical writers it is followed by the genitive.

πολιάς] Cf. Prov. xx 23 δόξα δὲ πρεσβυτέρων πολιαί.

ἔχων] for ἔχοντα. For similar breaches of concord in the papyri see Moulton *Proleg.* p. 60.

27. μιανθῶσιν] so Witk. for μὴ ἀνθῶσιν (Edd.). Cf. Tit. i. 15, Heb. xii. 15.

7. LETTER OF APOLLONIUS

P. PAR. 47.   c. B.C. 153.

Discovered at Memphis and edited by Brunet de Presle, *Notices et Extraits* XVIII. 2, p. 314 ff., and with a revised text, which is followed here, by Witkowski, *Ep. Gr. Priv.* p. 63 ff.

Several letters written by or to Apollonius, a κάτοχος in the Serapeum (see No. 4), have been recovered (P. Par. 40—47.), and of these the following exhibits various points of interest though its general meaning is far from clear. All we can gather is that Apollonius was at the time in sore straits of some sort (l. 9 ff.), and felt that he had been deceived even by the gods (ll. 6 ff., 28): hence the singular and ironical address πρὸς τοὺς τὴν ἀλήθε(= ει)αν λέγοντε(= α)ς.

Gerhard (*Untersuchungen*, p. 65) cites this letter as the only example of a Greek papyrus known to him with a personal greeting in the outside address (Πτολεμαίῳ χαίρειν).

Ἀπολλώνιος Πτολεμαίωι
τῶι πατρὶ χαίρειν. ὀμνύ-
ο τὸν Σαρᾶπιν,—ἰ μὴ μικρόν
τι ἐντρέπομαι, οὐκ ἄν με
ἶδες τὸ π<ό>ρσωπόν μου   5
πόποτε,—ὅτι ψευδῆι
πάντα καὶ οἱ παρὰ σὲ
θεοὶ ὁμοίως, ὅτι ἐν-
βέβληκαν ὑμᾶς εἰς ὕλην
μεγάλην καὶ οὐ δυνάμε-   10
θα ἀποθανεῖν· κὰν ἰδῆς,
ὅτι μέλλομεν σωθῆναι,
τότε βαπτιζώμεθα.
γίνωσ<κε>, ὅτι πιράσεται

Apollonius to Ptolemaeus his father greeting. I swear by Serapis,—but for the fact that I am a little ashamed, you would never yet have seen my face—that all things are false and your gods with the rest, because they have cast us into a great forest, where we may possibly die: and even if you know that we are about to be saved, just at the moment we are immersed in trouble. Know that the

2. πατρί] The exact relationships of the various persons in this group of papyri (see introd.) are by no means clear, but it is possible that throughout both πατήρ and ἀδελφός refer not to family connexion, but to membership in the same religious community: see Otto *Priester* I, p. 124, note 3, who for this use of πατήρ refers to Ziebarth *Griechisches Vereinswesen*, p. 154: for the religious connotation of ἀδελφός see 1 Thess. i 4 (note).

ὀμνύο(=ω) τ. Σαρᾶπιν] Cf. P. Oxy. 239. 5 (A.D. 66) ὀμνύω Νέρωνα, and the same acc. of invocation in Jas. v 12. For the transition from the Ptolemaic Σαρᾶπις to Σεράπις in the Roman age, see Mayser *Gramm.* p. 57, and cf. Thackeray *Gramm.* I,

p. 73 f.

4. ἐντρέπομαι] 'am ashamed': for this late metaphorical use of ἐ., found both in the LXX and N.T., cf. 2 Thess. iii 14 (note), and for the use of the *present* in the protasis, as in Lk. xvii 6, see Moulton *Proleg.* p. 200 note 2.

8. ἐνβέβληκαν κτλ.] Cf. Lk. xii 5 ἐμβαλεῖν εἰς τ. γέενναν. Ὕλην is apparently used metaphorically here much in the sense of Dante's 'selva oscura.' Ὑμᾶς stands for ἡμᾶς by a common confusion.

13. βαπτιζώμεθα] another metaphorical usage, recalling strikingly the language of Mk x 38 δύνασθε... τὸ βάπτισμα ὃ ἐγὼ βαπτίζομαι βαπτισθῆναι;

ὁ δραπέ[τη]ς μὴ ἀφῖναι   15
ἡμᾶς ἐ[πὶ τ]ῶν τόπων
ἴναι, χάριν γὰρ ἡμῶν
ἠζημίοται εἰς χαλκοῦ
τ(άλαντα) ιε'. ὁ στρατηγὸς ἀνα-
βαίν<ει> αὔριον εἰς τὸ Σαραπι-   20
ῆν καὶ δύο ἡμέρας ποι-
εῖ ἐν τῷ Ἀνουβιείωι
πινῶν. οὐκ ἔστι ἀνακύ-
ψα<ι με> πόποτε ἐν τῇ Τρικομίαι
ὑπὸ τῆς αἰσχύνης, ἰ καὶ   25
αὑτοὺς δεδώκαμεν
καὶ ἀποπεπτώκαμεν
πλανόμενοι ὑπὸ τῶν
θεῶν καὶ πιστεύοντες
τὰ ἐνύπνια.   εὐτύχει.   30

runaway will try not to allow us to remain on the spot, for on our account he has been fined to the amount of 15 bronze talents. The strategus goes up tomorrow to the Serapeum and spends two days in the Anubeum fasting. It is not possible ever to look up again in Tricomia for very shame, now that we have collapsed and fallen from hope, being deceived by the gods and trusting in dreams. Farewell.

15. ὁ δραπέ[τη]ς] The reference according to Witkowski, to whom the reading (for the Editor's ὅπ[ως] ἀπέ[χῃ]) is due, is to a runaway slave Menedemus, whom Apollonius mentions in P. Par. 45. 6, ὁρῶ ἐν τῷ ὕπνῳ τὸν δραπέδην Μενέδημον ἀντικείμενον ἡμῖν.

17. χάριν] For χάριν before the word it governs, as in 1 Jo. iii 12, cf. P. Tebt. 34. 6 (c. B.C. 100) χάριν τοῦ παρ' αὐτοῦ ἀπηγμένου, P. Oxy. 743. 29 (B.C. 2) χάριν τῶν ἐκφορίων.

18. ἠ(=ἐ)ζημίο(=ω)ται] cf. Phil. iii 8 τὰ πάντα ἐζημιώθην.

22. Ἀνουβιείωι] the smaller temple within the precincts of the Serapeum dedicated to Anubis.

23. πινῶν] l. πεινῶν.

ἀνακύψαι] For a similar metaphorical use cf. Job x 15, Lk. xxi 28.

24. Τρικο(=ω)μίαι] the name of a village (Wilcken, Witk.). Cf. Τρεῖς Ταβέρναι, Ac. xxviii 15.

27. ἀποπεπτώκαμεν] Witkowski compares Polyb. i. 87. 1 πίπτω ταῖς ἐλπίσιν.

30. ἐνύπνια] See the introd. to No. 6.

On the *verso*

(in small letters)	(in larger letters)
πρὸς τοὺς	Πτολε[μ]αί-
τὴν ἀλή-	ωι χαίρειν.
θεαν λέγοντες.	

(Addressed) To those that speak the truth. To Ptolemaeus greeting.

8. A LETTER OF INTRODUCTION

P. Goodspeed 4.   ii/b.c.

Edited by Goodspeed in *Greek Papyri from the Cairo Museum*, p. 8.
See also Witkowski, *Ep. Gr. Priv.* p. 70 f.

A letter from Polycrates to Philoxenus introducing to his notice one Glaucias, who was in all probability the bearer of the letter: cf. P. Oxy. 292 (= No. 14).

> Πολ[υ]κράτης Φ[ιλ]οξένω
> χαίρειν. εἰ ἔρρωσαι καὶ
> τἄλλα σοι κατὰ λόγον ἐστίν,
> εἴη ἂν ὡς αἱρούμεθα, καὶ
> αὐτοὶ δ' ὑγιαίνομεν.   5
> ὑπὲρ ὧν ἠβουλόμεθα,
> ἀπεστάλκαμεν πρὸς σὲ

Polycrates to Philoxenus greeting. If you are well and things in general are going right, it will be as we desire. We ourselves are in health. As regards those things we wished, we have sent to

3. κατὰ λόγον] Cf. P. Brit. Mus. 42. 2 (= No. 4).
4. αἱρούμεθα] Cf. P. Par. 26. 51 (= No. 5).
6. ὑπὲρ ὧν] For this weakened use of ὑπέρ, in which the original meaning of 'in the interest of' is practically lost sight of, cf. 2 Thess ii 1 (note).

Γλαυκίαν ὄντα ἡμῶν
ἴδιον κοινολογησόμενόν σοι.
χαριεῖ οὖν ἀκούσας   10
αὐτοῦ καὶ περὶ ὧν παρα-
γέγονεν ὑποδείξας,
μάλιστα δὲ σαυτοῦ ἐπι-
μελόμενος ἵν᾿ ὑγιαίνῃς.
ἔρρωσο. (ἔτους) κθ᾿ Φαμενώ(θ) η[15

On the *verso*

Φιλοξένωι.

you Glaucias who is ours to consult you. Please therefore give
him a hearing, and instruct him concerning those things he has
come about. But above all take care of yourself that you may be
in health. Good-bye. The 29th year, Phamenoth....
(Addressed)   To Philoxenus.

9. ἴδιον] practically = ἑαυτῶν, in
accordance with a common usage in
late Gk: cf. Job vii 10, Mt. xxii 5,
1 Cor. vii 2, 1 Thess. ii 14 (note);
but see also P. Oxy. 37. ii. 1 (= No.
18), note.
    κοινολογησόμενον] Cf. 1 Macc.
xiv 9, xv 28 (ἀπέστειλε...Ἀθηνό-
βιον...κοινολογησόμενον αὐτῷ), and
for the corresponding subst. see
2 Macc. xiv 22 and P. Fay. 12. 15 f.

(c. B.C. 103) ἐκ κοινολογ[ί]α[ς] τ[ῆ]ς
συνσταθείσης πρὸς αὐτούς.
    12. ὑποδείξας] Cf. 2 Chron. xv 3 A
καὶ οὐχ ἱερέως ὑποδεικνύοντος 'without a teaching priest,' Aristeas 112
(ed. Wendland) διὰ τὸ καλῶς ἡμῖν
τὸν Ἐλεάζαρον ὑποδεδειχέναι τὰ
προειρημένα.
    15. ἔτους κθ᾿] the 29th year either
of Philometor, i.e. B.C. 152, or of
Euergetes II, i.e. B.C. 141.

9. A PROMISE OF REWARD

P. GOODSPEED 5.   ii/B.C.

From Gebelên. Edited by Goodspeed in *Greek Papyri from the Cairo Museum*, p. 9.

Goodspeed understands the following note as a promise on the part of Peteuris to pay his contribution towards the στέφανος, or present which was made to the King on his accession or some other notable occasion (cf. 1 Macc. x 29 and see Wilcken *Gr. Ostr.* I, p. 295 ff.). But Wilcken (*Archiv* II, p. 578 f.) has shown good grounds for believing that it is rather a reward which Peteuris offers to his unnamed correspondent for assistance in releasing him from some obligation, perhaps military service.

> Παρὰ Πετεύριος
> διεθέντος μου
> διὰ τῆς σῆς σπ-
> ουδῆς ὑπάρξει
> σοι εἰς στέφανον
> χαλκοῦ (τάλαντα) πέν-
> τε γ(ίνεται) (τάλαντα) ε΄.
> εὐτύχει.

From Peteuris. On my being released through your efforts, there will fall to you by way of reward five talents of copper. Total 5 talents. Farewell.

2. διεθέντος] not = διαθέντος (Goodspeed), but 1 aor. part. pass. of διίημι according to Wilcken, who compares the use of the verb in Xen. *Hell.* ii. 4. 39 διῆκε τὸ στράτευμα. Add P. Petr. II 19 (1 *a*) 8 f. (iii/B.C.) διέσθαι [ἀπὸ τῆς] φυ[λα]κῆς, 'to set free from prison.'

5. στέφανον] 'reward.' For this wider use of the word cf. P. Par. 42. 11 f. where a certain Apollonius is promised a στεφάνιον ('gratification') of 3 talents for services rendered to the police of Memphis. For the more special application indicated above (cf. introd.) see further 1 Thess. ii 19 (note).

10. PETITION OF A TAX-FARMER

P. TEBT. 40.   B.C. 117.

Discovered at Tebtunis, and edited by Grenfell, Hunt, and Smyly in *Tebtunis Papyri* I, p. 140 ff.

A petition from a tax-farmer of Kerkeosiris asking that he should be placed under the protection of the royal scribe of the village. A docket appended to the petition shows that it was forwarded by the scribe to Menches the komogrammateus with the request that it should be given effect to. For similar advantages derived from official 'protection' see P. Tebt. 34 (quoted in note on l. 9); while as showing how even the officials themselves had recourse to bribery to secure the goodwill of their superiors, it may be noted that this very Menches, according to P. Tebt. 9, undertook to make certain payments in kind to the village on condition of his reappointment as komogrammateus.

ἐλ(άβομεν) ἔτους νγ´ Τῦβι ιε´.

2nd hand Ἀμεννεῖ βασιλικῶι γραμματεῖ
          παρὰ Πνεφερῶτος τοῦ Παοῦτος
          τοῦ ἐξειληφότος τὴν ζυτηρὰν
          καὶ νιτρικὴν Κερκεοσίρεως τῆς   5
          Πολέμωνος μερίδος εἰς τὸ νγ´ (ἔτος).
          σαφέστερον μετειληφὼς τοὺς

Received in the 53rd year, Tubi 15.

To Amenneus, royal scribe, from Pnepheros son of Paous, the contractor for the beer and nitrate tax at Kerkeosiris in the division of Polemon for the 53rd year. Having gained undoubted informa-

---

4. ζυτηράν] Beer, like oil, was probably a government monopoly, and the Editors think it very likely that the sale of nitrate, which was used for washing purposes (ἡ νιτρικὴ πλύνου, see Wilcken *Gr. Ostr.* I, p. 264), was also controlled by the state.

ἐκ τῆς κώμης ὁμοθυμαδὸν
ἀντέχεσθαι τῆς σῆς σκέπης,
καὶ αὐτὸς προθυμούμενος εἶναι   10
ἐκ τῆς οἰκίας διὰ τὸ μάλιστα
ἐπιβάλλειν προνοεῖσθαι τῶν
βασιλικῶν, ἀξιῶ συντάξαι
γράψαι Δημητρίωι τῶι τῆς
κώμης ἐπιστάτει καὶ Νικάνορι   15
ἀρχιφυλακίτει καὶ Μεγχεῖ κωμο-
γραμματεῖ καὶ τοῖς πρεσβυτέροις
τῶν γεωργῶν ἐπαναγκάσαι
τοὺς ἐκ τῆς κώμης κατακολου-

tion that the inhabitants of the village are with one accord holding
fast to your protection, and being myself eager to be a member
of your house because it chiefly falls to you to look after the
interests of the Crown, I beg you to give orders to write to
Demetrius the epistates of the village and to Nicanor the archi-
phylacites and to Menches the village-scribe and to the elders of
the cultivators, to compel the inhabitants of the village to follow

8. ὁμοθυμαδόν] 'with one accord'
as in the N.T., e.g. Ac. i 14 ἦσαν
προσκαρτεροῦντες ὁμοθυμαδὸν τῇ
προσευχῇ.

9. ἀντέχεσθαι κτλ.] Cf. P. Tebt.
34 (*c.* B.C. 100), a letter urging steps
to be taken for the release of a debtor
from prison, on the ground that he
was ὑπὸ σκέπην (under the 'protection') of a certain Demetrius, apparently an official of high rank.
For ἀντέχομαι, which in the N.T.
always retains its primary sense of
'hold firmly to' (Mt. vi 24, &c.),
cf. P. Par. 14. 22 f. (ii/B.C.) οὐθενὸς
δικαίου ἀντεχόμενοι.

10. προθυμούμενος] Cf. P. Tebt.
23. 10 f. (*c.* B.C. 119 or 114) καλῶς
ποιήσεις φιλοτιμότερον προθυμηθείς,
and for the use of the subst., as in
Ac. xvii 11, see Deissmann *BS.*
p. 254 f.

11. ἐκ τ. οἰκίας] The same phrase
is found in P. Tebt. 54. 4 f. (B.C. 86)

παρὰ Μέλανος τῶν ἐκ τῆς σῆς οἰκία[s].

12. ἐπιβάλλειν] a legal word; for
exx. of its use, as in Lk. xv 12 τὸ
ἐπιβάλλον μέρος, see Deissmann *BS.*
p. 230.

προνοεῖσθαι] For the compound
phrase πρόνοιαν ποιεῖσθαι c. gen., as
in Rom. xiii 14, cf. P. Hib. 79. 3
(*c.* B.C. 260) ὧν πρόνοιαν ποιεῖ.

17. τοῖς πρεσβυτέροις κτλ.] an
early example of the title π. as
applied to the holders of a civil
office, see further Deissmann *BS.*
p. 154 ff., and for the later religious connotation of the word *ibid.*
p. 233 ff., and Otto *Priester* I, p. 49.
The γεωργοί were cultivators of
crown lands, who paid rent in kind.

19. κατακολουθεῖν] Ci. LXX,
Dan. ix 10 κατακολουθῆσαι τῷ
νόμῳ σου. In the N.T. (Lk. xxiii
55, Ac. xvi 17) the verb is only
found in its literal sense.

θεῖν τοῖς ἐξ ἀρχῆς ἐθισμοῖς   20
ὅπως δύνωμαι τὰ καθήκοντα
ἀπευτακτεῖν.   εὐτύχει.

3rd hand   Μεγχῆι κωμογρ(αμματεῖ).   γενηθήτω
τῶι ὑποτελεῖ τὸ δίκαιον
κατὰ τοὺς τῆς κώμης   25
ἐθισμούς.   (ἔτους) νγ΄ Τῦβι ιγ΄.

On the *verso*
3rd hand   Μεγχῆι.

the ancient customs, that I may be able to pay my dues regularly.
Farewell.

To Menches village-scribe. Let justice be done to the tax-
payer in accordance with the customs of the village. The 53rd
year, Tubi 13.

(Addressed) To Menches.

20. τοῖς ἐξ ἀρχῆς ἐθισμοῖς] Cf.
P. Par. 16. 23 f. (B.C. 127) κα[τα]κο-
λουθεῖν τοῖς ἐξ ἀρχῆς ἐθισμοῖς καὶ
μη[θὲν ἐνκαινί]ζειν.
24. ὑποτελεῖ] 'a wide term ap-

plied to classes who contributed in
different capacities to the revenues
derived from the royal monopolies'
(Edd.).

11. PREPARATIONS FOR A ROMAN VISITOR

P. TEBT. 33.   B.C. 112.

Discovered at Tebtunis, and edited by Grenfell, Hunt, and Smyly
in *Tebtunis Papyri* 1, p. 127 ff.

A letter announcing the approaching visit to the Fayûm
of a Roman senator Lucius Memmius, who may perhaps be
identified with the father of C. Memmius Gemellus to whom
Lucretius dedicated the *De Rerum Natura*. The local authorities are instructed to show him every attention, and to let him
see the ordinary sights, the sacred crocodiles, the labyrinth,

&c., all of which are described by Strabo on the occasion of his visit about 100 years later. After the Roman occupation no person of senatorial rank was allowed to set foot in Egypt without the express permission of the Emperor (Tac. *Ann.* ii 59).

Ἑρμ(ίας) Ὥρωι χαί(ρειν). τῆς πρὸς Ἀσκλη(πιάδην)
ἐπισ(τολῆς) ἀντίγρ(αφον) ὑπόκι(ται).
[φρόν]τισον οὖν ἵνα γένη(ται) ἀκολούθως. ἔρρω(σο).
[(ἔτους)] ε′ Ξαντικοῦ ιζ′ Μεχεὶρ ιζ′.

Ἀσκλη(πιάδει). Λεύκιος Μέμμιος Ῥωμαῖος τῶν ἀπὸ
συνκλήτου ἐν μίζονι ἀξιώματι κα[ὶ] τιμῆι
κείμενος τὸν ἐκ τῆς πό(λεως) ἀνάπλουν ἕως τοῦ Ἀρσι(νοί-
τον) νο(μοῦ)   5
ἐπὶ θεωρίαν ποιούμενος μεγαλο{υ}πρεπέστερον
ἐγδεχθήτωι, καὶ φρόντισον ὡς ἐπὶ τῶν
καθηκόντων τόπων αἵ τε αὐλαὶ κατασκευασ-

Hermias to Horus, greeting. Appended is a copy of the letter to Asclepiades. Take care therefore that action is taken in accordance with it. Goodbye. The 5th year, Xandicus 17, Mecheir 17.

To Asclepiades. Lucius Memmius a Roman Senator, who occupies a position of highest rank and honour, is making the voyage from the city as far as the Arsinoite nome to see the sights. Let him be received with the utmost magnificence, and take care that at the proper places the guest-chambers be got ready, and the

---

2. ἀκολούθως] Cf. P. Brit. Mus. 177. 14 (=II, p. 169) (A.D. 40—1) ἀκολούθως τῇ τοῦ πατρὸς ἡμῶν διαθήκῃ.

Ξαντ(=δ)ικοῦ κτλ.] The date shows that by this time the Macedonian and Egyptian calendars had been equated, cf. p. xviii.

3 f. Ῥωμαῖος τῶν ἀπὸ συνκλήτου] With this use of ἀπό, where in classical Gk we should expect ἐκ, cf. Ac. xii 1 τινὰς τῶν ἀπὸ τῆς ἐκκλησίας.

6. θεωρίαν] Cf. 3 Macc. v 24, Lk. xxiii 48.

μεγαλοπρεπέστερον] The adj.,

which occurs several times in the LXX, is found in the N.T. only in 2 Pet. i 17. The adv. is not infrequent in the inscriptions, e.g. *O.G.I.S.* 513. 11 (of a priestess—iii/A.D.) ἱερασαμένην ἐνδόξως καὶ μεγαλοπρεπῶς.

8. αὐλαί] apparently 'guest-chambers' (Edd.), a usage which supports the N.T. application of the word to the *house* itself, or *palace*, as distinguished from the *court*, e.g. Mt. xxvi 3 (as against Meyer *ad l.*).

κατασκευασ[θ]ῇ[ο]ῦται] Cf. Heb. iii 4 πᾶς γὰρ οἶκος κατασκευάζεται ὑπό τινος.

[θ]ήσ[ο]νται καὶ αἱ ἀπὸ τούτων ἐγβα(τηρίαι) ε[·]ιε[···

π····συντελεσθήσονται καὶ αὐτῶι προσ-   10
ενεχθήσεται ἐπὶ τῆς ἐγβα(τηρίας) τὰ ὑπογεγρ(αμμένα)
ξένια,
καὶ τ[ὰ] εἰς τὸν τῆς αὐλῆς καταρτισμὸν
καὶ τὸ γεινόμενον τῶι Πετεσούχωι καὶ τοῖς κροκο(δείλοις)
ψωμίον καὶ τὰ πρὸς τὴν τοῦ λαβυρίνθου θέαν
καὶ τὰ·[··]·[··σ]ταθησόμενα θύματα καὶ τῆς   15
θυσί[α]ς·····χ·ηκ·ν[···]ται, τὸ δ' ὅλον ἐπὶ πάν[των
τὴν μεγίστην φροντίδα ποιουμένου τοῦ εὐδοκοῦν[τ]α
τὸν ἄνδρα κατασταθῆ[ναι] τὴν πᾶσαν προσενέγκαι
σπουδὴ[ν]····

Several much mutilated lines follow.

landing-stages to them be completed, and that there be brought
to him at the landing-stage the appended gifts of hospitality, and
that the things for the furnishing of the guest-chamber, and the
customary tit-bits for Petesuchus and the crocodiles, and the
necessaries for the view of the labyrinth, and the offerings and
sacrifices, be provided. In short, take the greatest care on all
points that the visitor may thereby be well satisfied, and display
the utmost zeal....'

9. ἐγβα(τηρίαι)] Cf. P. Petr. II,
4 (1), where certain quarry-men ἀπὸ
τῆς ἐγβατηρίας complain that they
have been ill-treated by the 'over-
seer' or 'taskmaster' (τοῦ ἐργο-
διώκτου, as Exod. iii 7).
12. καταρτισμόν] Cf. Eph. iv
12 (with Robinson's note), and for
the corresponding verb cf. 1 Thess.
iii 10 (note).
13. τοῖς κροκο(δείλοις)] Ci. Strabo
xvii 811 σφόδρα γὰρ ἐν τῷ νομῷ
τούτῳ τιμῶσι τὸν κροκόδειλον καὶ
ἔστιν ἱερὸς παρ' αὐτοῖς ἐν λίμνῃ καθ'
αὑτὸν τρεφόμενος, χειροήθης τοῖς
ἱερεῦσι· καλεῖται δὲ Σοῦχος· τρέ-
φεται δὲ σιτίοις καὶ κρέασι καὶ οἴνῳ,

προσφερόντων ἀεὶ ὧν ξένων τῶν ἐπὶ
τὴν θέαν ἀφικνουμένων.
14. ψωμίον] an early instance of
this N.T. diminutive (Jo. xiii 26 ff.):
cf. P. Grenf. II, 67. 14 (= No. 45).
λαβυρίνθου] Herodotus (ii 148)
describes the pyramids as λόγου
μέζονες 'passing description,' but
adds ὁ δὲ δὴ λαβύρινθος καὶ τὰς
πυραμίδας ὑπερβάλλει. Strabo (l.c.),
on the other hand, calls it πάρισον
ταῖς πυραμίσιν ἔργον.
17. εὐδοκοῦντα] The verb is
confined to later Greek writers,
and in the N.T. has usually the
idea of hearty goodwill associated
with it; cf. 1 Thess. ii 8 (note).

12. HILARION TO HIS WIFE ALIS

P. OXY. 744.　　　　　　　　　　　　　　B.C. I.

Discovered at Oxyrhynchus and edited by Grenfell and Hunt in
Oxyrhynchus Papyri IV, p. 243 f.　See also Lietzmann, *Gr. Papyri*,
p. 8 f.; Witkowski, *Ep. Gr. Priv.* p. 97 f.; and Deissmann, *Licht vom
Osten²*, p. 109 f. (E. Tr. p. 154 ff.).

A letter from a man, who had gone to Alexandria, to his
wife regarding certain domestic matters.

Ἰλαρίων[α] Ἄλιτι τῆι ἀδελφῆι πλεῖστα χαίρειν καὶ Βεροῦτι τῇ κυρίᾳ μου καὶ ᾿Απολλω-
νάριν. γίνωσκε ὡς ἔτι καὶ νῦν ἐν ᾿Αλεξαν-
δρε(ί)ᾳ ⟨ἐ⟩σμέν· μὴ ἀγωνιᾷς ἐὰν ὅλως εἰσ-
πορεύονται, ἐγὼ ἐν ᾿Αλεξανδρε(ί)ᾳ μένω.　　　　5
ἐρωτῶ σε καὶ παρακαλῶ σε ἐπιμελή-

Hilarion to Alis his sister, heartiest greetings, and to my dear
Berous and Apollonarion.　Know that we are still even now in
Alexandria.　Do not worry if when all the others return I remain
in Alexandria.　I beg and beseech of you to take care of the little

1. ἀδελφῆι] 'sister,' and no
doubt 'wife' (GH.): cf. P. Brit.
Mus. 42. 1 (= No. 4), note.

2. τ. κυρίᾳ] an address of
courtesy, as in 2 Jo. 1, 5; cf. from
a later date P. Leip. 110. 1, 24 f.
(c. iii/iv A.D.) Σαραπίω]ν τῇ κ[υ]ρίᾳ
μου μητρί...τὴν κυρίαν μου ἀδελφὴν
πολλὰ προσαγόρευε Ταῆσιν.

4. ἐὰν ὅλως εἰσπορεύονται] with
reference apparently to the return
of the writer's fellow-workmen from
Alexandria to Oxyrhynchus (Deissmann).

6. ἐρωτῶ] 'beg,' 'request,' as

frequently in late Gk.　Both alone
and in conjunction with παρακαλῶ
it is a common epistolary phrase;
cf. 1 Thess. iv 1 (note).

ἐπιμελήθητι] c. dat., as in P.
Tebt. 58. 62 f. (B.C. 111) ἐπειμένου
(= ἐπιμέλου) τοῖς ἐν οἴκωι; cf. Xen.
Hell. v. 4. 4 ἐπεμελεῖτο τοῖς πολε-
μάρχοις.　In the N.T. (Lk. x 34 f.,
1 Tim. iii 5) the word is construed
regularly with the gen., and similarly
in the LXX (except 1 Esdr. vi 26
προσέταξεν δὲ ἐπιμεληθῆναι Σισίννῃ):
cf. P. Par. 32. 30 f. (ii/B.C.) ἐπιμέλου
δὲ τοῦ σώματος.

θ⟨ητ⟩ι τῷ παιδίῳ καὶ ἐὰν εὐθὺς ὀψώνιον λάβωμεν ἀποστελῶ σε ἄνω. ἐὰν
πολλαπολλῶν τέκῃς, ἐὰν ἦν ἄρσε-
νον, ἄφες, ἐὰν ἦν θήλεα, ἔκβαλε.   10
εἴρηκας δὲ Ἀφροδισιᾶτι ὅτι μή με
ἐπιλάθῃς· πῶς δύναμαί σε ἐπι-
λαθεῖν; ἐρωτῶ σε οὖν ἵνα μὴ ἀγω-
νιάσῃς.

(ἔτους) κθ' Καίσαρος Παῦνι κγ'.   15

On the *verso*

Ἱλαρίων Ἄλιτι ἀπόδος.

child, and as soon as we receive wages I will send them to you.
If—good luck to you!—you bear a child, if it is a boy, let
it live; if it is a girl, expose it. You told Aphrodisias, 'Do not
forget me.' How can I forget you? I beg you therefore not to
worry.

The 29th year of Caesar, Pauni 23.

(Addressed)
Hilarion to Alis, deliver.

7. ὀψώνιον λάβωμεν] The same
phrase is found in 2 Cor. xi 8, and
for a similar use in the inscriptions
see Deissmann *BS.* p. 266. To the
examples given there of ὀψ. = 'wages,'
'salary,' add B.G.U. 621. 12, P.
Oxy. 514. 3 (both ii/A.D.), and for
its more limited *military* application,
as in Lk. iii 14, 1 Cor. ix 7, cf. B.G.U.
69. 7 f. (a soldier's letter, A.D. 120)
ἃς καὶ ἀποδώσω σοὶ τῷ ἔγγιστα δοθη-
σομένῳ ὀψωνίῳ, 'with my next pay.'

8. σε] for σοι, in accordance
with a common tendency in the
vernacular: cf. P. Oxy. 119. 4
(= No. 42).

9. πολλαπολλῶν] according to

Witkowski a word of good omen,
'quod bene vertat'; but the meaning
is far from clear.

ἄρσενον] For the form cf. P.
Gen. 35. 6 (ii/A.D.) ἄρσενας, and
the derivative in *Ostr.* 1601 παιδίου
ἀρσενικοῦ. WH. read ἄρσην (for
ἄρρην) throughout in the N.T.: cf.
the note on P. Oxy. 37. 7 (= No. 18).

10. ἔκβαλε] The heathen practice of exposing children is rebuked
by Justin *Apol.* i, 27.

11, 12. μή με ἐπιλάθῃς] On μή
c. aor. subj. 'do not (in future)
forget me,' see Moulton *Proleg.* p.
122 f. For ἐ. c. acc. cf. Phil. iii.
13.

M.

13. LETTER FROM ALEXANDRIA

P. OXY. 294.　　　　　　　　　　　　　A.D. 22.

Discovered at Oxyrhynchus, and edited by Grenfell and Hunt in *Oxyrhynchus Papyri* II, p. 294 ff.

The writer of this letter, Sarapion, has gone to Alexandria in connexion with some case in which he was interested, but hearing on arrival there that his house has been searched in his absence, he applies to his brother Dorion for further information. At the same time he takes the opportunity of sending particulars regarding the case, and concludes with a facetious reference to certain friends.

'Ο διαλογι[σμὸς··········
Σαραπίων Δω[ρίωνι τῷ ἀδελφῷ χαίριν καὶ διὰ παντὸς ὑ[γιαίνιν. ἐπὶ τῷ γεγο-
νέναι ἐν 'Αλεξανδρίᾳ [τῇ·· τοῦ ὑπογε-
γραμμένου μηνὸς ἔμ[αθον παρά τινων　　　　5
ἁλιέων εἰς 'Αλεξάνδρι[αν········· ὅ-
τι Σα[··]ειλλα προσοινθ[··········

The inquiry....
Sarapion to his brother Dorion, greeting and perpetual health. On my arrival in Alexandria on the...of the undernoted month, I learned from certain fishermen at Alexandria that...and that

1. διαλογισμός] a legal term, denoting an 'inquiry' or 'session' for the hearing of cases: cf. P. Tebt. 27. 35 (B.C. 113) ἐπὶ τοῦ συσταθέντος πρὸς σὲ διαλογισμοῦ, 'at the inquiry instituted against you,' and see Wilcken *Gr. Ostr.* I, p. 622, note 2.

4. ἐν 'Αλεξανδρίᾳ] Cf. l. 6 εἰς Αλεξ., the two passages illustrating the frequent misuse and interchange of the two prepositions in the vernacular: see Moulton *Proleg.* pp. 234, 245, Thackeray *Gramm.* I, p. 25.

6. ἁλιέων] Ἁλιεύς is the regular form in the Ptolemaic papyri as compared with ἁλεεύς in the best MSS. of the LXX and N.T.

παρ' ἐμοῦ ἐν αὐλῇ, καὶ ὁ ο[ἶκος········
Σεκόνδας ἠραύνηται κ[αὶ··········
ὁ ἐμ[ὸς] οἶκος ἠραύνητ[αι··········   10
καὶ σεσύνηται εἰ ταῦτα οὕτως ἔχι ἀσφα-
λῶς. εὖ οὖν ποιήσις γράψας μοι ἀντιφώνη[σ]ιν
περὶ τούτων εἴνα καὶ ⟨ἐ⟩γὼ αὐτὸς ἐπιδῶ ἀνα-
φόριον τῷ ἡγεμόνι. μὴ οὖν ἄλλως ποιήσις, ἐγὼ
δὲ αὐτὸς οὔπω οὐδὲ ἐνήλεπα ἕως ἀκούσω φάσ-   15
ιν παρὰ σοῦ περὶ ἁπάντων. ἐγὼ δὲ βιάζο-
μαι ὑπὸ φίλω[ν] γενέσθαι οἰκιακὸς τοῦ ἀρχι-
στάτορος Ἀπολλωνίου εἴνα σὺν αὐτῷ ἐπὶ δι-
αλογισμὸν ἔλ[θ]ω. [ὁ] μὲν ἡγούμενος τοῦ στρα-
[τ]ηγοῦ κ[αὶ] Ἰού]στος ὁ μαχαιροφόρος ἐν κοσ-   20
[τ]ωδε[ίᾳ εἰσί], ὡς ἐπέταξεν ὁ ἡγεμών, ἕως

the house of Secunda has been searched and...my house has
been searched..., and...whether these things are really so. Please
therefore write me an answer regarding these things, in order
that I may myself present a petition to the Prefect. Do not
fail to do so. I am not so much as anointing myself, until I
shall hear a report from you on all points. I am being pressed
by my friends to·become a member of the household of the chief-
usher Apollonius, in order that I may come along with him to the
inquiry. The marshal of the strategus and Justus the sword-
bearer are in prison, as the Prefect ordered, until the inquiry,

9. ἠραύνηται] from ἐραυνάω (not
an Alexandrinism, Thumb *Hellen.*
p. 176 f.), which is regularly found
in the N.T., Jo. v 39, &c.: see
WH. *Notes³*, p. 157, Blass *Gramm.*
p. 21, Thackeray *Gramm.* I, p.
78 f. The subst. ἔραυνα is found
in P. Oxy. 67. 18 (iv/A.D.) τὴν ἔραυ-
ναν ποιούμενον.

11. σεσύνηται] perhaps for σεσύ-
ληται 'was plundered', εἰ ταῦτα κτλ.
being then taken as an elliptical
indirect question (Edd.).

15. ἐνήλεπα]=ἐναλήλιφα sc. ἐμαυ-
τόν. Cf. the curious letter P. Oxy.

528 (ii/A.D.), where the husband
declares that he has neither washed
nor anointed himself (οὐκ ἐλουσάμην
οὖς ἤλιμ<μ>ε) for a month in the
hope of persuading his wife, who
had left him, to return. The two
passages throw an interesting side-
light on Mt. vi 16 ἀφανίζουσιν γὰρ
τὰ πρόσωπα αὐτῶν.

17. οἰκιακός] By entering the
chief usher's service Sarapion evidently hoped to further his own
interests at the impending inquiry:
see the introd. to No. 10. For οἰκ.
cf. Mt. x 36.

ἐπὶ διαλ[ογισ]μός, ἐὰν μή τι πίσωσι τὸν αρχι-
στάτορα δο[ῦν]αι εἰκανὸν ἕως ἐπὶ διαλο-
γισμόν. περὶ δ[ὲ] τοῦ φαλακροῦ γράψον μοι πῶς
πάλιν ἄνω λαλαχεύεται. μὴ οὖν ἄλλως ποι-   25
ήσῃς. εἶπον δὲ Διογένι τῷ φίλῳ σου μὴ ἀδικῆ-
σαί με πε[····] εἰς δαπάνην οὗ ἔχι μου·
συνανακ[···γ]ὰρ τῷ ἀρχιστάτορι. ἐρωτῶ δέ σε
καὶ παρακαλ[ῶ γρά]ψει μοι ἀντιφώνησιν περὶ
τῶν γενομέν[ων. πρ]ὸ μὲν πάντων σεαυτοῦ   30
ἐπιμέλου εἴν᾽ ὑ[γιαίνῃς]. ἐπισκωποῦ Δημητροῦ[ν
καὶ Δωρίωνα [τὸν πατ]έρα. ἔ[ρ]ρωσο.
(ἔτους) θ᾽ Τιβερίου Καίσαρ[ος Σεβαστοῦ. Χο]ιάκ ιε᾽.

On the *verso*

ἀπόδο(ς) Δωρίωνι   τῷ ἀδελφῶι.

unless indeed they shall persuade the chief-usher to give security
for them until the inquiry. As regards the bald-headed man write
me how his hair is growing again on the top. Do not fail to do
so. I told Diogenes your friend not to wrong me with reference
to the expense of what he has belonging to me.... I beg and
entreat you to write me an answer regarding what has happened.
Above all take care of yourself that you may be in health. Look
after Demetrius and our father Dorion. Good-bye. The 9th year
of Tiberius Caesar Augustus, Choiak 15.

(Addressed) Deliver to Dorion my brother.

23. δοῦναι εἰ(=ἰ)κανόν] *satis dare*,
cf. P. Brit. Mus. 196. 3 (=II, p. 153)
(ii/A.D.) and the new verb ἰκανο-
δοτέω in the same sense in P. Oxy.
259. 29 (A.D. 23). For the corre-
lative λαμβάνειν τὸ ἱκανόν *satis ac-*

cipere see Ac. xvii 9, and the
passages quoted in *Thess.* p. xxix,
note 2.

25. λαλαχεύεται] a new verb,
having the sense of λαχνόω 'grow
hairy' (Edd.).

14. A LETTER OF COMMENDATION

P. OXY. 292.   C. A.D. 25.

Discovered at Oxyrhynchus, and edited by Grenfell and Hunt
in *Oxyrhynchus Papyri* II, p. 292.

Theon recommends his brother Heraclides to the notice of
Tyrannus. For a somewhat similar ἐπιστολὴ συστατική (cf.
2 Cor. iii 1) see P. Goodspeed 4 (= No. 8).

Θέων Τυράννωι τῶι τιμιωτάτωι
    πλεῖστα χαίρειν.
Ἡρακλείδης ὁ ἀποδιδούς σοι τὴν
ἐπιστολὴν ἐστίν μου ἀδελφός·
διὸ παρακαλῶ σε μετὰ πάσης δυνά-   5
μεως ἔχειν αὐτὸν συνεσταμέ-
νον. ἠρώτησα δὲ καὶ Ἑρμί[α]ν
τὸν ἀδελφὸν διὰ γραπτοῦ ἀνηγεῖ[σθαί

Theon to his most esteemed Tyrannus, heartiest greetings.
Heraclides, the bearer of this letter to you, is my brother. Therefore I beg you with all my power to hold him as one recommended
to you. I have also asked Hermias my brother in writing to

1. Τυράννωι] From the *verso*
(cf. P. Oxy. 291) we learn that
Tyrannus (cf. Ac. xix 9) occupied
the position of διοικητής, apparently
here a local finance-officer, responsible to the central bureau in Alexandria: cf. Wilcken *Gr. Ostr.* I,
p. 492 ff.
    6. ἔχ. αὐτὸν συνεστάμενον] For
συνίστημι = 'commend,' which is

common in the papyri, cf. 2 Cor.
iii 1, &c., and for the form of the
above phrase cf. Lk. xiv 18, 19 ἔχε
με παρῃτημένον.
    8. διὰ γραπτοῦ] 'in writing' as
distinguished from 'by word of
mouth': cf. P. Oxy. 293. 5 f.
(A.D. 27) οὔτε διὰ γραπτοῦ οὔτε διὰ
σημε<ί>ου 'neither by letter nor
by message' (GH.).

σοι περὶ τούτου. χαρίεσαι δέ μοι τὰ μέγιστα
ἐάν σου τῆς ἐπισημασίας τύχηι.   10
πρὸ δὲ πάντων ὑγια(ί)νειν σε εὔχ[ο-
μαι ἀβασκάντως τὰ ἄριστα
πράττων.   ἔρρω(σο).

On the *verso*

Τυράννωι διοικ(ητῆ).

communicate with you regarding this. You will do me the greatest
favour if he [Heraclides] gains your notice. But above all I pray
that you may be in health unharmed by the evil eye and faring
prosperously. Goodbye.

(Addressed)   To Tyrannus, dioecetes.

9. χαρίεσαι] = χαριεῖσαι, cf. P.
Grenf. II, 14 (c). 7 (iii/B.C.) χαριεῖσαί
μοι τοῦτο ποιήσας, and see Moulton
Proleg. p. 53 f., where it is shown
that the similar N.T. formations
καυχᾶσαι, ὀδυνᾶσαι have been formed
'with the help of the -σαι that an-
swers to 3rd sing. -ται in the perfect.'
    10. ἐπισημασίας κτλ.] In P. Tebt.
23. 4 ff. (ii/B.C.) the writer complains
regarding his correspondent's conduct towards a protégé of his own—

καθ' ὑπερβολὴν βεβαρυμμένοι ἐπὶ τῷ
{σε} μὴ δι' ἡμᾶς ἐπισημασίας αὐτὸν
τετευχέναι, 'I am excessively vexed
that he should have gained no
special consideration from you on
my account' (Edd.).
    12. ἀβασκάντως] a common for-
mula in closing greetings, e.g. P.
Leip. 108. 9 ἄσπασε τὰ ἀβάσκαντά
σου παιδία, P. Oxy. 930. 23, P. Fay.
126. 10 (all ii/iii A.D.).

15. LETTER TO A MAN IN MONEY-DIFFICULTIES

B. G. U. 1079.   A.D. 41.

Edited by Viereck in *Berliner Griechische Urkunden* IV, p. 123 f.
See also Wilcken, *Archiv* IV, p. 567 f.

It is not easy to determine the exact circumstances of this
interesting letter, but it would appear that Heraclides was in
money-difficulties, Ptollarion being one of his creditors. Accordingly a certain Sarapion, who was connected with him in

some way (cf. l. 1 f. Ἡρ. τῷ ἡμετέρῳ), writes advising him to do his utmost to win over Ptollarion, lest he should be driven out of house and home. In any case he bids him 'beware of the Jews' (l. 24 ff.), apparently in their character of money-lenders.

Σαραπίων Ἡρακλείδῃ τῷ
ἡμετέρῳ χα(ίρειν). Ἔπεμψά σοι
ἄλλας δύο ἐπιστολάς,
διὰ Νηδύμου μίαν, διὰ
Κρονίου μαχαιροφόρου   5
μίαν· λοιπὸν οὖν ἔλα-
βον παρὰ το(ῦ) Ἄραβος τὴν
ἐπιστολὴν καὶ ἀνέ-
γνων καὶ ἐλυπήθην.
Ἀκολούθει δὲ Πτολλ-   10
αρίωνι πᾶσαν ὥραν· τά-
χα δύναταί σε εὔλυτ-
ον ποῖσαι. Λέγε αὐτῷ· ἄ-
λλο ἐγώ, ἄλλο πάντες,
ἐγὼ παιδάριν εἰμί· παρὰ   15
τάλαντόν σοι πέπρακα

Sarapion to our Heraclides, greeting. I sent you two other letters, one by the hand of Nedymus, one by the hand of Cronius the sword-bearer. Finally then I received from the Arabian the letter, and I read it and was grieved. Stick to Ptollarion constantly: perhaps he can set you free. Say to him: 'I am not like anyone else, I am a lad. With the exception of a talent I have made you to pay

4. διὰ Νηδύμου] Cf. Ac. xv 23 γράψαντες διὰ χειρὸς αὐτῶν, 1 Pet. v 12.

6. λοιπὸν οὖν] See 1 Thess. iv 1 (note).

8. ἀνέγνων] Contrary to the general use of the verb both in classical and late Gk for 'read aloud,' 'read publicly,' d. must here mean simply 'read': cf. 1 Thess.

▼ 27 (note).

11. τάχα] 'perhaps,' as often: cf. Rom. v 7, Philem. 15.

16. πέπρακα] 'have made to pay': cf. P. Tebt. 58. 48 f. (B.C. 111) τοὺς δὲ λοιποὺς κω(μο)γρ(αμματεῖς) πρᾶξαι...'that the rest of the komogrammateis should be made to pay...' (Edd.).

τὰ φο[ρτ]ία μου· οὐκ οἶδα
τιμ[··]μτρων ·οτο··
πολλοὺς δανιστὰς ἔχο-
μεν· μὴ ἵνα ἀναστατώ-   20
σῃς ἡμᾶς. Ἐρώτα αὐτὸ·
καθ᾽ ἡμέραν· τάχα δύνα-
ταί σε ἐλεῆσαι·\ ἐὰν μή, ὡς
ἂν πάντες καὶ σὺ βλέ-
πε σατὸν ἀπὸ τῶν Ἰου-   25
δαίων./Μᾶλλον ἀκολουθῶ·
αὐτῷ δύνῃ φιλιάσαι αὐτῷ·
ἰδέ, ἢ δύναται διὰ Διοδώρου
ὑπογραφῆναι ἡ τάβλα ⟨ἢ⟩ διὰ
τῆς γυναικὸς τοῦ ἡγεμ-   30
όνος· ἐὰν τὰ παρ(ὰ) σατοῦ ποί-
σῃς, οὐκ εἰ μεμπτός.
Ἀσπάζου Διόδωρον μ[ετ᾽] ἄλων.
Ἔρρω(σο). Ἀσπάζου Ἁρποχράτη[ν].

my burdens. I do not know…we have many creditors: do not
drive us out.' Ask him daily: perhaps he can have pity on
you: if not, do you, like all, beware of the Jews. Rather stick
to him (Ptollarion), and so you may become his friend. Notice that
the document can be signed either by Diodorus or by the wife of the
ruler. If you manage your own affairs, you are not to be blamed.
Greet Diodorus with the others. Goodbye. Greet Harpocrates.

19. δανιστάς] Cf. Lk. vii 41 δυὸ χρεοφιλέται ἦσαν δανιστῇ τινί.
20. ἀναστατώσῃς] 'drive us out,' i.e. from hearth and home. Cf. the metaphorical usage in Gal. v 12 οἱ ἀναστατοῦντες ὑμᾶς, and see P. Oxy. 119. 10 (= No. 42).
24. βλέπε σατὸν (=σεαυτὸν) ἀπό] With this construction, hitherto believed to be a Hebraism, cf. Mk viii 15 βλέπετε ἀπὸ τῆς ζύμης τῶν Φαρισαίων, xii 38 βλέπετε ἀπὸ τῶν γραμματέων.

Wilcken (*Archiv* IV, p. 567) finds here the earliest known reference to the Jews as money-lenders, the description of them as the ' bankers of Egypt,' which Sayce and Mahaffy draw from the v/B.C. Assuan papyri, not being established in his view by these documents.

27. φιλιάσαι] Cf. Sir. 37. 1 ἐφιλίασα αὐτῷ κἀγώ.
29. τάβλα] Cf. P. Par. 18 (*bis*) 5 f. [σῶμα]…ἔχω(= ο)ν τάβλαν κατὰ τοῦ τραχήλου.

(Ἔτους) αʹ Τιβερίου Κλαυδίου Καίσαρο(ς)   35
Σεβα(στοῦ) Γερμανικοῦ Αὐτοκρά(τορος) μηνὸ(ς)
Καισαρείου ιαʹ.

On the *verso* are three much effaced lines.

The 1st year of Tiberius Claudius Caesar Augustus Germanicus
Emperor, the 11th of the Caesarean month.

33. ἅλων] l. ἄλλων.   37. Καισαρείου] = Mesore, cf. p. xviii.

16. DEED OF DIVORCE

B. G. U. 975.   A.D. 45.

From the Fayûm. Edited by Schubart in *Berliner Griechische
Urkunden* III, p. 299.

A rather illiterate deed of separation between husband and
wife, in which they mutually declare that each renounces all
claim on the other, and the wife on her part acknowledges
the repayment of her dowry and super-dowry.

No reason for the separation is assigned here, but in
P. Grenf. II, 76. 3 f. (iv/A.D.) a couple renounce their wedded
life ἐκ τινὸς πονηροῦ δαίμονος 'owing to some evil deity,' and in
the late P. Flor. 93 (vi/A.D.) a similar cause is assigned for the
dissolution of a union which had been entered into ἐπὶ χρησταῖς
ἐλπίσι, and in the belief that it would last ἐφʼ ὅλον τὸν τῆς ἐξ
ἀμφοῖν ζωῆς χρόνον.

For similar deeds see P. Oxy. 266 (A.D. 96), C. P. R. 23 and
P. Leip. 27 (both ii/A.D.), and P. Oxy. 906 (ii/iii A.D.), and
the discussion of the whole question in its legal bearings by
Lesquier *Revue de Philologie* 1906, p. 25 ff.

Μεχ⟨ὶ⟩ρ κε΄.

Ἔτους τετάρτου Τιβερίου Κλαυδίου
Καίσαρος Σεβαστοῦ Γερμανικοῦ
Αὐτοκράτορος μηνὸς Μεχὶρ πέμπτῃ
καὶ εἰκάτῃ ἐν τῇ Σοκνοπαίου Νή-   5
σου τῆς Ἡρακλίδου μερίδος τοῦ Ἀρσ[ι-]
νοείτου νομοῦ. Ὁ[μ]ολουγῖ⟨α⟩ Πα[ο]ῦς
Παοῦτος ὡς ἐτῶν εἴκοσι πένδε [οὐλ]ὴ
μετόπο ἀριστερὸ γεγενεμένη αὐτοῦ
γυνὴ Τεσενοῦφις τῆς Ὀννώφρις ὡς   10
ἐτῶν εἴκοσι οὐλὴ καστροκνημίῳ ⟨ἐ⟩κ-
ξ ἀριστερὸ(ν) μετὰ γυρίου τοῦ ἑ(α)υτῆς
συνγηνὸς Σαταβοῦς τοῦ Ἐρ[ι]έως ὠ[ς]
ἐτῶν [τ]ριάκοντα οὐλὴ κασ[τ]ροκ[νη-]

Mechir 25.

The fourth year of Tiberius Claudius Caesar Augustus Germanicus Emperor, the twenty-fifth day of the month Mechir, in
Socnopaei Nesus of the Heraclides district of the Arsinoite nome.
Agreement of Paous son of Paous, about twenty-five years old, a
scar on the left forehead, with his wife Tesenouphis the daughter
of Onnophris, about twenty years old, a scar on the calf of the leg
on the left side, along with her guardian and kinsman Satabous,
the son of Erieus, about thirty years old, a scar on the calf of the

6. μερίδος] a geographical division,
as frequently in the papyri and in later
Greek generally (cf. Ramsay *Exp.* v
vi, p. 320). The use of the word in
Ac. xvi 12 πρώτη τῆς μερίδος Μακε-
δονίας πόλις is now therefore fully
justified as against WH. *Notes²*,
p. 96.

9. μετόπο κτλ.] l. μετώπῳ ἀρι-
στερῷ < τῇ > γεγενημένῃ (Wilcken).

10. γυνὴ κτλ.] l. γυναικὶ...τοῦ
Ὀννώφρεως.

11, 12. καστροκνημίῳ κτλ.] l. γα-
στροκνημίῳ ἐξ ἀριστερῶν μετὰ κυρίου.
For κύριος in its legal sense of
'guardian,' see especially *Archiv* iv,
p. 78 ff.

13. συνγηνὸς Σαταβοῦς] = συγ-
γενοῦς Σαταβοῦτος. On the forms
συγγενής takes in the N.T. see
Moulton *Proleg.* p. 244, and for its
use as an honorific title in the O.T.
Apocrypha see Deissmann *BS.*
p. 159.

μίο ἐκ δεξιô(ν) συνῆρσθαι τὴν πρὸς   15
ἀλλήρους συνβίοσιν, ἥτ[ι]ς αὐτοὺς
συνε[σ]τήκι κατὰ συνγραφὴ(ν) κά-
μοι, καὶ μηδὲν ἀλλήλο[ι]ς ἐνκ[α-]
λεῖν μηδ' ἐνκαλέσειν περὶ μη[δε-]
νὸς ἀπ[λῶς πράγ]μạτọς [···]··[·]·ς ᾽κ[αὶ ἀ-]   20
πέχι ἡ Τεσεν[ο]ῦφις τὴν ὀφιλη[μένην]
ὁ Πα[ο]ῦς φερνὴ[ν ἀ]ργυρίου καὶ τὰ [παρά-]
φερν[α········]ỵτῇ Τεσεν[ούφει]
[···]ẹṛỵ[········]·ẹτεṛạỵ·[·····]

Two much mutilated lines follow.

leg on the right side,—to the effect that there is dissolved the
mutual union which had brought them together in accordance with
the contract of marriage, and that they neither make nor will make
any claim against one another regarding any matter whatsoever...
and Tesenouphis acknowledges receipt of the dowry of silver owed
by Paous, and the *parapherna*....

15, 16.   συνῆρσθαι κτλ.] l. συνῆρ-
θαι τὴν πρὸς ἀλλήλους συμβίωσιν.
This passage may be taken as con-
firming Wessely's restoration in
C.P.R. 23. 17 συνῆρμαι τὴν πρ[ὸς
Σύρον συνβίωσι]ν (as against GH.
Oxy. Papyri, II p. 239). In P.
Grenf. II 76 the husband declares
that he will make no claim on his wife
μηδὲ περὶ συμβιώ[σεως μη]τὲ περὶ ἕ͂δνου
('wedding-gifts'), but that she will
be free ἀποστῆ[ναι καὶ] γαμηθῆναι ὡς
ἂν βουληθῇ.
    17.   συνγραφὴν κάμοι] l. συγγρα-
φὴν γάμου.
    20.   ἀπέχι(=ει)]   The return of

the dowry is an essential feature in
all divorce-contracts: cf. especially
P. Brit. Mus. 178 (= II, p. 207)
(A.D. 145), which is simply an
ἀποχή on the woman's part for
400 drachmas out of 1000 which
had formed her dowry. On ἀπέχω
= 'I have received' (as in Mt. vi
2 ff., Lk. vi 24, Phil. iv 18) see
Deissmann *BS.* p. 229, and the
addenda in *Lex. Notes, Exp.* VII vi,
p. 91.
    22 f.   παράφερνα] 'super-dowry,'
that which a married woman brings
over and above her dower.

17. CENSUS RETURN

P. Oxy. 255.   A.D. 48.

Discovered at Oxyrhynchus, and edited by Grenfell and Hunt in
Oxyrhynchus Papyri II, p. 215 f.

Few official documents amongst the papyri have awakened
greater interest than the census returns or house-to-house
enrolments (κατ' οἰκίαν ἀπογραφαί), of which a large number
have now been recovered, extending over a period of nearly
two and a half centuries. It is impossible here to enter into
the many important questions that these returns raise, but one
or two particulars regarding them may be mentioned. Thus
it has been established beyond a doubt that the enrolments
followed a cycle of fourteen years, and that they were sent in
during, and generally towards the end of, the first year of the
new census-period—the census-paper, for example, of A.D.
48—49 containing the facts required for the enrolment of A.D.
47—48. As yet we are not in possession of a return for any
period earlier than A.D. 19—20, but there is general agreement
that the whole system was originated by Augustus, perhaps as
early as B.C. 10—9, and that probably in this, as in so many
other details of his administration, he made use on a similar
system already in existence in Egypt. In any case it is
interesting to notice that not only have we numerous instances

of closely allied rating papers, dating from the time of the
Ptolemies, but also an actual return, belonging to the same
period, in which the names of the owner and the other
occupants of each house are given, and then the total number
of inhabitants and the number of males (P. Petr. III, 59 (*d*)).

In the main the Imperial ἀπογραφαί follow the same form.
Beginning with a statement as to the house, or part of a house,
which belongs to him, the writer goes on to specify the
number and ages of its inhabitants, whether members of his
own family or slaves or tenants, including in his return both
males and females, apparently always in that order. The
whole then concludes with some such formal phrase as διὸ
ἐπιδίδωμι and the date.

The uses to which such returns could be put were various.
For not only did they contain a record of the whole population
in any given year, but they also furnished a basis for the dis-
tribution of various public burdens (λειτουργίαι), and more
particularly for the levying of the poll-tax (λαογραφία), to
which all males in Egypt were liable from the age of fourteen
to sixty.

These and other kindred points are fully discussed by
Kenyon in *British Museum Papyri* II, p. 17 ff., by Grenfell
and Hunt in *Oxyrhynchus Papyri* II, p. 207 ff., and by Wilcken
in *Gr. Ostr.* I, p. 435 ff., while for the important bearing these
census returns have upon the historical accuracy of Luke ii,
1—4, it is sufficient to refer to Sir W. M. Ramsay's brilliant
monograph, *Was Christ born in Bethlehem?* I have not seen
A. Mayer's study, *Die Schätzung bei Christi Geburt in ihrer
Beziehung zu Quirinius* (Innsbruck, F. Rauch, 1908).

The present papyrus is a census return addressed by a
woman called Thermoutharion to the officials of Oxyrhynchus
in Oct., A.D. 48. Apart from the usual features, it contains a
curious declaration, made on oath, that 'neither a stranger,
nor an Alexandrian citizen, nor a freedman, nor a Roman
citizen, nor an Egyptian' was living in the house.

Δωρ[ίωνι σ]τρατηγῶι κ[αὶ·]ην [····]νω[ι

βα[σι]λικῷ γρ[α(μματεῖ)] καὶ Διδύμωι [καὶ·]·[·]ο·( )
τοπογρα(μματεῦσι) καὶ κωμογρα(μματεῦσι) παρὰ
    Θερ[μου-
θαρίου τῆς Θοώνιος μετὰ κυρίου
Ἀπολλω(νίου) τοῦ Σωτάδου. εἰσὶν   5
[οἱ] καταγεινόμενοι ἐν τῇ ὑπαρ-
χο[ύσῃ μοι οἰκίᾳ λαύρ]ας νότου [··

·   ·   ·   ·   ·   ·   ·

Θερμου[θάριον ἀπελ(ευθέρα) τοῦ προ-
γ[εγ]ρα(μμένου) Σωτάδ[ου] ὡς (ἐτῶν) ξε΄,
μέση μελίχ(ρως) μακροπ(ρόσωπος) οὐλ(ὴ) γόνα(τι)
  δε[ξι]ῷ[ι.   10
    (γίνεται) γ΄ ||
Θερμουθάρι[ον] ἡ προγεγρα(μμένη) μ[ετὰ

To Dorion strategus and...royal scribe and Didymus and...
topogrammateis and komogrammateis from Thermoutharion the
daughter of Thoonis with her guardian Apollonius the son of
Sotades. There are living in the house which belongs to me in
the South Lane...

Thermoutharion, a freedwoman of the above-mentioned Sotades,
about 65 years of age, of medium height, dark-complexioned, long-
visaged, a scar on the right knee. Total—three persons.

I the above-mentioned Thermoutharion along with my guardian

---

3. τοπογρα(μματεῦσι) κτλ.] The
topogrammateis were scribes of the
toparchies, into which the nomes
were divided (Wilcken *Gr. Ostr.* I,
p. 428 ff.). During the Roman
period their functions appear to have
become merged in those of the
komogrammateis or village-scribes,
although originally these were subor-
dinate officials: see the Editors' note
on P. Oxy. 251. 2.

4. κυρίου] See the note on B.G.U.
975. 12 (= No. 16).

8. Θερμουθάριον] Two names

(cf. l. 11) of which no trace is left,
must have preceded that of the
owner, who, contrary to the practice
of the Fayûm lists, returns herself
last.

ἀπελ(ευθέρα)] Not only freed persons but slaves were included in the
census returns, e.g. B.G.U. 137. 10
(ii/A.D.). For ἀ. cf. 1 Cor. vii 22.

11. γ΄] The two strokes following
γ΄ are apparently intended simply to
draw attention to the fact that γ is a
number.

κυρίου τοῦ α[ὐτο]ῦ Ἀπολλω(νίου) ὀμνύω
[Τ]ιβέριον Κλαύδιον Καίσαρα Σεβ[αστὸν
Γερμανικὸν Αὐτοκράτορα εἰ μὴν   15
[ἐ]ξ [ὑ]γιοῦς καὶ ἐπ' ἀληθείας ἐπι-
δεδωκέναι τὴ[ν π]ροκειμένην
[γρα]φὴν τῶν παρ' ἐμοὶ [ο]ἰκούν[των,
καὶ μηδένα ἕτερον οἰκ⟨ε⟩ῖν παρ' ἐμοὶ
μήτε ἐπ[ί]ξ[ενον μή]τε Ἀλεξανδ(ρέα)   20
μηδὲ ἀπελεύθερον μήτε Ῥωμαν⟨ὸν⟩
μηδὲ Αἰγύπ[τιον ἐ]ξ⟨ω⟩ τῶν προ-
γεγραμμένω[ν. εὐορ]κούσῃ μέν μοι
εὖ ε]ἴη, ἐφ]ιορκοῦντι δὲ τ[ὰ ἐν]αντία.
[ἔτο]υς ἐνάτου Τιβερίου Κλαυδ[ίου   25
[Καίσαρο]ς Σεβαστοῦ Γερμανικοῦ
[Αὐτοκρά]τορος, Φαῶφι[··

the said Apollonius swear by Tiberius Claudius Caesar Augustus
Germanicus Emperor that assuredly the preceding document makes
a sound and true return of those living with me, and that there is
no one else living with me, neither a stranger, nor an Alexandrian
citizen, nor a freedman, nor a Roman citizen, nor an Egyptian, in
addition to the aforesaid. If I am swearing truly, may it be well
with me, but if falsely, the reverse.

In the ninth year of Tiberius Claudius Caesar Augustus Germanicus Emperor, Phaophi....

13. ὀμνύω κτλ.] Cf. P. Par. 47. 2
(= No. 7), note.
  15. εἰ(= ἦ) μὴν κτλ.] For the
same emphatic phrase cf. P. Brit.
Mus. 181. 13 (= II, p. 147) (A.D. 64),
and for the form see Moulton *Proleg.*
p. 46, Thackeray *Gramm.* I, pp. 54,
83 f.
  20. ἐπίξενον] This rare word is
found in an ostracon-receipt of
A.D. 32—33 for the tax (τέλος ἐπι-
ξένου) which strangers had to pay

on settling down in any town or
village; see Deissmann *LO.*² p. 78,
and cf. Wilcken *Archiv* I, p. 153.
  21. Ῥωμαν⟨όν⟩] Lat. for usual
Gk Ῥωμαῖον.
  24. ἐφ]ιορκοῦντι] to be so restored,
rather than the Editors' ἐπ]ιορκοῦντι,
in accordance with the aspirated form
generally found in the papyri, e.g. P.
Oxy. 240. 8, P. Flor. 79. 26 (both
i/A.D.). The verb (unaspirated) occurs in Mt. v 33 (LXX).

18.   REPORT OF A LAWSUIT

P. OXY. 37.   A.D. 49.

Discovered at Oxyrhynchus, and edited by Grenfell and Hunt in *Oxyrhynchus Papyri* I, p. 79 ff.   See also Lietzmann, *Gr. Papyri* p. 4 f.

The official report of the proceedings instituted by Pesouris against a nurse Saraeus for the recovery of a male foundling, Heraclas, whom he had entrusted to her care. For the defence it is urged that the foundling had died, and that the child whom Pesouris was seeking to carry off was Saraeus' own. This plea the strategus sustained on the ground of the likeness of the living child to Saraeus, and accordingly gave judgment that she should get back her child, on refunding the wages she had received as nurse.

COL. I.

Ἐξ ὑπομ[ν]ηματισμῶν Τι[βερίο]υ Κλαυδ[ίο]υ Πασίωνος στρατη(γοῦ).

(ἔτους) ἐνάτ[ο]υ Τιβερίου Κλαυδίου Καίσαρος Σεβαστοῦ Γερμανικοῦ

Αὐτοκ[ρά]τορος, Φαρμοῦθι γ΄. ἐπὶ τοῦ βήματος,

[Π]εσοῦρι[ς] πρὸς Σαραεῦν. Ἀριστοκλῆς ῥήτωρ

From the minutes of Tiberius Claudius Pasion, strategus.

In the ninth year of Tiberius Claudius Caesar Augustus Germanicus Emperor, Pharmouphi 3. In court, Pesouris *versus* Saraeus.

3. ἐπὶ τοῦ βήματος] Cf. Ac. xxv 10 ἐστὼς ἐπὶ τοῦ βήματος Καίσαρός εἰμι.

ὑπὲρ Πεσούριος· "Πεσοῦρις, ὑπὲρ οὗ λέγωι, ζ΄ (ἔτους) 5
Τιβερίου Κλαυδίου Καίσαρος τοῦ κυρίου ἀνεῖλεν
ἀπὸ κοπρίας ἀρρενικὸν σωμάτιον ὄνομα Ἡρα-
κ[λᾶν]. τοῦτο ἐνεχείρισεν τῆι ἀντιδίκωι. ἐγένετο ἐνθάδε ἡ τροφεῖτις εἰς υἱὸν τοῦ Πεσούριος.
τοῦ πρώτου ἐνιαυτοῦ ἀπέλαβεν τὰ τροφεῖα.   10
ἐνέστηι ἡ προθεσμία τοῦ δευτέρου ἐνιαυτοῦ,
κα[ὶ] πάλιν ἀπέλαβεν. ὅτι δὲ ταῦτα ἀληθῆι λέγωι,
ἔστιν γράμματα αὐτῆς δι' ὧν ὁμολογεῖ εἰλη-

Aristocles, advocate for Pesouris, (said): "Pesouris, my client,
in the 7th year of Tiberius Claudius Caesar the lord, picked up
from the dung-heap a male foundling named Heraclas. This child
he handed over to the care of the defendant. There took place in
this court a contract-arrangement for the nursing of the son of
Pesouris. In the first year she [the nurse] received her wages for
nursing. There arrived the appointed time for the second year,
and she again received them. And in proof that I am telling the
truth there are the documents in which she admits that she has

6. τοῦ κυρίου] an early instance
of the application of this title to the
Roman Emperor, for which from
the time of Nero onwards innumer-
able examples can be cited (see
e.g. No. 31. 4). Readers of Phil.
ii 11 and 1 Cor. viii 5 f. can hardly
have failed therefore to find there
a 'tacit protest' on S. Paul's part
against this misuse of a term which
throughout the Eastern world was
endowed with a deeply religious
significance: see further Deissmann
*LO.*² p. 263 ff.

7. ἀπὸ κοπρίας] Cf. Lk. xiv 35
οὔτε εἰς κοπρίαν εὔθετόν ἐστιν.

ἀρρενικόν] See the note on P.
Oxy. 744· 9 (= No. 12), and as
illustrating the present form, which
is found in the Attic inscriptions
(Meisterhans p. 100), cf. C.P.R.
28. 12 (A.D. 110) τῶν δὲ ἀρρένων
υἱῶν, B.G.U. 88. 6 (A.D. 147) κάμη-
λ(ον) ἄρρενον [λ]ευκόν.

M.

σωμάτιον] implying that the child
had been adopted as a *slave* by
Pesouris. For this sense of σῶμα,
as in Rev. xviii 13, see Deissmann
BS. p. 160, and add P. Tebt. 407· 5
(A.D. 199?) δουλικὰ σώμ[ατ]α.

9. ἡ τροφεῖτις] not the nurse
herself, but the contract entered
into to supply her with τροφεῖα (cf.
l. 10): see Wilcken *Archiv* I, p. 123,
and the confirmation of his view afforded by the συγγραφὴ τροφῖτις in
P. Tebt. 51 (*c.* B.C. 113), and the
numerous exx. in B.G.U. 1106 &c.

10. τροφεῖα] Cf. B.G.U. 297·
12 ff. (A.D. 50), where a nurse gives a
receipt for τὰ τροφεῖα καὶ τὰ ἔλαια
καὶ τὸν ἱματισμὸν καὶ τἆλλα ὅσα
καθήκει δίδοσθαι τροφῷ κτλ.

11. προθεσμία] frequent in contracts with reference to a fixed or
stipulated date, e.g. P. Oxy. 728. 18
(A.D. 142) τῇ ὡρισμένῃ προθεσμίᾳ: cf.
Gal. iv 2 ἄχρι τ. προθεσμίας τ. πατρός.

φέναι. λειμανχουμέν[ο]υ τοῦ σωματ[ί]ου ἀπέ-
σπασεν ὁ Πεσοῦρις. μετ[ὰ] ταῦτα καιρὸν εὑροῦσ[α   15
εἰσεπήδησεν εἰς τὴν τοῦ ἡμετέρου [ο]ἰκίαν
καὶ τὸ σωμάτιον ἀφήρπασεν καὶ βούλεται ὀν[ό-
ματι ἐλευθέρου τὸ σωμάτιον ἀπενέγκασ-
θαι. ἔχω[ι] πρῶτον γράμμα τῆς τροφείτιδος,
ἔχωι δεύτερο[ν] τῶν τροφείων τὴν [ἀ]ποχή[ν.   20
ἀξιῶι ταῦ[τα] φυλαχθῆ[ν]αι." Σα[ρα]εῦς·
"'Απεγαλάκ[τισά] μου τὸ [π]αιδίον, κα[ὶ] τούτων
σωμάτιόν μοι ἐνεχειρίσθη. ἔλαβ[ον] παρ' αὐτῶν τοὺ[ς] πάντας ὀκτὼι στατῆρας. μετὰ
ταῦτα [ἐτελεύ]τησεν τ[ὸ σ]ωμάτιο[ν β' στα-   25
τήρων π[ερ]ιόντων. νῦν βούλογ[ται τὸ

received them. As the foundling was being starved, Pesouris took it
away. Thereupon Saraeus, seizing a favourable opportunity, leapt
into my client's house, and carried the foundling off. And now she
wishes (to defend herself on the ground) that it was in virtue of its
being freeborn that the foundling was carried off. I have here,
first, the document of the nursing-contract. I have, secondly, the
receipt of the nurse's wages. I demand that these be preserved (in
the record)."

Saraeus (said): "I weaned my child, and the foundling of these
people was put into my hands. I received from them all the eight
staters (that were due). Thereupon the foundling died, two staters
remaining in my possession. And now they wish to carry off my
own child."

14. λειμανχουμέν[ο]υ] l. λιμαγ-
χουμένου. Cf. Deut. vi 3 ἐλιμαγ-
χόνησέ σε.
    ἀπέσπασεν] For the pass. of
the verb in a strong sense cf. Lk.
xxii 41 καὶ αὐτὸς ἀπεσπάσθη ἀπ'
αὐτῶν, Ac. xxi 1 ὡς δὲ ἐγένετο
ἀναχθῆναι ἡμᾶς ἀποσπασθέντας ἀπ'
αὐτῶν. See also P. Oxy. 275. 22
(= No. 20), note.
    16. εἰσεπήδησεν] Cf. Ac. xvi 29

αἰτήσας δὲ φῶτα εἰσεπήδησεν.
    17. ὀνόματι ἐλευθέρου] Cf. Mt. x
41 f. εἰς ὄνομα προφήτου.
    20. [ἀ]ποχή[ν]] the exact equiva-
lent for our 'receipt' in the papyri
and ostraca, as in the common phrase
κυρία ἡ ἀποχή 'the receipt is valid'
(e.g. P. Oxy. 91. 25, ii/A.D.). For
the corresponding verb see B.G.U.
975. 20 (= No. 16), note.

COL. II

ἴ[δι]όν μου τέκνον ἀποσπάσαι." Θέων·
"Γράμματα τοῦ σωματίου ἔχομεν."
ὁ στρατηγός· "Ἐπεὶ ἐκ τῆς ὄψεως φαίνεται τῆς
Σαραεῦτος εἶναι τὸ παιδίον, ἐὰν χιρογραφήσηι
αὐτήι τε καὶ ὁ ἀνὴρ αὐτῆς ἐκεῖνο τὸ ἐνχει-   5
ρισθὲν αὐτῆι σωμάτιον ὑπὸ τοῦ Πεσούριος
τετελευτηκέναι, φαίνεταί μοι κατὰ τὰ ὑπὸ
τοῦ κυρίου ἡγεμόνος κριθέντα ἀποδοῦσαν
αὐτὴν ὃ εἴληφεν ἀργύριον ἔχειν τὸ [ἴδιο]ν
τέκνον."   10

Theon: "We have the documents relating to the foundling."
The strategus: "Since from its features the child appears to be
the child of Saraeus, if she will make a written declaration, both
she and her husband, that the foundling handed over to her by
Pesouris is dead, I give judgment in accordance with the decision
of our lord the prefect that she receive her own child after she
has paid back the money she received."

II 1. ἴ[δι]ον] Notwithstanding
the common tendency in Hellenistic
Gk to weaken ἴδιος into a mere
possessive (cf. P. Goodspeed 4. 9
(= No. 8) note), this seems to be
one of the passages where it must
be allowed its full force: see further
Moulton *Proleg.* p. 87 ff.
3. ἐκ τ. ὄψεως] Cf. Jo. vii 24
μὴ κρίνετε κατ' ὄψιν.
Σαραεῦτος] An extended gen.,
not uncommon in profane Gk, but
found in the N.T. only in Mk vi 3
BDLΔ Ἰωσῆτος: see Blass *Gramm.*

p. 30.
4. χιρογραφήσηι] The corresponding subst. is very frequent not
only in the more technical sense of
'bond,' 'certificate of debt,' but
more generally of any written obligation or agreement—a point which
should be kept in view in determin-
ing its meaning in Col. ii 14.
8. ἀποδοῦσαν κτλ.] The reference
may be not to the whole of the wages
received, but only to what remained
over after the foundling's death
(Lietzmann).

19. PETITION TO THE PREFECT

P. Oxy. 38.   A.D. 49—50.

Discovered at Oxyrhynchus, and edited by Grenfell and Hunt in *Oxyrhynchus Papyri* I, p. 81 f. See also Lietzmann, *Gr. Papyri*, p. 6.

This document deals with the same circumstances as the preceding. Pesouris, or, as he is here called, Syrus, had apparently not complied with the judgment there recorded, and accordingly the husband of Saraeus petitioned the Prefect to aid him in the recovery of his rights.

For similar petitions addressed directly to the Prefect see P. Brit. Mus. 177 (= II, p. 167 ff.) (A.D. 40—41) and B. G. U. 113, 114 (both ii/A.D.).

Γναίωι Οὐεργελίωι Καπίτωνι[[ω]],
παρὰ Τρύφωνος Διονυσίου τῶν ἀπ᾽ Ὀξυρύγ-
χων πόλεως. Σύρος Σύρου ἐνεχείρισεν
τῇ γυναικί μου Σαραεῦτι Ἀπίωνος τῶι ζ΄ (ἔτει)
Τιβερίου Κλαυδίου Καίσαρος Σεβαστοῦ Γερμανικοῦ   5
Αὐτοκράτορος δι᾽ ἐνγύου ἐμοῦ ὃ ἀνείρηται ἀπὸ

To Gnaeus Vergilius Capito from Tryphon, son of Dionysius, of the inhabitants of the city of Oxyrhynchus. Syrus, son of Syrus, entrusted to my wife Saraeus, daughter of Apion, in the 7th year of Tiberius Claudius Caesar Augustus Germanicus Emperor, with me as security, a male foundling, who had been picked up

2. τῶν ἀπ᾽ Ὀ.] the regular phrase to denote the inhabitants of a town or village. By Heb. xiii 24 οἱ ἀπὸ τῆς Ἰταλίας we naturally understand, therefore, those who were *in* Italy at the time.

6. δι᾽ ἐνγύου ἐμοῦ] 'to render the act of a woman legal the concurrence of her guardian is necessary' (Lietzmann).

κοπρίας ἀρσενικὸν σωμάτιον, ᾧ ὄνομα Ἡρακλᾶς,
ὥστε τροφ[εῦσα]ι. τοῦ [οὖ]ν σωματίο[υ τε]τελευτηκό-
τος, καὶ τοῦ Σύρ[ου] ἐπικεχειρηκότος ἀποσπάσαι
εἰς δουλαγωγία[ν] τὸν ἀφήλικά μου υἱὸν Ἀπίωνα,   10
καθὰ π[α]ρῆλθον ἐπὶ τοῦ γενομένου τοῦ νομοῦ
στρατηγοῦ Πασίωνος, ὑφ' οὗ καὶ ἀποκατεστάθη μοι
ὁ υἱὸς Ἀπίων ἀκολούθως τοῖς ὑπὸ σοῦ τοῦ εὐερ-
γέτου προστεταγμένοις καὶ τοῖς γεγονόσι ὑπὸ τοῦ
Πασίωνος ὑπομνηματισμοῖς. τοῦ δὲ Σύρου   15
μὴ βουλομένου ἐνμεῖναι τοῖς κεκριμένοις

from the dunghill, by name Heraclas, so that she might bring it
up. The foundling having died, and Syrus having endeavoured to
carry off into slavery my young son Apion, I accordingly brought an
action before Pasion, who was ex-strategus of the nome, by whom
also my son Apion was restored to me, in accordance with what
had been enacted by you, my benefactor, and the minutes made
by Pasion. But as Syrus does not wish to abide by what has been

7. ἀρσενικόν] See P. Oxy. 744. 9
(= No. 12) and 37. 7 (= No. 18),
notes, and cf. Thackeray *Gramm.*
I, p. 123.

9. ἐπικεχειρηκότος] 'having attempted,' 'taken in hand,' any idea
of failure, though often suggested by
the context, not lying in the word
itself: cf. e.g. P. Par. 61. 15 f.
(ii/B.C.) μάλιστα δὲ τῶν συκοφαντεῖν
ἐπιχειρούντων [τελωνῶν] with reference to the exactions practised by
the tax-gatherers. The word, which
is frequent in the LXX, is found three
times in the Lucan writings (Lk. i 1,
Ac. ix 29, xix 13).

10. δουλαγωγία[ν]] Cf. 1 Cor.
ix 27.

11. καθά] 'if right, is superfluous' (Edd.).

12. ἀποκατεστάθη] Cf. Heb. xiii
19 ἵνα ἀποκατασταθῶ ὑμῖν. For the
double augment, which is found in

the N.T. (Mt. xii 13, Mk iii 5, viii
25, Lk. vi 10), cf. P. Tebt. 413. 4
(ii/iii A.D.) ἀπεκατέστησα, and see
WSchm. p. 103.

13. εὐεργέτου] The constant
occurrence of this word as a title
of honour in the inscriptions and
coins has suggested to Deissmann (*LO.*[2] p. 185 f.) that in Lk.
xxii 25 ff. our Lord may have used
it not without a certain sense of
irony: that His disciples should allow
themselves to be so designated was
incompatible with the idea of
brotherhood.

16. ἐνμεῖναι τ. κεκριμένοις] a legal
formula, cf. B.G.U. 600. 6 (ii/iii A.D.)
ἐνμένω πᾶσι ταῖς προγεγραμμέν[α]ις
[ἐν]τολαῖς, and see Deissmann *BS.*
p. 248 f. where S. Paul's use of
similar phraseology in Gal. iii 10
is discussed.

ἀλλὰ καὶ καταργοῦντός με χειρότεχνον ὄντα,
ἐπὶ σὲ τοευνω τὸν σωτῆρα τῶν δικαίων τυ-
χεῖν. •····   εὐτύχ(ει).

decided, but also hinders me in my handicraft, (I turn) to you, my
preserver, to obtain my just rights.   Farewell.

17. καταργοῦντος] 'hinders,'
'makes inactive,' as in P. Strass.
32. 7 (A.D. 261) τὸ ταυρικὸν μὴ
καταργῆται. For the generally
stronger sense 'abolish,' 'bring to
naught' in the N.T. cf. 2 Thess.
ii 8 (note).

χειρότεχνον] From P. Oxy. 39. 8
we learn that Tryphon was a weaver
(γέρδιος).

18. σωτῆρα] The use of this title
in a complimentary sense may be
illustrated by its constant applica-

tion to the Ptolemies and the Roman
Emperors, e.g. P. Petr. II 8 (2)
(of Euergetes I), or the Egyptian
inscription in *Archiv* II, p. 434
Νέρωνι...τῶι σωτῆρι καὶ εὐεργέτηι
(see above on l. 13) τῆς οἰκουμένης,
a passage which offers a striking
parallel and contrast to Jo. iv 42,
1 Jo. iv 14: see further Moulton,
Exp. VI viii, p. 438, and Wendland's valuable study in *Z.N.T.W.*
v (1904), p. 335 ff.

20. CONTRACT OF APPRENTICESHIP

P. OXY. 275.   A.D. 66.

Discovered at Oxyrhynchus, and edited by Grenfell and Hunt in
Oxyrhynchus Papyri II, p. 262 ff.

One of a number of interesting documents that have been
recovered relating to the family history of a certain Tryphon,
son of Dionysius. Tryphon was born in A.D. 8 (P. Oxy. 288. 40),
and when twenty-eight years of age was married for the second
time to Saraeus (P. Oxy. 267), his first marriage with a woman
named Demetrous having turned out unhappily. From this
second union a son, of whom we have already heard, was born
in A.D. 46-7 (P. Oxy. 37. i. 5, 22 = No. 18), and another son,
Thoönis, about A.D. 54. A weaver by trade, Tryphon desired
that this Thoönis should follow the same calling, but instead of
instructing him himself, perhaps, as the Editors suggest (*Ox.
Pap.* ii, p. 244), because at this time he was 'suffering from

cataract and shortness of sight' (ὑπο⟨κε⟩χυμένος ὀλίγον βλέπων, P. Oxy. 39. 9), he arranged to apprentice him for one year with another weaver, named Ptolemaeus, upon certain conditions that are fully stated in the document before us. For similar agreements cf. P. Oxy. 724 (A.D. 155), 725 (A.D. 183).

'Ο[μ]ο[λ]ογοῦσιν ἀλλή[λ]οις Τρύφων Διονυ[σίου
τοῦ Τρύφωνος μητρὸς [Θ]αμούν[ιο]ς τῆ[ς
'Οννώφριος καὶ Πτολεμαῖο[ς] Παυσιρίωνος
τοῦ Πτολεμαίου μητρὸς 'Ωφελοῦτος τῆς
Θέωνος γέρδιος, ἀμφότεροι τῶν ἀπ' 'Οξυ-   5
ρύγχων πόλεως, ὁ μὲν Τρύφων ἐγδεδόσ-
θαι τῷ Πτολεμαίῳ τὸν ἑαυτοῦ υἱὸν Θοῶ-
νιν μητρὸς Σαραεῦτος τῆς 'Απίωνος οὐδέ-
πω ὄντα τῶν ἐτῶν ἐπὶ χρόνον ἐνιαυτὸν
ἕνα ἀπὸ τῆς ἐνεστώσης ἡμέρας, διακονοῦ(ν)-   10
τα καὶ ποιο[ῦ]ντα πάντα τὰ ἐπιτασσόμε-
να αὐτῷ ὑπὸ τοῦ Πτολεμαίου κατὰ τὴν

Agreement between Tryphon, son of Dionysius, the son of Tryphon, his mother being Thamounis the daughter of Onnophris, and Ptolemaeus, son of Pausirion, the son of Ptolemaeus, his mother being Ophelous, the daughter of Theon, weaver, both parties belonging to the city of Oxyrhynchus. Tryphon agrees to apprentice to Ptolemaeus his son Thoönis, his mother being Saraeus the daughter of Apion, who is not yet of age, for a period of one year from the present day, to serve and to do everything commanded him by Ptolemaeus in accordance with the whole

5. γέρδιος] a frequent term for a 'weaver' in Egypt, though little known elsewhere.
τῶν ἀπ' 'Οξ.] See P. Oxy. 38. 2 (= No. 19), note.
6. ἐγδεδόσθαι] The word is a *terminus technicus* at the beginning of Oxyrhynchus marriage-contracts, e.g. the fragmentary P. Oxy. 372

(A.D. 74–5) ἐξέδοτο Ταοννῶφρις (the mother of the bride). Cf. the N.T. usage Mk xii 1 ἐξέδοτο αὐτὸν [*sc.* ἀμπελῶνα] γεωργοῖς.
7. ἑαυτοῦ] On this 'exhausted' use of the reflexive ἑ. see Moulton *Proleg.* p. 87 ff.
9. ὄντα τῶν ἐτῶν] i.e. fourteen years of age.

γερδιακὴν τέχνην πᾶσαν ὡς καὶ αὐτὸς
ἐπίστα⟨τα⟩ι, τοῦ παιδὸς ‾ρεφομένου καὶ ἱμα-
τι⟨σ⟩ζομένου ἐπὶ τὸν ὅλον χρόνον ὑπὸ   15
τοῦ πατρὸς Τρύφωνος πρὸς ὃν καὶ εἶναι
τὰ δημόσια πάντα τοῦ παιδός, ἐφ᾽ ᾧ
δώσει αὐτῷ κατὰ μῆνα ὁ Πτολεμαῖος
εἰς λόγον διατροφῆς δραχμὰς πέντε
καὶ ἐπὶ συνκλεισμῷ τοῦ ὅλου χρόνου   20
εἰς λόγον ἱματισμοῦ δραχμὰς δέκα δύο,
οὐκ ἐξόντος τῷ Τρύφωνι ἀποσπᾶν τὸν
παῖδα ἀπὸ τοῦ Πτολεμαίου μέχρι τοῦ
τὸν χρόνον πληρωθῆναι, ὅσας δ᾽ ἐὰν ἐν
τούτῳ ἀτακτήσῃ ἡμέρας ἐπὶ τὰς   25

weaving art, as also he himself knows it—the boy being supported and clothed during the whole time by his father Tryphon,
on whom also all the public dues for the boy shall fall, on condition
that Ptolemaeus shall give him monthly on account of his keep five
drachmas, and at the expiry of the whole period on account of his
clothing twelve drachmas, it not being permitted to Tryphon to
remove the boy from Ptolemaeus until the time is completed ; and
if there are any days during this period on which he [the boy] plays

17. τὰ δημόσια πάντα] Like
other trades weaving was subjected
to a regular tax, often described as
γερδιακόν, which seems to have
varied with the yearly profits of the
persons taxed ; but see Wilcken *Gr.
Ostr.* I, p. 172 f.

19. εἰς λόγον διατροφῆς] Cf.
Phil. iv 15 εἰς λόγον δόσεως καὶ
λήμψεως.

20. συνκλεισμῷ] Cf. P. Oxy.
502. 26 f. (ii/A.D.) ἐπὶ συνκλεισμῷ
ἑκάστης ἐξαμήνου, 'at the conclusion
of each period of six months.'

22. ἀποσπᾶν] In P. Petr. II 9
(3). I (iii/B.C.) ἔγραψάς μοι μὴ ἀποσπάσαι τὸ [πλήρωμα] the verb is
used with reference to the 'with-
drawing' of a set of workmen engaged

in copper mines: cf. Ac. xx 30
ἀποσπᾶν τοὺς μαθητὰς ὀπίσω ἑαυτῶν.
For a stronger sense see P. Oxy. 37.
i. 14 (= No. 18), note.

24. πληρωθῆναι] one of many
passages that might be cited showing
that the use of πληροῦσθαι in connexion with *time* is no 'Hebraism'
as Grimm asserts; cf. further P.
Brit. Mus. 1168. 10 (= III, p. 136)
(A.D. 18) πληρωθέντος δὲ τοῦ χρόνου
ἀποδότωι, P. Tebt. 374. 9 ff. (A.D.
131) ἦς ὁ χρόνος τῆς μισθώσεως ἐπ-
ληρό(= ώ)θη εἰς τὸ διελη[λ]υθὸς ιδ′
(ἔτος).

25. ἀτακτήσῃ] On the weakened
sense of ἀτακτέω in the Κοινή, and
its consequent meaning in 2 Thess.
iii 7, see *Thess.* p. 152 ff.

ἴσας αὐτὸν παρέξεται [με]τὰ τὸν χρόνον ἢ ἀ[πο]τεισάτω ἑκάσ[τ]ης ἡμέρας
ἀργυρίου [δρ]αχμὴν μίαν, [τ]οῦ δ' ἀποσπα-
θῆναι ἐντὸς τοῦ χρόν[ου] ἐπίτειμον
δραχμὰς ἑκατὸν καὶ εἰς τὸ ·δημόσιον   30
τὰς ἴσας. ἐὰν δὲ καὶ αὐτὸ[ς ὁ] Πτολεμαῖος
μὴ ἐγδιδάξῃ τὸν παῖ[δ]α, ἔνοχος
ἔστω τοῖς ἴσοις ἐπιτε[ί]μοις. κυρία
ἡ διδασκαλική. (ἔτους) ιγ′ Νέ[ρ]ωνος Κλαυδίου
Καίσαρος Σεβαστοῦ Γερμανικοῦ   35
Αὐτοκράτορος, μηνὸς Σεβαστοῦ κα′.

2nd hand Πτολεμαῖος [Πα]υσιρίωνος
τοῦ Πτολεμαίου μητρὸς Ὠφε-
λοῦτος τῆς Θέωνος ἕκαστα
ποιήσω ἐν τῷ ἐνιαυτῷ ἑνί.   40
Ζωίλος Ὥρου τοῦ Ζωίλου μητρὸς

truant, he [Tryphon] will produce him for an equal number of days
after the time, or let him pay back for each day one silver drachma,
and the penalty for removing him within the period shall be a
hundred drachmas and a like amount to the public treasury. But
if Ptolemaeus himself does not teach the boy thoroughly, let him
be liable to the like penalties. This contract of apprenticeship is
valid. The 13th year of Nero Claudius Caesar Augustus Germanicus Emperor, the month Sebastus 21.

I Ptolemaeus, son of Pausirion, the son of Ptolemaeus, my
mother being Ophelous the daughter of Theon, will carry out
each of these requirements in the one year.

I Zoilus, son of Horus, the son of Zoilus, my mother being

27. ἀ[πο]τεισάτω] stronger than
ἀποδότω, and implying repayment
by way of punishment or fine (cf.
Gradenwitz *Einführung*, p. 85,
note 4), a fact which lends additional emphasis to its use by S. Paul
in Philem. 19.

29. ἐπίτειμον] Cf. P. Gen. 20.
15 (ii/B.C.) προσαποτισάτω ἐπίτιμον
παραχρῆμα κτλ.

32. ἔνοχος κτλ.] an apt parallel
to Mt. v. 22 ἔ. τῇ κρίσει, which
Wellhausen (*Einl.* p. 33 f.) regards
as ' ungriechisch.'

Διεῦτος τῆς Σωκέως ἔγραψα
ὑπὲρ αὐτοῦ μὴ ἰδότος γράμματα.
ἔτους τρισκαιδεκάτου
Νέρωνος Κλαυδίου Καίσαρος   45
Σεβαστοῦ Γερμανικοῦ
Αὐτοκράτο[ρο]ς, μη(νὸς) Σεβαστοῦ κα'.

Dieus daughter of Soceus, write on his behalf seeing that he does not know letters. The 13th year of Nero Claudius Caesar Augustus Germanicus Emperor, the month Sebastus 21.

43. μὴ ἰδότος γράμματα] The phrase occurs in countless papyrus documents written either in whole or in part by a scribe on behalf of the 'unlettered' author. Cf. the use of the corresponding adjective ἀγράμματος in Ac. iv 13 (cf. Jo. vii 15, Ac. xxvi 24) = 'unacquainted with literature or Rabbinic learning.'

21. LETTER REGARDING THE PURCHASE OF DRUGS

P. BRIT. MUS. 356.   i/A.D.

Edited by Kenyon in *British Museum Papyri* II, p. 252.

A letter from Procleius to Pecusis, asking that certain drugs should be sent to him at Alexandria by the hand of his friend Sotas, and warning him that they must be of good quality.

Προκλήιος Πεκύσει τῶι
φιλτάτωι χαίρειν.
καλῶς ποιήσεις ἰδίωι

Procleius to his dearest Pecysis greeting. Be so good as to

κινδύνῳ τὸ καλὸν πω-
λήσας ἐξ ὧν ἐάν σοι εἴ-   5
πῃ φαρμάκων ἔχειν
χρείαν Σώτας ὁ φίλος
μου ὥστε ἐμοὶ κατε-
νεγκεῖν αὐτὸν εἰς Ἀλε-
ξάνδρειαν. ἐὰν γὰρ ἄλ-   10
λως ποιήσῃς ὥστε σα-
πρὸν αὐτῷ δοῦναι τὸ
μὴ χωροῦν ἐν τῇ Ἀλε-
ξανδρείᾳ γείνωσκε
σαυτὸν ἔξοντα πρὸς ἐμὲ   15
περὶ τῶν δαπανῶν.
ἄσπασαι τοὺς σοὺς πάντας.
ἔρρωσο

On the *verso*

Πεκύσει.

sell at your own risk good quality of those drugs of which my
friend Sotas says that he has need, so that he may bring them
down for me to Alexandria. For if you do otherwise, and give
him stale stuff, which will not pass muster in Alexandria, understand that you will have to settle with me with regard to the
expenses. Greet all your family. Farewell.

(Addressed) To Pecysis.

5. ἐάν] On the vernacular use
of ἐάν for ἄν, of which examples still
survive in the best MSS. of the N.T.
(WM. p. 390), see Moulton *Proleg.*
pp. 42 f., 234, and cf. Thackeray
Gramm. 1 p. 65 ff. for the significance of ὃς ἄν (ὃς ἐάν) in the LXX.

11. σαπρόν] 'stale,' 'worthless,'
opposed to καλόν as here in Mt. xii

33, xiii 48: cf. P. Fay. 119. 4
(*c*. A.D. 100) χόρτου...δύσμην σαπράν
'a stale bundle of hay.'

13. χωροῦν] For this use of
χωρέω cf. Polyb. xxviii. 15. 12 τὰ
πράγματα χωρεῖ κατὰ λόγον.

15. ἔξοντα κτλ.] Cf. Ac. xix. 38
ἔχουσιν πρός τινα λόγον, also Heb.
ii 13.

22. LETTER OF REMONSTRANCE TO
A DILATORY SON

i/A.D.

From the Fayûm. Edited by Krebs in *Berliner Griechische
Urkunden* II, p. 174, cf. p. 357. See also Erman and Krebs,
p. 215 f. ; Preisigke, *Familienbriefe*, p. 104 f.

This letter gives us a clear glimpse into the anxieties of a
small landholder. He is dependent upon the assistance of his
son for the care of his lot of land, but that assistance has been
withheld, and for some reason or other the son has left his
father's and mother's letters unanswered. The father accordingly writes him again in peremptory terms telling him
that he must return, as otherwise the lot will be ruined, and
it will be impossible to find a tenant for it.

'Ερμοκράτη[ς Χαιρᾷ]
τῷ υἱῷι [χαίρειν].
Πρ[ὸ] τῶ[ν ὅλων ἐρρῶσθαί
[σ]ε εὔχο[μαι·········]
[δ]έομε σε ε[········]   5
[γ]ράφειν π[ερὶ] τῆς
ὑγίας σου καὶ [ὅ],τι βούλι,
καὶ ἄλλοτέ σοι ἔγραψα
περὶ τῆς τ[··]ψνα καὶ οὔ-

Hermocrates to Chaeras his son, greeting. First of all I pray
that you may be in health...and I beg you...to write regarding your
health, and whatever you wish. Already indeed I have written you

τε ἀντέγραψας οὔτε   10
ἦλθας, καὶ νῦν, αἰὰν
μὴ ἔλθῃς, κινδινεύ-
ω ἐκστῆναι οὗ ἔχω
[κλή]ρου. Ὁ κοινωνὸς ἡ-
μῶν οὐ συνηργάσα-   15
το, ἀλλ' οὐδὲ μὴν τὸ
ὕδρευμα ἀνεψήσθη,
ἄλλως τε καὶ ὁ ὑδρα-
γωγὸς συνεχώσθη ὑ-
πὸ τῆς ἄμμου καὶ τὸ   20
κτῆμα ἀγεώργητόν
ἐστιν. Οὐδεὶς τῶν γεωρ-
γῶν ἠθέλησεν γεωρ-
γεῖν αὐτό, μόνον δια-

regarding the..., and you neither answered nor came, and now, if you do not come, I run the risk of losing the lot (of land) which I possess. Our partner has taken no share in the work, for not only was the well not cleaned out, but in addition the water-channel was choked with sand, and the whole land is untilled. No tenant was willing to work it, only I continue paying the

14. [κλή]ρου] as restored by Viereck for the Editors' [και]ροῦ.
κοινωνός] Cf. Lk. v 10, Heb. x 33.
17. ὕδρευμα] This rare word is found in Th. Jer. xxxix (xlvi) 10.
ἀνεψήσθη] C . P. Brit. Mus. 131, 631 (= 1, p. 188) (A.D. 78–9) ἀνα-ψῶντ[ες] τὸ ἔνδον φρέαρ, B. G. U. 530¹⁷ (i/A.D.).
18. ὑδραγωγός] the channel by which the Nile overflow was conducted to the fields. So essential was this inundation (βροχή) that in leases special provision was usually made for any years in which it might not take place (cf. P. Oxy. 280. 5, note).
20. ἄμμου] Cf. P. Tebt. 342. 27 (late ii/A.D.) εἰς ἐκσκαφὴν χοὸς καὶ

χαυνογείου καὶ ἄμμου 'for the digging of earth and porous clay and sand.'
21. κτῆμα] 'land,' 'field,' as in Prov. xxiii 10: cf. also Ac. ii 45, where κτήματα are apparently to be understood in the same sense, as distinguished from the vaguer ὑπάρ-ξεις 'goods.'
24. διαγράφω] 'pay,' as frequently in the ostraca, see Wilcken Gr. Ostr. I, p. 89 ff., where, following Peyron (P. Tor. I, p. 144 ff.), reference is also made to Esth. iii 9 κἀγὼ διαγράψω εἰς τὸ γαζοφυλάκιον τοῦ βασιλέως ἀργυρίου τάλαντα μύρια, 2 Macc. iv 9 πρὸς δὲ τούτοις ὑπισχνεῖτο καὶ ἔτερα (sc. τάλαντα) διαγράφειν κτλ.

γράφω τὰ δημόσια   25
μηδὲν συνκομιζόμε-
νος. μόλις γὰρ μίαν πρα-
σεὰν ποτίζι τὸ ὕδωρ,
ὅθεν ἀνανκαίως ἐλ-
θέ, ἐπὶ κινδυνεύει   30
τὰ φυτὰ διαφωνῆσαι.
Ἀσπάζεταί σε ἡ ἀδελ-
φή σου Ἑλένη καὶ ἡ μή-
τηρ σου μέμφεταί σε,
ἐπὶ μὴ ἀντέγραψας αἰ-   35
τῇ. Ἄλλως τε καὶ ἀπαι-
τῖται ὑπὸ τῶν πρακτό-
ρων ἱκανὸν ὅτι οὐκ ἔ-
πεμψας πρὸς σὲ τοὺς πρά-

public taxes without getting back anything in return. There is
hardly a single plot that the water will irrigate. Therefore you
must come, otherwise there is a risk that the plants perish.
Your sister Helene greets you, and your mother reproaches you
because you have never answered her Especially security is
demanded by the taxgatherers because you did not send the tax-

26. συνκομιζόμενος] Cf. P. Flor.
58. 5 (iii/A.D.) τοὺς φόρους συνκομι-
ζομένη. The use of the verb in Job
v 26 ὥσπερ θιμωνιὰ ἅλωνος καθ᾽
ὥραν συνκομισθεῖσα prepares us for
the semi-metaphorical application
in Ac. viii 2, the only other passage
in the Bibl. writings where it is
found.

27. μίαν πρασε(= ι)άν] one of the
plots or beds of which the κτῆμα was
made up: cf. Sir. xxiv 31 μεθύσω μου
τὴν πρασιάν, and the striking use of
the figure in Mk vi 40 ἀνέπεσαν
πρασιαὶ πρασιαί—the different 'com-
panies' presented the appearance of
so many garden beds dotted over the
green grass.

31. διαφωνῆσαι] 'perish.' For

this late sense of the verb, as several
times in the LXX (e.g. Exod. xxiv
11, Ezek. xxxvii 11), cf. P. Petr. 11
13 (3), where the fall of a wall is
attended with the risk of the death
of certain prisoners, κινδυνεύει πεσόν-
τος αὐτοῦ διαφωνῆσαί τι τῶν σωμάτων.

36. ἀπαιτῖται] = ἀπαιτεῖται 'is
demanded': cf. P. Fay. 39. 14 ff.
(A.D. 183) ἐκ τίνος ἀπαιτεῖται τὸ
προκείμενον ἀπότακτον, where the
Editors state that ἀ. 'may imply
that the payment was in arrear or
have a quite general meaning.'

37. πρακτόρων] the general term
for collectors of revenue in imperial
times. In Lk. xii 58 it denotes
rather a lower 'officer of the court':
see Deissmann *B.S.* p. 154.

κτορες, ἀλλὰ καὶ νῦν πέμ-   40
ψον αὐτῇ. Ἐρρῶσθαί σε εὐ-
χ[ομ]αι. Παοῖνι θ'.

On the *verso*

Ἀ[πόδ]ο-
ς ἀπὸ Ἑρμοκράτους Χ Χαιρᾷ υἱῶι.

gatherers to you (?): but now also send to her. I pray that you
may be well. Pauni 9.
   (Addressed)
   Deliver from Hermocrates to Chaeras his son.

42. Παοῖνι θ'] = June 3. This date explains the urgency of the letter, as the Nile overflow began about the middle of June, and consequently all preparations for utilizing it had to be completed before that date (Erman and Krebs).

23. AN INVITATION TO A FESTIVAL

B. G. U. 596.   A.D. 84.

From the Fayûm. Edited by Krebs in the *Berliner Griechische Urkunden* II, p. 240.

Didymus invites his friend Apollonius to return along with
the bearer of the letter, in order that he may take part in an
approaching feast. For another letter of invitation see No. 39.

Δίδυμος Ἀπολλωνίωι
τῶι τιμιωτάτωι
χαίρειν.

Didymus to his most esteemed Apollonius greeting.

7

Καλῶς ποιήσεις συνελθὼν
[Α]ἰλουρίωνι τῶι κομίζον-   5
τί σοι τὸ ἐπ[ι]στ[ό]λιον, ὅπως
εἰς τὴν ἑορτὴν περιστε-
ρείδια ἡμεῖν ἀγοράσηι,
καὶ ἐρωτηθεὶς κατελ-
θὼν συνευωχηθῇ[ι]   10
ἡμεῖν. Τοῦτ[ο] οὖν ποιή-
σας ἔσῃ μοι μεγάλην
χάριταν κατ[α]τεθειμ[έ]νο(ς).
Ἀσπασαι τοὺς σοὺς πάντας.
Ἔρρωσο.   15
(Ἔτους) τρίτου Αὐτοκράτορος
Καίσαρος Δομιτιανοῦ
Σεβαστοῦ Γερμανικοῦ Παχ(ὼν) ιε΄.

On the *verso*

Εἰς Βακχιάδα [ἀπόδος Ἀπολλωνίωι] τῶι τιμιωτ[ά(τωι)].

Please accompany Ailourion, who conveys this letter to you, in order that he may buy for us young pigeons for the feast, and being invited may come down and feast along with us. If you do this, you will have laid up a great store of gratitude at my hands. Greet all your household. Goodbye.

The third year of the Emperor Caesar Domitian Augustus Germanicus, Pachon 15.

(Addressed)

Deliver at Bacchias to the most esteemed Apollonius.

---

4. συνελθών] The word is used several times in the same sense of 'accompany' in the Lucan writings (e.g. Lk. xxiii 55, Ac. ix 39).

5. κομίζοντι] Cf. P. Brit. Mus. 42. 7 (= No. 4), note.

7. περιστερείδια] = περιστερίδια. The diminutive occurs several times in P. Goodsp. 30 (A.D. 191-2) a roll of accounts from Karanis.

10. συνευωχηθῇι] Cf. Jude 12,

2 Pet. ii 13. For the simple verb see *O.G.I.S.* 383. 157 (i/B.C.) ἀσυκοφάντητον ἔχῃ τὴν ἑορτὴν εὐωχούμενος ὅπου προαιρεῖται.

13. χάριταν κατ[α]τεθειμ[έ]νο(ς)] the same phrase as in Ac. xxiv 27, xxv 9. For χάριτα, for χάριν, cf. Jude 4. Both forms occur in the same document, B.G.U. 48 (ii/A.D.): see further Crönert *Mem. Gr. Herc.* p. 170 note 6.

24. GEMELLUS TO EPAGATHUS

P. FAY. III.   A.D. 95-6.

From the Fayûm. Edited by Grenfell and Hunt in *Fayûm Towns and their Papyri*, p. 165 f.

One of a family budget of fourteen letters which were discovered by Drs Grenfell and Hunt in a house at Kaṣr el Banât, a village in the Fayûm. They are for the most part addressed by the head of the family, a certain Lucius Bellenus Gemellus, to his son Sabinus or to Epagathus, perhaps his nephew, who seem to have managed his affairs for him. The letters extend over sixteen years, and the latest, written by Gemellus when he was seventy-seven years old, bears traces of his advancing age in the 'shaky and illegible' character of the handwriting. The general impression the Editors have formed of the character of Gemellus, as they tell us in their delightful introduction to the letters (*Fayûm Papyri* p. 261 ff.), is that 'of a shrewd old man of business, somewhat wilful and exacting, but of a kind and generous disposition.' The following letter, the earliest in the series written by Gemellus' own hand, proves that he was no great scholar, his spelling in particular often leaving much to be desired.

M.

Λούκι[ος Βελ]λῆνος Γέμελλος
Ἐπαγα[θῶι τ]ῶι ἰδίωι χαίριν.
μένφομαί σαι μεγάλως ἀπο-
λέσας χ[υ]ρίδια δύω ἀπὸ τοῦ
σκυλμοῦ τῆς ὡδοῦ ἔχων   5
ἐν τῇ [κ]όμῃ ἐργατικὰ κτήνη δέκα. Ἡρακλίδας ὁ [ὀν]η-
λάτης τὼ αἰτίωμα περι-
επύησε λέγον ὥτι σὺ εἴρηχας
πεζῶι [τὰ χ]υρίδια ἐλάσαι.   10
περισὸν [ἐν]ετιλάμ[η]ν συ
εἰς Διο[νυσι]άδα μῖναι δύ-
ωι ἡμέρας ἕως ἀγοράσης

Lucius Bellenus Gemellus to his own Epagathus, greeting. I blame you greatly for having lost two little pigs owing to the fatigue of the journey, seeing that you have in the village ten beasts able to work. Heraclidas the donkey-driver shifted the blame from himself, saying that you had told him to drive the little pigs on foot. I gave you strict charges to remain at Dionysias for two days until you had bought 20 artabas of

2. τῶι ἰδίωι] Cf. Jo. xiii 1, Ac. iv 23, xxiv 23, 1 Tim. v 8.

5. σκυλμοῦ] Cf. the use of the verb in Mt. ix 36 ἐσκυλμένοι 'worn out,' 'distressed.' In P. Tebt. 41. 7 (c. B.C. 119) the subst. is used metaphorically [μ]ετὰ τοῦ παντὸς σκυλμοῦ 'with the utmost insolence,' cf. 3 Macc. iii 25 μετὰ ὕβρεως καὶ σκυλμῶν.

6. ἐργατικὰ κτήνη] evidently the pigs might have been carried in a cart and thereby their loss averted. For κτήνη cf. Lk. x 34, Ac. xxiii 24.

8. αἰτίωμα] the same form, of which hitherto no other example has been produced, as the αἰτιώματα of the best codd. of Ac. xxv 7, though in the present instance little stress can be laid on the orthography,

owing to the generally illiterate nature of the document (cf. e.g. the preceding τώ).

περιεπύησε] 'shifted.' In support of this undoubtedly unusual meaning of π., adopted by the Editors in view of the context, Dr Hunt thinks that σοι must be understood, and refers to the somewhat similar passage in Isocr. p. 150 E, where the common reading is μεγάλην αἰσχύνην τῇ πόλει περιποιοῦσιν (ποιοῦσιν Blass, περιάπτουσιν Cobet), and to Polyb. v 58. 5 αἰσχύνης ἦν περιποιεῖ νῦν τῇ βασιλείᾳ. For the subst., as in Eph. i 14, cf. P. Tebt. 317, 25 f. (ii/A.D.) τὸ τῆς περιποιήσεως δίκαιον 'claim of ownership.'

11. περισὸν...συ] l. περισσόν...σοι.

λωτίνου (ἀρτάβας) κ΄. λέγουσι εἶναι τὼ λώτινον ἐν τῇ Διο-   15
νυσιά[δι] ἐγ (δραχμῶν) ιη΄. ὡς ἐὰν βλέ-
πῃς [τ]ὴν τιμὴν πάν-
τος ἀγόρασον τὰς τοῦ λοτίνου
(ἀρτάβας) κ΄, [ἀ]νανκαῖν ἡγήσα[ς.
τὸν λ[ι]μνασμ[ὸν] δ[ί]οξον   20
τῶν [ἐ]λα[ι]ών[ων τ]ῶν πάν-
τον [καὶ] τάξον τ[··]ον Σέν-
[θεως] ἐργάτην χρ····
λιμνάζειν, καὶ τὼν στί-
χον τὸν φυτὸν τῶν   25
ἐν τῷ προφήτῃ πότισον.
μὴ οὖν ἄλλως πυήσῃς.

lotus. They say that there is lotus to be had at Dionysias at
the cost of 18 drachmas. As soon as you discover the price,
by all means buy the 20 artabas of lotus, considering that it is
essential. Hurry on the flooding of all the oliveyards...and water
the row of trees in 'the prophet.' Do not fail in this. Goodbye.

16. ἐγ]=ἐκ. For this usage of
ἐκ for the gen. of price see Ac. i 18
ἐκτήσατο χωρίον ἐκ μισθοῦ τῆς ἀδι-
κίας, and cf. Mt. xx 2 συμφωνήσας
δὲ μετὰ τῶν ἐργατῶν ἐκ δηναρίου τὴν
ἡμέραν with the simple gen. in v. 13.
ὡς ἐάν] = ὡς ἄν, 'as soon as,'
rather than 'however' (Edd.)—a
temporal use of the phrase, foreign
to classical Gk, but found both in
the LXX (Jos. ii 14) and the N.T.
(1 Cor. xi 34 ὡς ἄν ἔλθω, Phil. ii 23
ὡς ἄν ἀφίδω): Blass Gramm. p. 272.
19. (ἀρτάβας)] an Egyptian dry
measure of varying capacity: see
Wilcken Gr. Ostr. I p. 742 ff.
[ἀ]νανκαῖν ἡγήσα[ς] for ἀναγκαῖον
ἡγησάμενος, a Pauline phrase, 2 Cor.
ix 5, Phil. ii 25.

21. [ἐ]λα[ι]ών[ων]] Apart from
this passage, where the restoration
might be called in question, the
existence of the subst. ἐλαιών, -ῶνος,
which Blass (Gramm. pp. 32, 85)
denies even in Ac. i 12, is now
abundantly demonstrated from the
papyri. Moulton (Proleg. p. 49,
cf. pp. 69, 235) has found nearly
thirty examples between i/ and
iii/A.D.
26. τῷ προφήτῃ] 'apparently a
familiar name of a piece of land'
(Edd.).
πότισον] Cf. P. Petr. I 29 verso
(iii/B.C.) ὀχετεύομεν δὲ καὶ ποτίζομεν
'we are making conduits and water-
ing.' In this sense the word is
Biblical, Gen. xiii 10, 1 Cor. iii 6 ff.

68   GEMELLUS TO EPAGATHUS   No. 25

ἔρρωσο. (ἔτους) ιε΄ Αὐτοκράτορος
Καίσαρος Δομιτιανοῦ Σεβασ[τοῦ
Γερμανικοῦ, μηνὸς Γερμανικ(   )   30
ιε΄.

On the *verso*

'Επαγαθῶι τ]ῶι ἰδίωι
ἀπὸ Λουκίου Βελλήν]ου Γεμέλλου.

The 15th year of the Emperor Caesar Domitianus Augustus Germanicus, the 15th of the month Germanic....

(Addressed) To his own Epagathus from Lucius Bellenus
Gemellus.

30. Γερμανικ(   )] either Γερμα-   i.e. Pachon (Edd.): see further
νικ(οῦ), i.e. Thoth, or Γερμανικ(είου),   p. xviii.

25. QUESTION TO THE ORACLE

P. FAY. 137.   i/A.D.

From the temple of Bacchias in the Fayûm. Edited by Grenfell
and Hunt in *Fayûm Towns and their Papyri*, p. 292 f.

The practice of consulting the local oracle in times of
difficulty seems to have been widely extended, and was
doubtless encouraged by the priests as a fruitful source of
gain. Both the following document and P. Fay. 138 were
actually found within the temple of Bacchias, which leads
Wilcken (*Archiv* I, p. 553) to recall the interesting notice by
Ammian. Marcell. xix 12 of the oracle of Besa in Abydos
(*c.* A.D. 359): *chartulae seu membranae, continentes quae pete-
bantur, post data quoque responsa interdum remanebant in fano.*

For similar questions or petitions see B. G. U. 229, 230,
P. Oxy. 923 (all ii/iii A.D.), also the interesting Christian
counterpart, P. Oxy. 925 (= No. 54).

Σοκωννωκοννῖ θεῶι με⟨γά⟩λο μεγά-
λωι. χρημάτισόν μοι, ἦ μείνωι
ἐν Βακχιάδι ; ἢ μέλ⟨λ⟩ω ἐντυνχ-
άνιν ; τούτωι ἐμοὶ χρημάτισον.

To Sokanobkoneus the great, great god. Answer me, Shall I
remain in Bacchias? Shall I meet (him)? Answer me this.

1. Σοκωννῳκοννῖ κτλ.] = Σοκανοβ-
κονεῖ θεῷ μεγάλῳ, the local deity
of Bacchias. For μεγ. μεγ.=μεγ·
ίστου, see Moulton, *Proleg.* p. 97.

2. χρημάτισον] of a divine command or response, as frequently in
the LXX (e.g. Job xl 3) and N.T.
(e.g. Mt. ii 12). In P. Fay. 138. 1
κρεῖ(=ι)νεται is the technical term
for the decision of the oracle.

ἢ μείνωι] In P. Tebt. 284 (i/B.C.)
a brother informs his sister that he
will not start before a certain date,
seeing that it has been so determined
(ἐπικέκριται) for him by the god.
For ἢ cf. the question in B.G.U.
229. 3 ἢ μὲν σοθήσωι (=σωθήσομαι)
ταύτηι ἧς(=τῆς) ἐν ἐμοὶ ἀσθενεία
(=ας);

26. LETTER DESCRIBING A JOURNEY UP THE NILE

P. BRIT. MUS. 854.   i/ii A.D.

Edited by Kenyon and Bell in *British Museum Papyri* III,
p. 205 f., cf. p. XL. See also Wilcken, *Archiv* IV p. 554; Deissmann,
Licht vom Osten², p. 116 ff. (E. Tr. p. 162 f.).

This letter, the first part of which is unfortunately much
mutilated, is interesting not only from its mention of the
legendary source of the Nile and the oracle of Jupiter
Ammon, but from its very 'modern' reference to the practice
of inscribing one's own and one's friends' names on sacred
spots.

Νέαρχος α[
πολλῶν τοῦ κα[
καὶ μέχρι τοῦ πλεῖν ε·[

Nearchus...Since many [go on journeys] and even [betake them-
selves] to a journey by ship, in order that they may visit works of art

μένων, ἵνα τὰς χε[ι]ροπ[οι]ή[τους τέ-]

χνας ἱστορήσωσι, ἐγὼ παρεπο[ιησ]ά-   5

μην, καὶ ἀράμενος ἀνάπλο[υν π]αρ[α-]

γενόμενός τε εἴς τε Σοήνας καὶ ὅθεν τ[υγ]χά-

νει Νεῖλος ῥέων, καὶ εἰς Λιβύην ὅπου

Ἄμμων πᾶσιν ἀνθρώποις χρησμῳδεῖ.

[καὶ] εὔ⟨σ⟩τομα ἱστόρ[η]σα, καὶ τῶν φίλων   10

[ἐ]μ[ῶν τ]ὰ ὀνόματα ἐνεχάραξα τοῖς ἱ[ε]-

ροῖς ἀειμνή⟨σ⟩τως. τὸ προσκύνημα

Two lines are washed out.

On the *verso*

Ἡλιοδώρῳ.

made by hands, I have followed their example, and having undertaken the voyage up the stream have arrived at Syene, and at the spot
whence the Nile happens to flow out, and at Libya where Ammon
chants his oracles to all men, and I have learned things of good
omen, and have engraved the names of my friends on the sanct-
uaries for perpetual remembrance. The prayer... (Addressed) to
Heliodorus.

4. χε[ι]ροϝ[οι]ή[τους]] The word
is applied to material temples and
their furniture in Ac. vii 48, xvii 24,
Heb. ix 11, 24: in the LXX it
occurs fifteen times, always with
reference to idols.

5. ἱστορήσωσι] For the Hellenistic sense 'visit,' 'see,' as in
Gal. i 18, cf. Letronne *Recueil des
inscriptions grecques* 201 τὴν δὲ τοῦ
Μέμνονος ταύτην (σύριγγα) ἔτι ἱστο-
ρήσας ὑπερεθαύμασα (cited *Exp.* VII
vii, p. 115).

παρεπο[ιησ]άμην] So Wilcken,
GH., for the Editors' παρεπ[λευσ]-
άμην. The verb is found in the
same sense of 'copy,' 'imitate,' in
Athenaeus 513A.

7. ὅθεν κτλ.] Cf. Herod. ii. 28,
where the fountains of the Nile are
similarly placed at Elephantine-
Syene, and also the Syene inscr.
O.G.I.S. 168. 9 (ii/B.C.) ἐν αἷς ἡ τοῦ
Νείλου πηγὴ ὀνομαζομέ[νη], where
the addition of ὀνομαζομέ[νη] shows,
as Dittenberger has pointed out,
that the 'reputed' origin was no
longer believed in.

10. εὖ < σ > τομα] In justification
of the insertion of σ, Wilcken cites
Herod. ii. 171, where it is said of
the mysteries, εὔστομα κείσθω.

11. ὀνόματα ἐνεχάραξα] For
similar προσκυνήματα, the Editors
refer to *C.I.G.* 4897–4947, &c.,
and for the general practice of consulting the local temple oracle, see
the introd. to No. 25.

27. COPY OF A PUBLIC NOTICE

P. FLOR. 99.   i/ii A.D.

From Hermopolis Magna. Edited by Vitelli in *Papiri Fiorentini*
I, p. 188 f., cf. p. xvi.

The copy of a public notice which the parents of a prodigal
youth requested the strategus of the Hermopolite nome to set
up, to the effect that they will no longer be responsible for
their son's debts.

Γ'Αν]τίγραφον ἐκθέματος

.....[·].... ωι καὶ Ἡρακλείδηι στρατηγῶι Ἑρμο[π(ολίτου)].

Παρὰ ['Α]μμωνίου πρεσβυτέρου τοῦ Ἑρμαίου καὶ

τῆς..... γενομένης γυναικὸς Ἀ··πασίης Ἀρείο[υ]

μετ[·] · τοῦ συνόντος ἀνδρὸς Καλλιστράτου   5

τοῦ Ἀ··αεως Ἑρμοπολίτων. Ἐπεὶ ὁ υἱὸς ἡμῶν

Κάστωρ μεθ' ἑτέρων ἀσωτευόμενος ἐσπάνισε

Copy of a Public Notice.

...to Heraclides, strategus of the Hermopolite nome, from
Ammonius, elder, the son of Ermaeus, and his former wife A...,
the daughter of Areius, along with her present husband Callis-
tratus, the son of A..., inhabitants of Hermopolis. Since our son
Castor along with others by riotous living has squandered all his

---

1. ἐκθέματος] Ἔκθεμα 'public
notice' or 'edict' is found in Polyb.
xxxi. 10. 1; in Esther viii 14, 17 A
it is used to translate the Persian
loan-word רִנ. For the verb cf.
P. Tebt. 27. 108 (B.C. 113) ἐκθεμα-
τισθῆι 'be proclaimed as a defaulter.'

5. τοῦ συνόντος ἀνδρὸς Κ.] Castor's
mother would seem to have been
divorced, and then to have married
again. For a similar joint-action
on the part of a divorced couple,

though in their case the wife had
not remarried, Vitelli refers to P.
Gen. 19. In Lk. ix 18, Ac. xxii 11,
σύνειμι = 'company with.'

7. ἀσωτευόμενος] Cf. Lk. xv 13
διεσκόρπισεν τὴν οὐσίαν αὐτοῦ ζῶν
ἀσώτως. For the subst., as in Eph.
v 18, Tit. i 6, 1 Pet. iv 4, cf. P.
Par. 63, col. 10, 37 (ii/B.C.) [ἀ]να-
τετραμμένης δι' ἀσ[ω]τίας, P. Fay.
12. 24 (c. B.C. 103) πρὸς ἀσωτείαν.

τὰ αὐτοῦ πάντα καὶ ἐπὶ τὰ ἡμῶν μεταβὰς βούλεται ἀπολέσαι, οὗ χάριν προορώμεθα μήποτε
ἐ[π]ηρεάσηι ἡμεῖν ἢ ἕτερο[ν] [[ἢ]] ἄτοπόν τι πράξη[ι].   10
ἀ[ξιοῦμεν? π]ρογραφῆναι[·········] δεις αὐτῷ[·].

own property, and now has laid hands on ours and desires to
scatter it, on that account we are taking precautions lest he
should deal despitefully with us, or do anything else amiss—we
beg, therefore, that a proclamation be set up (that no one any
longer should lend him money)....

9. προορώμεθα] The verb occurs
literally in Ac. xxi 29, and metaphorically in Ac. ii 25 (from Ps. xv
(xvi) 8).
10. ἐ[π]ηρεάσηι] Cf. Lk. vi 28
προσεύχεσθε περὶ τῶν ἐπηρεαζόντων
ὑμᾶς. A good example of the verb is
found in P. Fay. 123. 7 (c. A.D. 100)
διὰ τὸ ἐπηρεᾶσθαι 'owing to having
been molested': cf. P. Brit. Mus. 846.
6 (=III, p. 131) (A.D. 140), P. Gen.
31. 18 (ii/A.D.).
ἄτοπον] From its original meaning 'out of place,' 'unbecoming,'
ἄτοπος came in late Greek to be

used ethically = 'improper,' 'un-
righteous'; and it is in this sense
that, with the exception of Ac.
xxviii. 6, it is always used in the
LXX and N.T.; cf. 2 Thess. iii 2
(note).
11. προγραφῆναι] 'announced as
a magisterial edict,' 'placarded':
cf. the significant use of the verb in
Gal. iii 1 οἷς κατ᾽ ὀφθαλμοὺς Ἰησοῦς
Χριστὸς προεγράφη ἐσταυρωμένος.
In the present passage the sense
must be filled up with some such
words as [ὅπως μη]θεὶς αὐτῷ[ι] [εἰς
τὸ πέραν δανείζῃ] (Vitelli).

28.   ORDER TO RETURN HOME FOR THE CENSUS

P. BRIT. MUS. 904.   A.D. 104.

> Edited with another fragment from an official letter-book by Kenyon
> and Bell in *British Museum Papyri* III, p. 124 ff. Various amended
> readings suggested by Wilcken, and in many cases confirmed by a fresh
> examination of the original by Grenfell and Hunt, are introduced in
> the transcription given below: see *Archiv* IV p. 544 f., and cf. Deiss-
> mann, *Licht vom Osten*², p. 201 f.

This extract from a rescript of the Prefect Gaius Vibius
Maximus contains an order for all persons who happen to be
residing out of their homes to return at once in view of the
census about to be held in the seventh year of Trajan,

A.D. 103-4 (cf. No. 17 intr.).   The document thus presents an interesting analogy to Luke ii 1-4, and confirms the fact that Herod, when he issued his command, was acting under Roman orders (cf. Ramsay, *Luke the Physician*, p. 244).

Along with the reference to the census the Prefect takes the opportunity of reminding the absentees of a certain λειτουργία, which as other edicts (e.g. B. G. U. 159, P. Gen. 16, P. Fay. 24) show, was sometimes evaded by leaving home (ll. 26, 27).

Γ[άιος Οὐί]βιο[ς Μάξιμος ἔπα]ρχ[ος]

    Αἰγύπτ[ου λέγει]·

τῆς κατ' οἰ[κίαν ἀπογραφῆς συ]νεστώ[σης]   20

ἀναγκαῖόν [ἐστιν πᾶσιν τοῖ]ς καθ' ἥ[ντινα]

δήποτε αἰτ[ίαν ἐκστᾶσι τῶν ἑαυτῶν]

νομῶν προσα[γγέλλε]σθαι ἐπα[νελ-]

θεῖν εἰς τὰ ἑαυ[τῶν ἑ]φέστια, ἵν[α]

καὶ τὴν συνήθη [οἰ]κονομίαν τῆ[ς ἀπο-]   25

γραφῆς πληρώσωσιν, καὶ τῇ προσ[ηκού-]

σῃ αὐτοῖς γεωργίαι προσκαρτερήσω[σιν].

Gaius Vibius Maximus, Prefect of Egypt (says): Seeing that the time has come for the house to house census, it is necessary to compel all those who for any cause whatsoever are residing out of their nomes to return to their own homes, that they may both carry out the regular order of the census, and may also attend diligently to the cultivation of their allotments.

18. Γ[άιος] κτλ.] For the recovery of the Prefect's name the Editors refer to B.G.U. 329 and P. Amh. 64.

20. τῆς κατ' οἰ[κίαν ἀπογραφῆς] Cf. the introd. to P. Oxy. 255 (= No. 17).

25. οἰ]κονομίαν] For the wide sense attaching to this word in late Gk see Robinson's note on Eph. i 10.

26. πληρώσωσιν] 'carry out,' 'accomplish,' as frequently in the N.T., e.g. Ac. xii 25, Col. iv 17.

27. προσκαρτερήσω[σιν] Cf. P. Amh. 65 (early ii/A.D.) in which two brothers who had been chosen as δημόσιοι γεωργοί, cultivators of the royal domains, petition that one of them should be released ἵνα δυνηθῶμεν καὶ τῇ ἑαυτῶν γεωργίᾳ προσκαρτερεῖν. The verb is also frequent in the papyri of 'attending' a court, e.g. P. Oxy. 260. 14 (A.D. 59), 261. 12 (A.D. 55). For the subst., as in Eph. vi. 18, see E. L. Hicks *J.T.S.* x p. 571 f.

29. PETITION REGARDING A ROBBERY

B. G. U. 22.   **A.D. 114.**

Edited by Krebs in the *Berliner Griechische Urkunden* I, p. 36.
See also Erman and Krebs, p. 137 f.

A petition by a woman to the Strategus, bringing a charge
of assault and robbery against another woman, and asking
that justice should be done.

Σαρα]πίωνι στρ(ατηγῷ) 'Αρσι(νοίτου) Ἡρακ(λείδου)
    με(ρίδος)

παρὰ Ταρμούθιος τῆς
Φίμωνος λαχανοπώλης
ἀπὸ κώμης Βακχιάδος
τὸ παρὸν μὴ ἔχουσα κύ-   5
ριον· Τῇ δ' τοῦ ἐνεσ-
τῶτος μηνὸς Φαρμοῦθι,
ἁπλῶς μηδὲν ἔχουσα
πρᾶγμα πρὸς ἐμέ, Ταορσε-

To Sarapion strategus in the division of Heraclides of the
Arsinoite nome from Tarmuthis, the daughter of Phimon, vegetable-
seller, belonging to the village of Bacchias, at present without a
guardian. On the 4th of the current month Pharmouthi, Taor-

3. λαχανοπώλης] Cf. B.G.U.
454. 12 f. (A.D. 193) ἐβάσταξαν ἡμῶν
θήκας λαχανοσπέρμ[ο]ν εἰς ἕτερον
ψυγμὸν (cf. Ezek. xxvi 5, 14) οὐκ
ἔλαττον θηκῶν δέκα δύο. The simple
λάχανον (l. 22) occurs several times
in the LXX and N.T.
5. τὸ παρόν] Cf. Heb. xii 11
πρὸς μὲν τὸ παρόν.
κύριον] 'guardian,' cf. B.G.U. 975.
12 (= No. 16). In the case of a married woman this was as a rule her

husband: cf. P. Grenf. II 15, col. i
13 (B.C. 139) μετὰ κυρίου τοῦ αὐτῆς
ἀνδρὸς Ἑρμίου, the earliest example
of this office that we have. In P.
Tebt. 397 (A.D. 198) a woman makes
formal application for a temporary
guardian owing to her husband's
absence (ἐπὶ ξένης εἶναι, cf. l. 34
below).
8. ἔχουσα πρᾶγμα] Cf. 1 Cor.
vi 1 τις ὑμῶν πρᾶγμα ἔχων πρὸς
τὸν ἕτερον.

νοῦφις, γυνὴ 'Αμμωνίου   10
τοῦ καὶ Φίμωνος πρεσβυ-
τέρου κώμης Βακχιάδο(ς),
ἐπελθοῦσα ἐν τὴν οἰ-
κία μου ἄλογόν μοι ἀη-
δίαν συνεστήσατο καὶ   15
περιέσχισέ μοι τὸν κι-
τῶνα καὶ τὸ πάλλιον
οὐ μόνον, ἀλλὰ καὶ ἀπε-
νέγκατό μου ἐν τῇ ἀη-
δίᾳ ἃς εἶχον κιμένας   20
ἀπὸ τιμῆς ὧν πέπρακον
λαχάνων (δραχμὰς) ις'. Καὶ τῇ
ε΄ τοῦ αὐτοῦ μηνὸς
ἐπελθὼν ὁ ταύτης
ἀνὴρ 'Αμμώνιος, ὁ καὶ Φί-   25

senouphis, the wife of Ammonius, also called Phimon, elder of
the village of Bacchias, although she had absolutely no ground
of complaint against me, came into my house and picked a
brutal quarrel against me. Not only did she strip off my tunic
and mantle, but also robbed me in the quarrel of the sum
which I had lying by me from the price of the vegetables I had
sold, namely 16 drachmas. And on the 5th of the same month
there came this woman's husband Ammonius, also called Phimon,

11. τοῦ καί] Cf. Ac. xiii 9, and
see Deissmann *BS.* p. 313 ff.

πρεσβυτέρου] a communal office,
the men so designated being generally responsible for the peace and
order of the village. Their number
varied, and as they do not seem to
have been entitled to a sum of more
than from 400—800 drachmas in
virtue of their office, their position
cannot have been one of great
importance: cf. Milne *Hist.* p. 7,
and see further B.G.U. 16. 6
(= No. 33).

13. ἐπελθοῦσα ἐν τὴν οἰκία(= ίαν)]
For ἐπελθοῦσα cf. Lk. xi 22 (ἐπελθὼν
νικήσῃ αὐτόν), and for the late use
of ἐν the note on P. Oxy. 294. 4
(= No. 13).

14. ἄλογον κτλ.] Cf. P. Brit.
Mus. 342. 6 (= II, p. 174) (ii/A.D.)
ἄλογον ἀηδίαν συνεστήσαντο, and P.
Tebt. 304. 9 (ii/A.D.) ἀητ(= δ)ίαν
συ<ν>ῆψαν 'they picked a quarrel'
(Edd.), and see further the note on
P. Brit. Mus. 42. 14 (= No. 4).

18. ἀπενέγκατο] Cf. Mk xv 1.

μων, εἰς τὴν οἰκίαν μου
ὡς ζητῶν τὸν ἄνδρα μο(υ)
ἄρας τὸν λύχνον μου
ἀνέβη εἰς τὴν οἰκίαν
μου, ἀπενέγκατο οἰχό(μενος)   30
κίμενον ζεῦγος ψελλίω(ν)
ἀργυρῶν ἀσήμου ὁλκῆς
(δραχμῶν) μ΄, τοῦ ἀνδρός μου ὄν-
τος ἐπὶ ξένης. Διὸ ἀξιῶ
ἀκθῆναι τοὺς ἐνκαλου-   35
μένους ἐπί σε πρὸς δέ-
ουσ(αν) ἐπέξοδον. Εὐτύχι··
    Ταρμοῦθις ὡς (ἐτῶν) λ΄, οὐ(λὴ)
ποδὶ δεξιῷ.
(ἔτους) ιζ΄ Αὐτοκράτορος   40
Καίσαρος Νερούα Τραιανοῦ
Σεβαστοῦ Γερμανικοῦ
Δακικοῦ. Φαρμοῦθι ϛ΄.

into my house as if seeking my husband. Seizing my lamp, he
went up into my house, and stole and carried off a pair of bracelets
of unstamped silver of the weight of 40 drachmas, my husband
being at the time away from home. I require therefore that you
will cause the accused to be brought before you for fitting punishment. May good fortune attend you.

Tarmuthis about 30 years old, a mark on the right foot.

The 17th year of the Emperor Caesar Nerva Trajanus Augustus
Germanicus Dacicus.   Pharmouthi 6.

32. ἀσήμου] 'unstamped': hence
constantly in the papyri to denote a
man 'not distinguished' from his
neighbours by any convenient marks
(e.g. P. Oxy. 73. 29 (A.D. 94)). In
medical language it is used of a
disease 'without distinctive symp-
toms' (e.g. Hipp. *Epid.* I 938), and
is found in a metaphorical sense
in Ac. xxi 39.

34. ἐπὶ ξένης] c1. the note on
l. 5.
35. ἀκ(=χ)θῆναι] The verb is
frequent in this legal sense, e.g. Mt.
x 18, Ac. xviii 12 (ἤγαγον αὐτὸν ἐπὶ
τὸ βῆμα).
37. ἐπέξοδον] 'punishment,' as
in Philo II, p. 314 M.
43. Φαρμοῦθι ϛ΄]=April 1.

30. WILL OF THAËSIS

P. TEBT. 381.   A.D. 123.

Edited by Grenfell, Hunt and Goodspeed in *Tebtunis Papyri* II, p. 227 f.

Will of Thaësis, in which she bequeaths all her property, with a nominal exception (cf. 1. 15), to her daughter, Thenpetesuchus, on condition that she makes her funeral arrangements and discharges her private debts.

As is generally the case with wills, the writing is across the fibres of the papyrus, and consequently the lines are of great length: cf. P. Oxy. 105.

Ἔτους ὀγδόου Αὐτοκράτορος Καίσαρος Τραιανοῦ
   Ἀδριανοῦ Σεβαστοῦ Χοίαχ κβ′ ἐν
Τεβτύνι τῆς Πολέμονος μερίδος τοῦ Ἀρσινοείτου
   νομοῦ. ὁμολογεῖ Θαῆσις
Ὀρσενούφεως τοῦ Ὀννώφρεως μητρὸς Θενοβάστιος
   ἀπὸ τῆς προκιμένης κώμης
Τεβτύνεως ὡς ἐτῶν ἑβδομήκοντα ὀκτὼι οὐλὴι πήχι
   δεξιῶι μετὰ κυρίου τοῦ
ἑαυτῆς συνγενοῦς Κρονίωνος τοῦ Ἀμείτος ὡς ἐτῶν
   εἴκοσι ἑπτὰ οὐλὴ μεσοφρύῳ   5

In the 8th year of the Emperor Caesar Trajanus Hadrianus Augustus, Choiak 22, at Tebtunis in the division of Polemon of the Arsinoite nome. Thaësis daughter of Orsenouphis son of Onnophris, her mother being Thenobastis, of the aforesaid village of Tebtunis, being about seventy-eight years of age, with a scar on the right forearm, acting along with her guardian, her kinsman Cronion son of Ameis, being about twenty-seven years of age, a

---

4. μετὰ κυρίου κτλ.] For κυρίου
see the notes on B.G.U. 975. 12
(= No. 16) and on B.G.U. 22. 5
(= No. 29); for ἑαυτῆς the note on

P. Oxy. 275. 7 (= No. 20); and for
συνγενοῦς the note on B.G.U. 975.
13 (= No. 16).

5. ὡς ἐτῶν] Cf. Lk. viii 42.

συνκεχωρηκέναι τὴν ὁμολογοῦσαν Θαῆσιν μετὰ τὴν
ἑαυτῆς τελευτὴν
εἶναι τῆς γεγονυείης αὐτῆι τοῦ γεναμένου καὶ μετηλ-
λαχότος αὐτῆς ἀνδρὸς
Πομσάιος θυγατρὶ Θενπετεσούχωι ἔτι δὲ καὶ τῶι
τῆς τετελευτηκυείης αὐτῆς
ἑτέρας θυγατρὸς Ταορσέως υἰῶι Σανσνεῦτι Τεφερσῶτος
τοῖς δυσί, τῇ [μὲν
Θενπετεσούχωι μόνηι τὴν ὑπάρχουσαν αὐτῆι Θαῆσι
ἐν τῇ προκιμένῃ [κ]ώμῃ   10
Τεβτύνι ἀγοραστὴν παρὰ Θενπετεσούχου τῆς
Πετεσούχου οἰκίαν καὶ
αὐλὴν καὶ τὰ συνκύρωντα πάντα καὶ τὰ ὑπ' αὐτῆς
Θαήσιος ἀπολειφθεισό-
μενα ἐπίπλοα καὶ σκεύηι καὶ ἐνδομενίαν καὶ ἱματισμὸν
καὶ ἐνοφιλόμ[ε-
ν⟨α⟩ αὐτῆι ἢ καὶ ἕτερα καθ' ἣν δήποτε οὖν τρόπον,
τ[ῷ] δὲ Σανσνεῦτι διατε[τα-

scar between his eyebrows, declares that she, the declarer, Thaësis,
has agreed that after her death there shall belong to Thenpetesuchus, the daughter born to her by her late departed husband
Pomsais, and also to Sansneus son of Tephersos, the son of her
other daughter Taorseus, now dead, to the two of them, (property
as follows): to Thenpetesuchus alone, the house belonging to
Thaësis in the aforesaid village of Tebtunis, as purchased from
Thenpetesuchus daughter of Petesuchus, and the court, and all its
appurtenances, and the furniture which will be left by Thaësis, and
utensils, and household stock, and clothing, and the sums due to
her, and other things of whatsoever kind, while to Sansneus she has

---

7. τῆς γεγονυείης]=τῇ γεγονυείῃ.
13. ἐπίπλοα]=ἔπιπλα. The longer
form is almost universal in the
papyri.
σκεύηι] Cf. Mk iii 27, Lk. xvii

31.
ἐνδομενίαν] The word is common
in testamentary dispositions, e.g. P.
Oxy. 105. 4, 10, P. Gen. 3. 9, 14
(both ii/A.D.).

χέναι ἀργυρίου δραχμὰς ὀκτὼι ἀς καὶ κομιε(ῖ)ται
   ὁ Σανσνεὺς παρὰ [τῆς   15
Θενπετεσούχου μετὰ τὴν τῆς Θαήσ[ι]ος τελευτήν,
   ἐφ' ὧι ἡ θυγάτηρ Θενπετ[ε-
σούχος ποιήσεται τὴν τῆς μητρὸς κηδίαν καὶ
   περιστολὴν ὡς καθή-
κει καὶ διευλυτώσει ὧν ἐὰν φανῆι ἡ Θαῆσις ὀφίλ-
   ουσα ἰδιοτικῶν
χρεῶν· ἐφ' ὃν δὲ χρόνον περίεστιν ἡ μήτηρ Θαῆσις
   ἔχειν αὐτὴ[ν

.   .   .   .

bequeathed eight drachmas of silver, which Sansneus shall receive
from Thenpetesuchus after the death of Thaësis, on condition that
the daughter Thenpetesuchus shall perform the obsequies and
laying out of her mother as is fitting, and shall discharge whatever private debts Thaësis shall be proved to be owing: but as
long as her mother Thaësis lives she shall have power to...

15. δραχμὰς ὀκτώι] From the
parallel in B.G.U. 183. 23 cited by
the Editors, it would seem that 'this
sum was a conventional legacy where
a serious bequest was not intended':
cf. our 'cut off with a shilling.'
  17. κηδί(=εἰ)αν] Cf. 2 Macc.
iv 49, v 10.
  18. διευλυτώσει] Cf. P. Oxy. 268.
15 (A.D. 58) περὶ τῆς διευλυτημένης

φερνῆς, with reference to a 're-
funded' dowry.
  ἐάν]=ἄν, see the note on P. Brit.
Mus. 356. 5 (= No. 21).
  ἰδιο(=ω)τικῶν χρεῶν] Cf. P. Brit.
Mus. 932. 8 (=III, p. 149) (iii/A.D.)
δάνεια ἤτοι ἰδιωτικὰ ἢ δημόσια.
  19. ἐφ' ὃν δὲ χρόνον κτλ.] Cf.
1 Cor. vii 39 ἐφ' ὅσον χρόνον ζῇ ὁ
ἀνὴρ αὐτῆς.

31. A REGISTER OF PAUPERS

P. BRIT. MUS. 911.   A.D. 149.

Edited by Kenyon and Bell in *British Museum Papyri* III, p. 126 f.

The existence of a poor-rate (μερισμὸς ἀπόρων) in Roman Egypt, by means of which the well-to-do contributed to the relief of those lacking means, conjectured by Wilcken (*Gr. Ostr.* I, p. 161) on the evidence of an ostracon of A.D. 143, has now been strikingly confirmed by the discovery of the following document. It is the copy, unfortunately much mutilated, of an official list of persons, described as ἄποροι and presumably entitled to relief, amongst whom the only name preserved is that of a certain Petesorapis.

> ἀντίγραφον γραφῆς ἀπόρων
> κατα[κε]χωρισμένων ιβ′ (ἔτους)
> Ἀντ[ων]εί[νου Καίσ]αρος τοῦ
> κυρί[ου], Μεσορὴ ιβ′.
>
> Δ[·····]ια [5
> ἐστι δὲ ἐν ἀπόροις.
>
> Πετεσόραπις Πεναῦτος
> τοῦ Πετεσόραπις μητρὸς
> [   ].

Copy of a register of paupers recorded in the 12th year of Antoninus Caesar the lord, Mesore 12.

There is among the paupers Petesorapis the son of Penaus, the son of Petesorapis, his mother being...

1. γραφῆς ἀπόρων] The Editors prefer the translation 'a certificate of poverty,' but admit the possibility of the meaning given above.

2. κατακεχωρισμένων] 'recorded,' as in 1 Chron. xxvii 24 οὐ κατεχωρίσθη ὁ ἀριθμὸς ἐν βιβλίῳ λόγων.

4. Μεσορὴ ιβ′]= Aug. 5.

32. NOTICE OF BIRTH

P. FAY. 28.   A.D. 150–1.

Edited by Grenfell and Hunt in *Fayûm Towns and their Papyri*, p. 137 f.

The exact object of this and similar Birth Notices (P. Gen. 33 and B. G. U. 28, 110, 111) has not yet been determined. They were apparently not compulsory, or, as the Editors here point out, the common formula κατὰ τὰ κελευσθέντα would hardly have been so consistently omitted. It is also noteworthy that the ages of the boys so announced (in none of the documents is there any mention of girls) vary from one to seven years. Wilcken (*Gr. Ostr.* I, p. 451 ff.) considers that their purpose was primarily military, and not fiscal.

Σωκράτῃ καὶ Διδύμῳ τῷ καὶ Τυράννῳ
    γραμματεῦσι μητροπόλεως
παρὰ Ἰσχυρᾶτος τοῦ Πρωτᾶ τοῦ Μύσθου
[μ]ητρὸς Τασουχαρίου τῆς Διδᾶ ἀπ[ὸ ἀ]μ-
φόδου Ἑρμουθιακῆς καὶ τῆς τούτου γυ-   5
ναικὸς Θαισαρίου τῆς Ἀμμωνίου [τ]οῦ
Μύσθου μητρὸς Θαισᾶτος ἀπὸ τοῦ αὐτοῦ

To Socrates and Didymus also called Tyrannus, scribes of the metropolis, from Ischyras, son of Protas, son of Mysthes, his mother being Tasucharion, daughter of Didas, from the quarter Hermuthiace, and from his wife Thaisarion, daughter of Ammonius, son of Mysthes, her mother being Thaisas, from the same quarter

4. ἀ]μφόδου] the regular word in the papyri to denote the 'quarter,' *vicus*, of a city. In the N.T. it is found only in Mk xi 4 (where see the examples collected by Wetstein), and in the D text of Acts xix 28. In Jer. xvii 27, xxx (xlix) 27, it is used to translate אַרְמוֹן 'citadel,' 'palace.'

M.

ἀμφόδου Ἑρμουθιακῆς. ἀπογραφόμεθα
τὸν γεννηθέντα ἡμεῖν ἐξ ἀλλήλων υἱὸν
Ἰσχυρᾶ[ν] καὶ ὄντα εἰς τὸ ἐνεστὸς ιδ΄ (ἔτος) Ἀντω-
νείνο(υ)   10
Κα[ί]σαρος τοῦ κυρίου (ἔτους) α΄· διὸ ἐπιδίδωμ[ι] τὸ
τῆς ἐπιγενήσεως ὑπόμνημα.
[Ἰσχυρ]ᾶς (ἐτῶν) μδ΄ ἄσημος.
Θαισάριον (ἐτῶν) κδ΄ ἄσημος.
ἔγραψ[ε]ν ὑπὲρ αὐτῶν Ἀμμώνιος νομογ(ράφος).   15

Hermuthiace. We give notice of the son born to us mutually,
Ischyras, who is aged 1 year in the present 14th year of Antoninus Caesar the lord. I therefore give in the notice of his
birth.

(Signed) Ischyras, aged 44 years, having no distinguishing
mark.

Thaisarion, aged 24 years, having no distinguishing
mark.

Written for them by Ammonius, scribe of the nome.

9. γεννηθέντα] Cf. B.G.U. 28.
16 (ii/A.D.) γενηθέντα, and on the
fluctuations in the orthography see
Deissmann BS. p. 184.

10. ἐνεστός] On the form see
Mayser Gramm. p. 371. The strictly
present sense of the verb must be kept
in view in the translation of such a
passage as 2 Thess. ii 2 (note).

11. ἐπιδίδωμ[ι]] the ordinary formula for handing in a letter or report
to any royal or official authority, e.g.
Diodor. xiv. 47. 2 τὴν ἐπιστολὴν

ἐπέδωκε τῇ γερουσίᾳ: cf. Ac. xv 30.

12. ἐπιγενήσεως] On the form
see again Deissmann BS. p. 184 f.
ὑπόμνημα] a more general word
than ἔντευξις 'petition.' Its root-
sense comes well out in P. Lille 8
(iii/B.C.), a 'reminder' addressed to
a strategus with reference to an
ἔντευξις already presented to him:
see further Laqueur Quaestiones,
p. 8 ff.

13. ἄσημος] Cf. B.G.U. 22. 32
(=No. 29), note.

33. COMPLAINT AGAINST A PRIEST

B. G. U. 16.   A.D. 159—160.

From the Faiyûm. Edited by Wilcken in the *Berliner Griechische Urkunden* 1, p. 27; cf. Erman and Krebs, p. 185.

The following Report has reference to an inquiry which the five presbyter-priests of the Socnopaeus temple had been ordered to make into the conduct of a brother-priest Panephremmis, who was charged with letting his hair grow too long, and with wearing woollen garments. Unfortunately the papyrus breaks off without our learning the result of the investigation.

'Α[ν]τίγρ(αφον). Ἱέρακι στρ(ατηγῷ) καὶ Τειμαγένῃ
    βασιλ(ικῷ) γρ(αμματεῖ),
        'Αρσι(νοΐτου) Ἡρακλείδο(υ) μερίδος,
παρὰ Πακύσεως Σαταβοῦτος καὶ Πανούπιος Τεσε-
νούφιος καὶ Πανεφρέμμεως Στοτοήτιος καὶ Πακύσεως Πακύσεως καὶ Στοτοήτιος Στοτοήτιος τῶν ε΄   5
πρεσβυτέρων ἱερέων πενταφυλίας θεοῦ Σοκνο-
[π]αίου τοῦ ἐνεστῶτος κγ΄ (ἔτους). Πρὸς τὸ μεταδοθὲν

Copy. To Hierax strategus and Timagenes royal scribe of the Arsinoite nome, district of Heraclides, from Pacysis son of Satabus and Panupis son of Tesenuphis and Panephremmis son of Stotoetis and Pacysis son of Pacysis and Stotoetis son of Stotoetis, the five elder-priests of the five tribes of the god Socnopaeus in the present 23rd year. With regard to the report handed over to us for ex-

6. πρεσβυτέρων ἱερέων κτλ.] The priests of the Socnopaeus temple were divided into five phylae under the rule of presbyter-priests, the title referring not to age but to dignity.

These πρεσβύτεροι must be distinguished from the village-presbyters, see the note on B.G.U. 22. 11 (=No. 29), and cf. further Otto *Priester* 1 p. 47 ff.

εἰς ἐξέτασιν εἶδος τῆς τοῦ ἰδίου λόγου ἐπιτροπῆς
γ´ τόμου κολλή(ματος) γ´, δι᾽ οὗ δηλοῦται περὶ Πανεφρέμμεως Ὥρου συνϊερέως ἡμῶν εἰσαγγε-   10
λέντος ὑ[π]ὸ Πάσειτος Νείλου ὡς κομῶντος
[κ]αὶ χρω[μ]ένου ἐρεαῖς ἐσθήσεσι, ἐπιζητοῦσι
ὑμ[ῖ]ν εἰ [οὕ]τως ἔχει προσφωνοῦμεν ὀμνύ-
οντ[ες τ]ὴν Αὐτοκράτορος Καίσαρος Τίτου Αἰλίου
[Ἀδριανοῦ Ἀντων]είνου Σεβαστοῦ Εὐσεβοῦς τύχην/   15

.   .   .   .

amination from the acts of the idiologos' administration volume 3,
sheet 3, by which it is shown with regard to Panephremmis, son of
Horus, our fellow-priest, who has been informed against by Paseis,
son of Nilus, on the charge of letting his hair grow too long and of
wearing woollen garments, to your inquiries whether these things
are so we report on oath by the fortune of the Emperor Caesar
Titus Aelius Hadrianus Antoninus Augustus Pius....

8. ἐξέτασιν] forensic, as in Sap. i 9, 3 Macc. vii 5.

ἰδ. λόγ. ἐπιτροπῆς] The general revenues of the country were under the charge of the Idiologus, and as in a Rainer papyrus (see *Führer durch die Ausstellung*, p. 77) we find a report made to his bureau as well as to the high-priest's office, to the effect that none of the priests had absented themselves from the performance of their religious duties, it would appear that, had it been otherwise, it was in his power to stop supplies: cf. also P. Rain. 107 (ii/A.D.), where precautions are taken πρὸς τῷ ἰδίῳ λόγῳ...ἵνα μηκέτι αἱ τῶν θεῶν θρησκείαι (Jas. i 27) ἐμποδίζο(=ω)νται (1 Macc. ix 55) (Wessely *Karanis*, p. 56).

11. ὡς κομῶντος κτλ.] For the old Egyptian practice see Herod. ii. 36 οἱ ἱρέες τῶν θεῶν τῇ μὲν ἄλλῃ κομέουσι, ἐν Αἰγύπτῳ δὲ ξυρῶνται, and 37 ἐσθῆτα δὲ φορέουσι οἱ ἱερέες

λινέην μούνην καὶ ὑποδήματα βίβλινα. ἄλλην δέ σφι ἐσθῆτα οὐκ ἔξεστι λαβεῖν οὐδὲ ὑποδήματα ἄλλα. For the verb κομάω cf. 1 Cor. xi 14 f., and in connexion with the passage before us note that in the early Church short hair was considered the mark of the Christian teacher as compared with the unshorn locks of the heathen philosopher: see *Dict. of Chr. Antt.* I, p. 755.

12. ἐσθήσεσι] The double form is found according to the best MSS. in Ac. i 10 ἐν ἐσθήσεσι λευκαῖς.

13. προσφωνοῦμεν] 'report.' For this technical use of προσφωνέω, cf. P. Oxy. 51 (A.D. 173), with reference to the instructions given to a public physician to 'inspect the body of a man who had been found hanged' (ἐφιδεῖν σῶμα νεκρὸν ἀπηρτημένον) and to 'report' (προσφωνῆσαι) upon it.

ὀμνύοντες κτλ.] Cf. P. Par. 47. 2 (= No. 7), note.

34.   A MARRIAGE CONTRACT

P. OXY. 905.   A.D. 170.

Discovered at Oxyrhynchus, and edited by Grenfell and Hunt in *Oxyrhynchus Papyri* VI, p. 243 ff.

A contract of marriage between Apollonius, son of Heracles, and Thatres, daughter of Menodorus, inhabitants of the Oxyrhynchite village Psobthis.   The contract, as generally in the case of similar Oxyrhynchus documents, is in the form of a protocol, and includes the ordinary provisions with regard to the maintenance of the wife, and the return of her dowry in the event of a separation, though the mention of the bridegroom's father, as a consenting party (l. 17 ff.), is unusual. The differences of formula from the Elephantine contract (No. 1) will be at once remarked.

[·········· Ἀντωνί]νου καὶ Φαυστείνας Σεβαστῶν.

[ἐξέδοτο Μηνόδωρο]ς Ὥρου μητ(ρὸς) Τακαλλίππου
      ἀπὸ κώμης Ψώβθεως

[τὴν αὐτοῦ θυγατ]έραν Θατρῆν μητρὸς Θατρῆτος
      Ἀπολλωνίῳ

[Ἡρακλέους μητρὸ]ς Ταυσοράπιος ἀπὸ τῆς αὐτῆς
      κώμης πρὸς γάμου κοι-

[νωνίαν. ἡ δ' ἔκδοτ]ος φέρει τῷ ἀνδρὶ [εἰς φε]ρνὴν
      λόγου [χ]ρυσοῦ μὲν κοινοῦ σταθμῷ   5

...Antoninus and Faustina, Augusti.   Menodorus son of Horus, his mother being Tacallippus, of the village of Psobthis, has given for partnership of marriage his daughter Thatres, her mother being Thatres, to Apollonius son of Heracles, his mother being Tausorapis. The bride brings to her husband for dowry of common gold on the

1. The Editors think that the opening formula may be filled up with some such words as τῇ τύχῃ Ἀντωνί]νου, and compare the ἀγαθῇ τύχῃ common in wills.

4. πρὸς γάμου κοι[νωνίαν]] Cf. B.G.U. 1051. 8 f. (a marriage contract—time of Augustus) συνεληλυθέναι ἀλλ[ήλοις] πρὸς βίου κοινωνίαν.

['Οξυρυγχείτη] μναγαῖον ἐν [[τέταρτον]] ἐν εἴδεσι
συντιμηθέν,

[καὶ ἔτι ἐν παρ]αφέρνοις ἱματίων σουβροκομαφόρτια
δύο,

[ἐν μὲν‥‥‥]νον τὸ δὲ ἕτερον λευκόν. [ονουν]]
συμβιούτωσαν

[οὖν ἀλλήλοις οἱ γ]αμοῦντες φυλάσσοντες τὰ τοῦ
γάμου δίκαια,

[καὶ ὁ γαμῶν ἐπι]χορηγείτω τῇ γαμουμένῃ τὰ δέοντα
κατὰ δύνα-   10

μιν [τοῦ βίου. ἐ]ὰν δ[ὲ ἀ]παλλαγὴ γένητ[α]ι, τέκνων
ὄντων ἢ καὶ

[μὴ γενομένων, ἀποδότ]ω ὁ γαμῶν τὰ παράφερνα
πάντα

Oxyrhynchite standard one mina's weight, in kind, according to valuation, and in *parapherna* in clothing two outer veils, one...and the other white. Let the husband and wife therefore live together, observing the duties of marriage, and let the husband supply the wife with necessaries in proportion to his means. And if a separation takes place, whether there are children or none have been born, let the husband restore all the *parapherna* at the time

6. μναγαῖον]=μνααῖον. For the insertion of γ cf. P. Par. 51. 15 (=No. 6) κλάγω, and see Mayser *Gramm.* p. 167 f.

ἐν εἴδεσι] For εἴδος = ' kind,' 'class,' in popular Gk cf. P. Tebt. 58. 20 (B.C. 111) ἀπὸ παντὸς εἴδους, 289. 4 f. (A.D. 23) διαγεγρ(αμμένων) κατ' εἴδος 'classified,' and for the bearing of this usage on 1 Thess. v 22 see note *ad l.*

συντιμηθέν] The corresponding subst. is found several times in the LXX, e.g. Lev. xxvii 4 τῆς δὲ θηλείας ἔσται ἡ συντίμησις τριάκοντα δίδραχμα.

7. σουβρο(= ι)κομαφόρτια] For this new compound the Editors com-

pare P. Oxy. 921. 4 (an inventory—iii/A.D) σουρικοπάλλιον, and B.G.U. 327. 7 (ii/A.D.) σουβρικοπάλλιον.

10. ἐπι]χορηγείτω] Cf. P. Oxy. 282. 6 ff. (A.D. 30—35) ἐ]γὼ μὲν οὖν ἐπεχορήγησα αὐτῇ τὰ ἑξῆς καὶ ὑπὲρ δύναμιν ' I for my part provided for my wife in a manner that exceeded my resources'—a passage that may illustrate the 'generous' connotation of the word in Phil. i 19 ἐπιχορηγίας τοῦ πνεύματος 'Ιησοῦ Χριστοῦ (with Kennedy's note in the *Expositor's Greek Testament*).

τῇ γαμουμένῃ] For the survival of γαμεῖσθαι = *nubere* in legal contracts, see Moulton *Proleg.* p. 159.

μὲν ἄμ[α] τ[ῇ ἀπ]αλλαγῇ τὴν δ[ὲ] φερνὴν ἐν ἡμέραις ἑξή-
κοντα ἀ[φ᾽ ἧ]ς ἐ[ὰν ἡ ἀ]παλλαγὴ γένηται, τῆς πράξεως
⟦αυ⟧ οὔσης
τῷ ἐκδιδόν[τ]ι Μηνοδώρου παρὰ τοῦ γαμοῦντος καὶ ἐκ   15
τῶν ὑπαρχ[ό]ντων αὐτῷ πάντων. παρὼν δὲ ὁ πατὴρ
τοῦ
γαμοῦντος Ἡρ[α]κλῆς Μώρου μητ(ρὸς) Ἀπ[ολ]λωνίας
ἀπὸ τῆς αὐτῆς κώμης
    εὐδοκεῖ τῷ [τε] γάμῳ καὶ ἐνγυᾶται εἰς ἔκτισιν
τὴν προκειμένην φερνήν. κυρία ἡ συνγραφὴ δισσὴ γρα-
φεῖσα πρὸς τὸ ἑκάτερον μέρος ἔχειν μοναχόν, καὶ
ἐπερωτη-   20
[θέν]τες ἑαυτοῖς ⟦ἀλλήλοις⟧ ὡμολόγησαν. (ἔτους) ι᾽
Φαμενὼθ ιη᾽.

of the separation, and the dowry in sixty days from the day when
the separation takes place, the right of execution belonging to
Menodorus, the giver (of the bride), upon the husband and upon
all that belongs to him. The father of the husband, Heracles, son
of Morus, his mother being Apollonia, of the same village, being
present assents to the marriage, and is surety for the payment of
the aforesaid dowry. The contract is valid, being written in
duplicate in order that each party may have one: and in answer
to the formal question they declared to each other their consent.
The 10th year, Phamenoth 18.

13, 14. ἐν ἡμέραις ἑξήκοντα] 'in
Roman marriage-contracts thirty
days is a commoner limit' (Edd.).
    16. τῶν ὑπαρχ[ό]ντων κτλ.] a
common N.T. phrase, e.g. Mt. xix
21, Ac. iv 32, 1 Cor. xiii 3.
    18. εὐδοκεῖ] For this late Gk
word cf. P. Tebt. 33. 17 (=No. 11),
and for its construction with the
dative cf. 2 Thess. ii 12 (note).
    ἐνγυᾶται] Cf. P. Oxy. 259. 7
(A.D. 23) ὃν ἐνγεγύημαι…ἐκ [τ]ῆς

πολιτικῆς φυλα[κ]ῆς 'the man whom
I bailed out of the public prison,'
and for the corresponding adj. (as
Heb. vii 22), cf. P. Tebt. 384. 12
(A.D. 10) ὄντες ἀλλήλων ἔγγυοι εἰς
ἔκτισιν 'who are mutual security for
payment.'
    20, 21. ἐπερωτη[θέν]τες…ὡμολό-
γησαν] 'a remarkably early example
of the use in Egypt of the stipulatory
formula, which only becomes common in the third century' (Edd.).

35. NOTICE OF DEATH

P. OXY. 79.   A.D. 181—192.

Discovered at Oxyrhynchus, and edited by Grenfell and Hunt in
Oxyrhynchus Papyri I, p. 142 f.

To ensure the proper keeping of the census-returns it was
customary to make official notice of all cases of death, that the
names of the deceased persons might be struck off the lists.
The earliest of these certificates that has been recovered
is P. Brit. Mus. 281 (= II, p. 65 f.) belonging to the year
A.D. 66, where a priest's death is notified to the ἡγουμένοις
ἱε[ρέων]. Other examples are Papyri 173, 208a, and 338 in
the same collection (p. 66 ff.), and B. G. U. 17, 79, 254—all of
the second century, and P. Oxy. 1030 (A.D. 212).

On the *verso* of the present document are several rudely
written lines, containing moral precepts such as μηδὲν ταπινὸν
μηδὲ ἀγενὲς μηδὲ ἄδοξ[ο]ν μη[[δὲ]] ἀνάλκιμον πράξῃς, 'do nothing
mean or ignoble or inglorious or cowardly.' From their
character and the corrections in the writing that have been
made, the Editors conjecture that they may have formed a
school composition. Similarly the *verso* of another certificate
(B. G. U. 583) has been utilized for a private letter (B. G. U.
594).

π

'Ιουλίῳ κωμογρ(αμματεῖ) Σέσφθά
παρὰ Κεφαλᾶτος Λεοντᾶτος
μητρὸς Πλουτάρχης ἀπὸ τῆ-
ς αὐ(τῆς) Σέσφθα. ὁ σημαινόμε-

To Julius, village-scribe of Sesphtha, from Cephalas, son of
Leontas, his mother being Ploutarche, from the same Sesphtha.

4. σημαινόμενος] The same sense
of *per litteras significare* is found in
Ac. xxv 27 τὰς κατ' αὐτοῦ αἰτίας
σημᾶναι. For other examples from

the papyri, cf. P. Grenf. I, 30. 5 f.
(B.C. 103) διὰ γραμμάτων ἐκρίναμεν
σημῆναι, B.G.U. 1078. 3 ff. (A.D. 39)
οὐ καλῶς δὲ ἐποίησας...μὴ σημᾶναί μοι.

νός μου υἱὸς Πανεχώτης   5
Κ[ε]φαλᾶ[τος] τοῦ Λεοντᾶτος
μητρὸς Ἡρ[α]ίδος ἀπὸ τῆς αὐ(τῆς)
Σέσφθα ἄτεχνος ὢν ἐτε-
λεύτησεν [τ]ῷ ἐνεστῶτι ἔτ-
ι μηνὶ Ἀθύρ. διὸ ἐπιδίδω-   10
μι [τὸ] βιβλείδιον ἀξιῶν ταγῆναι αὐτὸν ἐν τῇ τῶν τε-
τελευτηκότων τάξει ὡ-
ς καθήκει, καὶ ὀμνύω
Αὐτοκράτορα Καίσαρα Μᾶρ[κο]ν   15
Αὐρήλιον Κόμοδον Ἀντωνῖνον
Σεβαστὸν ἀληθῆ εἶν[αι] τὰ προ-
[γεγραμμένα   ]

.   .   .   .

My son who is here indicated, Panechotes, son of Cephalas, son of Leontas, his mother being Herais, from the same Sesphtha, died childless in the present year in the month Hathyr. I therefore send in this announcement, requesting that he be enrolled in the roll of the dead, as is fitting, and I swear by the Emperor Caesar Marcus Aurelius Commodus Antoninus Augustus that the above statements are true.

8. ἄτεχνος]=ἄτεκνος: cf. Lk. xx 28 ff.

10. μηνὶ Ἀθύρ] The notices of death refer regularly to the month as well as year in which the death took place, unlike the notices of birth (cf. P. Fay. 28 = No. 32) in which only the year is mentioned. In neither case is the exact day ever specified.

11. βιβλείδιον] a diminutive of βιβλίον, which in itself seems to have no diminutive sense attached to it: cf. also βυβλάριον (P. Lille 7. 7, iii/B.C.).

ταγῆναι αὐτόν κτλ.] In the 3rd century the corresponding formula was περιαιρεθῆναι (cf. Ac. xxvii 20, Heb. x 11) τοῦτο τὸ ὄνομα 'that this name be blotted out': see Wilcken *Gr. Ostr.* I, p. 455.

14. ὡς καθήκει] Cf. 1 Regn. 2. 16, Ac. xxii 22.

ὀμνύω κτλ.] Cf. P. Par. 47. 2 (= No. 7).

17. προ[γεγραμμένα]] Cf. Eph. iii 3 καθὼς προέγραψα ἐν ὀλίγῳ, where the temporal force of the preposition is again almost wanting. For a more technical usage of the verb see P. Flor. 99. 11 (= No. 27).

36.　A SOLDIER TO HIS FATHER

B. G. U. 423.　　　　　　　　　　　　　　　ii/A.D.

Edited by Viereck in the *Berliner Griechische Urkunden* II, p. 84 f., cf. p. 632. See also Deissmann, *Licht vom Osten*², p. 120 ff. (E. Tr. p. 167 ff.).

The soldier Apion who had been despatched to Italy writes from Misenum to his father Epimachus, to announce his safe arrival after a stormy passage. He mentions that he has received his travelling-pay, and that his army-name is Antoni(u)s Maximus, and takes the opportunity of forwarding a picture of himself.

The address is of interest as showing that the letter was sent in the first instance to the headquarters of the writer's cohort in Egypt, to be forwarded from there, as opportunity offered, to the residence of Epimachus at Philadelphia in the Fayûm.

In the original ll. 25, 26 are inserted in the margin.

'Απίων 'Επιμάχῳ τῷ πατρὶ καὶ
　κυρίῳ πλεῖστα χαίρειν. πρὸ μὲν πάν-
τῶν εὔχομαί σε ὑγιαίνειν καὶ διὰ παντὸς
ἐρωμένον εὐτυχεῖν μετὰ τῆς ἀδελφῆς
μου καὶ τῆς θυγατρὸς αὐτῆς καὶ τοῦ ἀδελφοῦ　　5
μου. εὐχαριστῶ τῷ κυρίῳ Σεράπιδι,
ὅτι μου κινδυνεύσαντος εἰς θάλασσαν

Apion to Epimachus his father and lord heartiest greetings. First of all I pray that you are in health and continually prosper and fare well with my sister and her daughter and my brother. I thank the lord Serapis that when I was in danger at sea he

2. κυρίῳ] a title of address, see P. Oxy. 744. 2 (= No. 12).

3. εὔχομαί σε ὑγιαίνειν] a common epistolary formula, cf. 3 Jo. 2 περὶ πάντων εὔχομαί σε εὐοδοῦσθαι καὶ ὑγιαίνειν.

7. κινδυνεύσαντος εἰς κτλ.] Cf. 2 Cor. xi 26 κινδύνοις ἐν θαλάσσῃ, and for the encroachment of εἰς on ἐν see P. Oxy. 294. 4 (= No. 13).

ἔσωσε. εὐθέως ὅτε εἰσῆλθον εἰς Μη-
σηνούς, ἔλαβα βιάτικον παρὰ Καίσαρος
χρυσοῦς τρεῖς. καὶ καλῶς μοί ἐστιν.   10
ἐρωτῶ σε οὖν, κύριέ μου πατήρ,
γράψον μοι ἐπιστόλιον πρῶτον
μὲν περὶ τῆς σωτηρίας σου, δεύ-
τερον περὶ τῆς τῶν ἀδελφῶν μου,
τρ[ί]τον, ἵνα σου προσκυνήσω τὴν   15
χέραν, ὅτι με ἐπαίδευσας καλῶς,
καὶ ἐκ τούτου ἐλπίζω ταχὺ προκό-
σαι τῶν θε[ῶ]ν θελόντων. ἄσπασαι
Καπίτων[α πο]λλὰ καὶ το[ὺς] ἀδελφούς
[μ]ου καὶ Σε[ρήνι]λλαν καὶ το[ὺς] φίλους μο[υ].   20

saved me. Straightway when I entered Misenum ·I received my
travelling money from Caesar, three gold pieces. And I am
well. I beg you therefore, my lord father, write me a few
lines, first regarding your health, secondly regarding that of my
brother and sister, thirdly that I may kiss your hand, because
you have brought me up well, and on this account I hope to be
quickly promoted, if the gods will. Give many greetings to
Capito, and to my brother and sister, and to Serenilla, and my

8. ἔσωσε. εὐθ. κτλ.] Deissmann
aptly recalls the account of Peter's
deliverance in Mt. xiv 30 f. ἀρξάμε-
νος καταποντίζεσθαι ἔκραξεν λέγων
Κύριε, σῶσόν με. εὐθέως δὲ ὁ
'Ἰησοῦς ἐκτείνας τὴν χεῖρα κτλ.

9. ἔλαβα βιάτικον] the viaticum
of the Roman soldier: cf. P. Goodspeed 30, col. xli, 18 (Karanis
accounts, A.D. 191-2) Ἑρμῆτι ὑ(πὲρ)
βιατίκου (δραχμὰς) ξς΄.

For the extension of the 'vulgar'
2nd aor. in a to the LXX and
in lesser degree to the N.T. see
Thackeray Gramm. 1 p. 210 ff., W.
Schm. p. 111 f., Blass Gramm.
p. 45 f. Numerous examples of
this usage from the papyri will be
found in Deissmann BS. p. 190 f.

10. χρυσοῦς τρεῖς] = 75 drachmas.

13. σωτηρίας] here used as frequently in the Κοινή in the general

sense of 'health,' 'well-being': cf.
B.G.U. 380. 6 (= No. 43).

16. χέραν] = χεῖρα. The late
Greek form in -αν is found in MSS.
of the N.T., e.g. χεῖραν Jo. xx
25 AB, 1 Pet. v 6 ℵA: see Blass
Gramm. p. 26.

17. προκόσαι] = προκόψαι: cf.
Lk. ii 52, Gal. i 14. A striking
parallel to the former passage occurs
in Syll. 325. 18 (i/B.C.), where a
certain Aristagoras is praised as
ἡλικίᾳ προκόπτων καὶ προαγόμενος
εἰς τὸ θεοσεβεῖν.

18. τῶν θε[ῶ]ν θελόντων] a common pagan phrase (examples in Deissmann BS. p. 252) which reappears
in its Christian form Ac. xviii 21 τοῦ
θεοῦ θέλοντος, cf. 1 Cor. iv 19, Jas.
iv 15; see further the note on
B.G.U. 27. 11 (= No. 41).

ἄσπασαι..πολλά] Cf. 1 Cor. xvi 19.

Ἔπεμψά σο[ι εἰ]κόνιν μ[ου] διὰ Εὐκτή-
μονος. ἔσ[τ]ι [δέ] μου ὄνομα Ἀντῶνις Μάξιμος.   Ἐρρῶσθαί σε εὔχομαι.
Κεντυρί(α) Ἀθηνονίκη.
ἀσπάζεταί σε Σερῆνος ὁ τοῦ Ἀγαθοῦ [Δα]ίμονος
    [καὶ····]ς ὁ τοῦ [···]   25
ρος· καὶ Τούρβων ὁ τοῦ Γαλλωνίου καὶ·[····] νη-
    σο·[·····] σεν [···]
                                        [····]·[···]·[   ]

On the *verso*

Ε[ἰς] Φ[ιλ]αδελφίαν Ἐπιμχάχῳ ἀπὸ Ἀπίωνος υἱοῦ.

In the opposite direction the following two lines have been added:

Ἀπόδος εἰς χώρτην πρίμαν\ /Ἀπαμηνῶν Ἰο[υλι]α[ν]οῦ Ἀν·[··]
λιβλαρίῳ ἀπὸ Ἀπίωνος ὤσ/ \ τε Ἐπιμάχῳ πατρὶ αὐτοῦ. 30

friends. I send you a little portrait of myself at the hands of
Euctemon. And my (military) name is Antoni(u)s Maximus. I
pray for your good health.

Company Athenonike.

Serenus the son of Agathos Daemon greets you...and Turbo
the son of Gallonius and...

(Addressed)

To Philadelphia for Epimachus from his son Apion.

Then the following addition:

Give this to the (office of the) first cohort of the Apamaeans to
Julianus...paymaster from Apion, so that (he may forward it) to
Epimachus his father.

21. [εἰ]κόνιν] = εἰκόνιον. This
happy reading for the Editors'
original [ὀθ]όνιν (= ὀθόνιον) is due
to Wilcken: see Deissmann *ad l.*
In B.G.U. 1059. 7 (i/B.C.) εἰκόνες is
the name given to the personal
descriptions which accompany an
IOU, receipt, &c.: see Moulton
Proleg. p. 235.

22. ὄνομα κτλ.] When foreigners
entered the Roman army, it was
customary for them to receive a new

name. In a subsequent letter from
the same soldier to his sister
(B.G.U. 632), he describes himself
simply as Antonius Maximus, and
makes mention of his wife Aufidia
and his son Maximus.

29. ἀπόδος] Cf. Mt. xviii 28
ἀπόδος εἴ τι ὀφείλεις.

30. λιβλαρίῳ] l. λιβελλαρίῳ, with
reference apparently to the secretary
or paymaster of the cohort.

37. LETTER OF A PRODIGAL SON

B. G. U. 846.   ii/A.D.

From the Fayûm. Edited by Krebs in *Berliner Griechische Urkunden* III, p. 170 f., cf. *ibid. Berichtigungen*, p. 6, for various emendations by Schubart. See also Deissmann, *Licht vom Osten²*, p. 128 ff. (E. Tr. p. 176 ff.).

A son writes to tell his mother of the pitiful state into which he has fallen. He is ashamed to come home, but he does not forget her in his prayers, and if he had only dared to hope that she would actually seek him in the metropolis, he would have met her there. As it is, he begs her forgiveness, and at the same time inveighs against a certain acquaintance, Postumus, who had met her on her way home from Arsinoe, and retailed the whole sad story. The letter is very illiterate, and though unfortunately the concluding lines are much mutilated, like the rest they testify to the depth of the writer's emotion.

Ἀντῶνις Λόνγος Νειλοῦτι

[τ]ῇ μητρὶ π[λ]ῖστα χαίρειν. Καὶ δι-
ὰ πάντω[ν] εὔχομαί σαι ὑγειαίνειν. Τὸ προσκύνη-
μά σου [ποι]ῶ κατ᾽ αἰκάστην ἡμαίραν παρὰ τῷ
κυρίῳ [Σερ]άπειδει. Γεινώσκειν σαι θέλω, ὅ-   5
τι οὐχ [ἤλπ]ιζον, ὅτι ἀναβένις εἰς τὴν μητρό-

Antonis Longus to Nilous his mother many greetings. Continually I pray for your health. Supplication on your behalf I direct each day to the lord Serapis. I wish you to know that I had no hope that you would come up to the metropolis. On this

6. [ἤλπ]ιζον] For the aspiration Deissmann, to whom the restoration is due, refers to such instances in N.T. Gk as ἀφελπίζοντες (Lk. vi 35 DP) and ἐφ᾽ ἐλπίδι (Ac. ii 26 אCD): see Blass *Gramm.* p. 15, Moulton *Proleg.* p. 44, and cf. Helpis, Helpidius in Lat. inscriptions.

πολιν. χ[ά]ρειν τούτο ούδ' έγὸ εἰσῆθα εἰς τὴν πόλιν. ' αἰδ[υ]σοπο[ύ]μην δὲ ἐλθεῖν εἰς Καρανίδα"
ὅτι σαπρῶς παιριπατῶ. ' Αἴγραψά σοι, ὅτι γυμνός
εἰμει. Παρακα[λ]ῶ σαι, μήτηρ, δ[ι]αλλάγητί μοι. Λοι-   10
πὸν οἶδα τί [ποτ'] αἰμαυτῷ παρέσχημαι.   παιπαίδ-
δευμαι, καθ' ὃν δὶ τρόπον.   οἶδα, ὅτι ἡμάρτηκα.
Ἥκουσα παρὰ το[ῦ Ποστ]ούμου τὸν εὑρόντα σαι
ἐν τῷ Ἀρσαινοείτῃ καὶ ἀκαίρως πάντα σοι δι-
ήγηται.   Οὐκ οἶδες, ὅτι θέλω πηρὸς γενέσται,   15

account neither did I enter into the city.   But I was ashamed to
come to Karanis, because I am going about in rags.   I write
you that I am naked.   I beseech you, mother, be reconciled to
me.   But I know what I have brought upon myself.   Punished
I have been every way.   I know that I have sinned.   I heard
from Postumus who met you in the Arsinoite nome, and un-
seasonably related all to you.   Do you not know that I would

7. χ[ά]ρειν τούτο]=χάριν τούτου:
see the note on P. Par. 47. 17
(=No. 7).
ἐγὸ εἰσῆθα]=ἐγὼ εἰσῆλθα: see the
note on B.G.U. 423. 9 (=No. 36).
8. αἰδ[υ]σοπο[ύ]μην]= ἐδυσωπού-
μην (Deissmann, but regarded as a
very uncertain restoration by Schubart). The verb is used several
times by the Gk translators of the
O.T., e.g. 8m. Gen. xix 21: cf.
also P. Fay. 112. 12 f. (A.D. 99)
καὶ εἶνα αὐτὸν μὴ δυσωπήσῃς 'don't
look askance at him' (Edd.).
9. σαπρῶς] The adj. is similarly used of what is 'decayed,'
'crumbling' in Dittenberger Syll.
587. 24 (B.C. 328) μισθωτεῖ τοῦ
διατειχίσματος ἀνελόνει τὰ σαπρὰ καὶ
τῶν πύργων κτλ. For the metaph.
sense, cf. Eph. iv 29 πᾶς λόγος
σαπρὸς ἐκ τοῦ στόματος ὑμῶν μὴ
ἐκπορευέσθω, and see the note on
P. Brit. Mus. 356. 11 (=No. 21).

παιριπατῶ] l. περιπατῶ, ethically
as Eph. v 15, &c.
γυμνός] probably = 'clad only with
the χιτών' as in Jo. xxi 7. This
sense is well illustrated by P. Magd.
6 (iii/B.C.) ὡς ἤμην γυμνὸς ὑπ' αὐτῶν,
where the complainant had just
been stripped of his ἱμάτιον.
10. δ[ι]αλλάγητί μοι] Cf. Mt. v
24 πρῶτον διαλλάγηθι τῷ ἀδελφῷ σου.
11. παιπαίδευμαι] evidently in
the familiar class. and Bibl. sense
of 'visited with punishment or
chastisement,' cf. e.g. Ps. vi 2, 1
Cor. xi 32, 2 Cor. vi 9.
12. καθ' ὃν δὶ τρόπον] καθ' ὃν δὴ
τρόπον, cf. καθ' ὅντινα οὖν τρόπον,
2 Macc. xiv 3, 3 Macc. vii 7
(Deissmann). Wilcken reads δῖ = δεῖ,
'punished as I ought.'
ἡμάρτηκα] Cf. Lk. xv 18, 21
πάτερ, ἥμαρτον....
15. θέλω] For θέλω followed by
ἤ (εἴ Pap.) cf. 1 Cor. xiv 19.

εἰ γνοῦναι, ὅπως ἀνθρόπῳ [ἔ]τ[ι] ὀφείλω ὀβολόν;

[......] ο [...........] σὺ αὐτὴ ἐλθέ.

[.............] χανκ[...]ον ἤγουσα, ὅτι··

[.............]·λησαι[··] παρακαλῶ σαι

[...................]···α[.]· αἰγὼ σχεδν   20

[..................]ῳ παρακαλῶ σαι

[..................]ωνου θέλω αἰγὼ

[..................]σει······οὐκ ε̄·

[..................]··· ἄλλως ποι[·]

[σεις···]   25

The papyrus is broken off here.

On the *verso*

[·····]μητρεὶ ἀπ' 'Αντωνίω Λόνγου νεἱοῦ.

rather be a cripple than be conscious that I am still owing any-
one an obolus?...come yourself...I have heard that...I beseech you...
I almost...I beseech you...I will...not...do otherwise...(Addressed)
To...his mother from Antonius Longus her son.

16. ὅπως] here used like πῶς   26. νεἱοῦ] This form is found
= ὡς = ὅτι, see Blass *Gramm.* p. 230 f.   also in Lycaonian inscriptions.

38. LETTER OF CONSOLATION

P. OXY. 115.   ii/A.D.

Discovered at Oxyrhynchus, and edited by Grenfell and Hunt in
Oxyrhynchus Papyri I, p. 181 f. See also Deissmann, *Licht vom
Osten²*, p. 118 ff. (E. Tr. p. 164 ff.).

The following beautiful letter is addressed by a certain
Irene to her friend Taonnophris and her husband Philon.
These latter have apparently just lost a son, and a bereave-
ment Irene herself had sustained (l. 4) leads her and all the
members of her household to mourn with those who mourn.
She is however bitterly conscious how little all that she can do
amounts to, and breaks off with the exhortation that they must
do their best to comfort one another.   How different Christian

9

consolation could be is clearly shown by such a passage as
1 Thess. iv. 14—18, which the letter before us so strikingly
recalls (l. 11). Deissmann (*op. cit.* p. 88) refers to the letter
as a good example of popular narration.

> Εἰρήνη Ταοννώφρει καὶ Φίλωνι
>   εὐψυχεῖν.
>
> οὕτως ἐλυπήθην ^{καὶ} ἔκλαυσα ἐπὶ
> τῶι
> εὐμοίρωι ὡς ἐπὶ Διδυμᾶτος
> ἔκλαυσα, καὶ πάντα ὅσα ἦν κα-   5
> θήκοντα ἐποίησα καὶ πάντες
> οἱ ἐμοί, Ἐπαφρόδειτος καὶ Θερμού-
> θιον καὶ Φίλιον καὶ Ἀπολλώνιος
> καὶ Πλαντᾶς. ἀλλ' ὅμως οὐδὲν
> δύναταί τις πρὸς τὰ τοιαῦτα.   10
> παρηγορεῖτε οὖν ἑαυτούς.
>   εὖ πράττετε. Ἀθὺρ α'.

On the *verso*

>   Ταοννώφρει καὶ Φίλωνι.

Irene to Taonnophris and Philo, good cheer! I was as much
grieved and wept over the blessed one, as I wept for Didymas, and
everything that was fitting I did and all who were with me,
Epaphroditus and Thermouthion and Philion and Apollonius and
Plantas. But truly there is nothing anyone can do in the face of
such things. Do you therefore comfort one another. Farewell.
Hathyr 1. (Addressed) To Taonnophris and Philo.

2. εὐψυχεῖν] in place of the customary χαίρειν on account of the character of the letter. The verb is found in an interesting 1st century letter from a woman to her husband, B.G.U. 1097. 15 οὐ^{χ°} ὀλιγωρῶ, ἀλλὰ εὐψυχοῦσα πα[ρα]μένω: cf. Phil. ii 19.

4. εὐμοίρωι] at first understood by the Editors as a proper name, but, as the interjected article proves, to be taken as an adjective describing the deceased. The word occurs in

a similar sense in a wooden-tablet published by Goodspeed in *Mélanges Nicole*, p. 180: cf. also *Archiv* IV, p. 250.

5. πάντα κτλ.] i.e. all the customary religious rites and prayers.

11. παρηγορεῖτε] For the corresponding subst. cf. Col. iv 11 (with Lightfoot's note).

ἑαυτούς]= ἀλλήλους, as in Col. iii 16: see Moulton *Proleg.* p. 87.

12. Ἀθὺρ α']=October 28.

39. INVITATION TO DINNER

P. Oxy. 523.   ii/A.D.

Discovered at Oxyrhynchus, and edited by Grenfell and Hunt in
Oxyrhynchus Papyri III, p. 260.

An invitation from Antonius to a friend (unnamed) to
dinner in the house of Claudius Sarapion; cf. B. G. U. 596
(= No. 23), and for similar formulas see P. Oxy. 110, 111,
P. Fay. 132.

From Jos. *Antt.* xviii § 65 ff., which implies that members
of the Isis-community were in the habit of being invited to
δεῖπνον in the Isis temple, Wilcken (*Archiv* IV, p. 211) considers that such a document, as P. Oxy. 110, is an invitation
to a ceremonial rather than a private feast. In this way the
general resemblance to the phraseology regarding the τράπεζα
κυρίου καὶ δαιμονίων in 1 Cor. x 21 becomes all the more
striking.

> Ἐρωτᾷ σε Ἀντώνιο(ς) Πτολεμ(αίου) διπνῆσ(αι)
> παρ᾽ αὐτῶι εἰς κλείνην τοῦ κυρίου
> Σαράπιδος ἐν τοῖς Κλαυδ(ίου) Σαραπίω(νος)
> τῆι ις᾽ ἀπὸ ὥρας θ᾽.

Antonius, son of Ptolemaeus, invites you to dine with him at
the table of the lord Serapis in the house of Claudius Serapion on
the 16th at 9 o'clock.

1. ἐρωτᾷ] 'Ἐρωτάω = *peto* is so
thoroughly established in the Κοινή
that all thought of the influence of
the Heb. שָׁאַל on its Bibl. usage
may be completely dismissed: cf.
1 Thess. iv 1 (note), and see Deissmann *BS.* pp. 195, 290.

2. κλει(= l)νην] Sophocles *Lex.*
s.v. cites Philo II, pp. 537 M. for

κλίνη = 'a convivial party.'

3. ἐν τοῖς κτλ.] An interesting
confirmation of the R.V. rendering
of Lk. ii 49 ἐν τοῖς τοῦ πατρός μου
'in my Father's house.'

4. ἀπὸ ὥρας θ᾽] The same hour
is fixed in P. Oxy. 110, 111, and P.
Fay. 132: it would correspond
generally to our 3 o'clock in the
afternoon.

M.

40. EXTRACTS FROM A DIPLOMA OF CLUB MEMBERSHIP

P. BRIT. MUS. 1178.   A.D. 194.

Edited by Kenyon and Bell in *British Museum Papyri* III, p. 214 ff.

The following extracts are taken from a diploma of membership granted to the boxer Herminus by the Worshipful Gymnastic Club of Nomads, and consist of (1) a letter from the Emperor Claudius to the Club acknowledging the 'golden crown' which they had sent him on the occasion of his victorious campaign in Britain (ll. 8—15), and (2) the formal notification to the members of the Club of the admission of Herminus on his payment of the statutory fee (ll. 37—44).

The whole document, whose 'unique' character is emphasized by the Editors, is dated at Naples in Italy at the 49th performance of the Augustan games, 22nd Sept. A.D. 194, and is signed in various hands by most of the Club officials.

Τιβέριος [Κλ]αύδιος Καῖσαρ Σεβαστὸς Γερμανικὸς Σαρ-
    ματικός, ἀρχιερεὺς
μέγι[στο]ς, δημαρχικῆς ἐξουσίας τὸ ϛ΄, ὕπατος ἀποδεδειγ-
    μένος
τὸ [δ΄, αὐτ]οκράτωρ τὸ ιβ΄, πατὴρ πατρίδος, συνόδ[ῳ]
    ξυστικῇ   10
    [περιπολιστικ]ῇ   χαίρειν.

Tiberius Claudius Caesar Augustus Germanicus Sarmaticus, the very great high-priest, in the 6th year of his tribunician power, consul-designate for the 4th time, (proclaimed) Emperor for the 12th time, father of his country, to the Gymnastic Club of Nomads, greeting.

9. ἀποδεδειγμένος] 'designated,' 'nominated,' as frequently in late Gk: cf. 1 Thess. ii 4 (note).

10. συνόδ[ῳ] κτλ.] For a description of this Club, which on the evidence of various inscriptions was apparently the principal athletic society of Rome, the Editors refer to Friedländer *Sittengeschichte Roms*⁶ II, p. 491 f.

Τὸν πεμ[φ]θέντ[α μο]ι ὑφ' ὑμῶν ἐπὶ τῇ κατὰ Βρετάννων
νείκῃ χρυ-
σοῦν σ[τέ]φ[α]νον ἡδέως ἔλαβον σύμβολον περιέχοντα
τῆς ὑμετέ-
ρας πρός με εὐσεβείας.   Οἱ πρεσβεύοντες ἦσαν Τιβ.
Κλ. Ἑρμᾶς
Τιβ. Κλ. Κῦρος Δίων Μικκάλου Ἀντιοχεύς. ἔρρωσθε.   15

.   .   .   .   .   .

Ἡ ἱερὰ ξυστικὴ περιπολιστικὴ Ἀδριανὴ Ἀντωνιανὴ
Σεπτιμιανὴ
σύνοδος τῶν περὶ τὸν Ἡρακλέα καὶ τὸν ἀγώνιον καὶ
αὐτοκράτορα
Καίσαρα Λ· Σεπτίμιον Σευῆρον Περτίνακα Σεβαστὸν τοῖς
ἀπο τῆς
[αὐτῆς συνό]δου χαίρειν.   40
[Γεινώσκετε] ὄντα [ἡμῶν] συνοδείτην Ἑρμεῖνον, τὸν καὶ
Μωρόν,

I received with pleasure the golden crown which was sent to
me by you on the occasion of my victory over the Britons, as an
expression of your loyal devotion towards me. The ambassadors
were Tib. Cl. Hermas, Tib. Cl. Cyrus, Dion son of Miccalus, an
Antiochene. Farewell.

The Worshipful Gymnastic Club of Nomads under the patron-
age of Hadrian Antoninus Septimius, who meet under the auspices
of Heracles and the umpire of games and Emperor Caesar Lucius
Septimius Severus Pertinax Augustus, to the members of the same
club greeting.

Know that we are adopting as member Herminus, also called

12. τῇ κατὰ Βρετ. νείκῃ] in
A.D. 43.

13. περιέχοντα] Cf. 2 Macc. xi
16 ἐπιστολαί...περιέχουσαι τὸν τρόπον
τοῦτον, Ac. xxiii 25 A ἐπιστολὴν πε-
ριέχουσαν (ἔχουσαν ℵB) τὸν τύπον
τοῦτον.

14. εὐσεβείας] To what Deissmann (*BS.* p. 364) says of the
religious connotation of this word,

add from the papyri such passages
as P. Par. 29. 9 f. (ii/B.C.) δι' ἣν
ἔχετε πρὸς τὸ θεῖον εὐσέβειαν, and
the payments made to the Socnopaeus temple ἐξ εὐσεβείας in P. Tebt.
298. 45 (A.D. 107–8).

πρεσβεύοντες] The regular use of
this verb in the Greek East in connexion with an Imperial embassy
lends fresh emphasis to the Pauline

['Ερμοπολείτην πύ]κτην ὡς ἐτῶν   καὶ ἀποδεδωκότα
 τὸ κατὰ
τὸν νόμ[ον ἐν]τάγιον πᾶν ἐκ πλήρους δηνάρια ἑκατόν.
 ἐγράψα-
μεν οὖν ὑμεῖν ἵνα εἰδῆτε.   ἔρρωσθε

Morus, boxer of Hermopolis, about   years old, on his payment
of the legal fee amounting altogether to a hundred denarii.   We
have written you accordingly that you may know.   Farewell.

claim in 2 Cor. v 20, Eph. vi 20:
see Deissmann *LO.*² p. 284.

42. ὡς ἐτῶν] The actual age of
Herminus has not been filled in
here, but from a census return of
A.D. 216 or 217 that has been
recovered, P. Brit. Mus. 935 (=III,
p. 29 f.), we know that it was 27.

43. ἐν]τάγιον] apparently here
='a fee for registration' (Edd.).
The word is found several times in
late papyri= 'receipt,' e.g. P. Oxy.
136, 142 (both vi/A.D.).
 ἐκ πλήρους] Cf. P. Par. 26. 8
(= No. 5).

---

41. LETTER FROM ROME

B. G. U. 27.   ii/A.D.

From the Fayûm.   Edited by Krebs in the *Berliner Griechische
Urkunden* I, p. 41, cf. p. 353.   See also Erman and Krebs, p. 213.

The ship-master Irenaeus, who had been sent with a cargo
of corn to Rome, writes from thence to his brother in the
Fayûm announcing his safe arrival.   According to our mode
of reckoning, he had reached Ostia on June 30th, finished unloading on July 12th, and arrived in Rome a week later, where
he was now awaiting his discharge.

Apart from its contents, the letter is interesting as one of
the few papyrus-documents, hitherto discovered in Egypt, but
not written there: cf. B. G. U. 423, 632, P. Amh. 3 (a) (all
from Rome), B. G. U. 316 (from Ascalon), ? 895 (from Syria),
and a Latin papyrus from Seleucia in Pieria (cf. Wessely *Taf.
Lat.* No. 7): see Wilcken *Archiv* II, p. 138 n.¹.

[Εἰρηναῖος Ἀπολι-   ]
[ναρίωι τ]ῶι ἀδε[λ]φ[ῶι] π[ολλὰ] χαίρ[ειν].
καὶ διὰ π[α]ντὸς εὔχομαί σε ὑγιένεν
καὶ [ἐγὼ?] αὐτὸς ὑγιένω. Γινώσκειν σε θέλω ὅτει εἰς γῆν   5
ἐλήλυθα τῇ ϛ' τοῦ Ἐπεὶφ
μηνός, καὶ ἐξε[κ]ένωσα μὲν τῇ
ιη' τοῦ αὐτοῦ μηνός, ἀνέβην
δὲ εἰς Ῥώμην τῇ κε' τοῦ αὐτοῦ μηνός, καὶ παρεδέξατο ἡ-   10
μᾶς ὁ τόπος ὡς ὁ θεὸς ἤθελεν,
καὶ καθ' ἡμέραν προσδεχόμ[ε-
θα διμι[σ]σωρίαν, ὥστε ἕως
σήμερον μηδέν' ἀπολε-
λύσθαι τῶν μετὰ σίτου.   15
Ἀσπάζομαι τὴν σύνβιόν σου

Irenaeus to Apolinarius his brother, many greetings. Continually I pray that you may be in health, even as I myself am in health. I wish you to know that I arrived at land on the 6th of the month Epeiph, and I finished unloading my ship on the 18th of the same month, and went up to Rome on the 25th of the same month, and the place welcomed us, as God willed. Daily we are waiting for our discharge, so that up till to-day no one of us in the corn service has been let go. I greet your wife

4. γινώσκειν κτλ.] Cf. the Pauline formula οὐ θέλω δὲ ὑμᾶς ἀγνοεῖν (Rom. i 13 etc.).

7. ἐξε[κ]ένωσα] Cf. the use of the verb in Song of Solomon i 3 μύρον ἐκκενωθὲν ὄνομά σου, and see the note by Dr J. H. Moulton in *Exp.* VI iii, p. 276.

10. παρεδέξατο] For the idea of 'welcome' underlying the word cf. Mk iv 20, Acts xv 4 παρεδέχθησαν

ἀπὸ τῆς ἐκκλησίας.

11. ὡς ὁ θεὸς ἤθελεν] This precise formula has not yet been discovered elsewhere, and has led to the idea that the writer was a Christian, cf. καθὼς (ὁ θεὸς) ἠθέλησεν in 1 Cor. xii 18, xv 38, and see further the note on B.G.U. 423. 18 (= No. 36).

13. διμι[σ]σωρίαν] Cf. Latin *litterae dimissoriae.*

πολλὰ καὶ Σερῆνον καὶ πάντες τοὺς φιλοῦντάς σε κατ᾽ ὄνο·
μα.

        Ἔρρωσο. Μεσορὴ θ᾽.

On the *verso*

    Ἀπολιναρί(ωι?) ✕ ἀπὸ Εἰρηναίου ἀδελφοῦ.

much, and Serenus, and all who love you, by name. Good-bye.
Mesore 9.

(Addressed) To Apolinarius from Irenaeus his brother.

18. κατ᾽ ὄνομα] Cf. 3 Jo. 15 ἀσπάζου τοὺς φίλους κατ᾽ ὄνο; α.

42. A BOY'S LETTER

P. OXY. 119.   ii/iii A.D.

Edited by Grenfell and Hunt in *Oxyrhynchus Papyri* I, p. 185 f.
For various emendations in the text which have been followed here, see
Wilamowitz-Moellendorf, *G. G. A.* 1898, p. 686, and Blass, *Hermes*,
XXXIV (1899), p. 312 ff. ; cf. also Deissmann, *Licht vom Osten²*,
p. 137 ff. (E. Tr. p. 187 ff.).

A letter from a boy to his father complaining that he had
not been taken to Alexandria. Notwithstanding the atrocious
spelling and grammar, which are on a level with the unfilial
tone of the contents, the letter is very instructive for the
student of the Greek vernacular.

Θέων Θέωνι τῷ πατρὶ χαίρειν.
καλῶς ἐποίησες. οὐκ ἀπένηχές με μετ᾽ ἐ-
σοῦ εἰς πόλιν. ἢ οὐ θέλις ἀπενέκκειν με-

Theon to Theon his father, greeting. You did a fine thing!
You have not taken me away along with you to the city ! If

1. Θέων] From the address we
learn that Theon *fils* was also known
as Θεωνᾶς.

2. ἀπένηχες]=ἀπήνεγκες, as ἀπενέκκειν (l. 3)=ἀπενεγκεῖν, and ἀπενέκαι l. 8)=ἀπενέγκαι. For a similar

use of the verb cf. P. Par. 49. 23 f.
(ii/B.C.) διὰ τὸ εἰς τὴν πόλιν με θέλειν
δοῦναι ἀπενεγκεῖν.
    ἐσοῦ] For the form see Moulton,
Proleg. p. 234.

τ' ἐσοῦ εἰς Ἀλεξανδρίαν, οὐ μὴ γράψω σε ἐ-
πιστολήν, οὔτε λαλῶ σε, οὔτε υἰγένω σε   5
εἶτα. ἀν δὲ ἔλθῃς εἰς Ἀλεξανδρίαν, οὐ
μὴ λάβω χεῖραν παρά [σ]ου, οὔτε πάλι χαίρω
σε λυπόν. ἀμ μὴ θέλῃς ἀπενέκαι μ[ε],
ταῦτα γε[ί]νετε. ˙ καὶ ἡ μήτηρ μου εἶπε Ἀρ-
χελάῳ, ὅτι ἀναστατοῖ με· ἀρρον αὐτόν.   10
καλῶς δὲ ἐποίησες. δῶρά μοι ἔπεμψε[ς]
μεγάλα, ἀράκια. ˙ πεπλάνηκαν ἡμῶς ἐκε[ῖ],
τῇ ἡμέρᾳ ιβ' ὅτι ἔπλευσες. λυπὸν πέμψον εἴ[ς]
με, παρακαλῶ σε. ἀμ μὴ πέμψῃς, οὐ μὴ φάγω, οὐ μὴ πείνω. ταῦτα.   15
        ἐρῶσθέ σε εὔχ(ομαι).
    Τῦβι ιη'.
On the *verso*
ἀπόδος Θέωνι [ἀ]πὸ Θεωνᾶτος υἱῶ.

you refuse to take me along with you to Alexandria, I won't
write you a letter, or speak to you, or wish you health. And
if you do go to Alexandria, I won't take your hand, or greet
you again henceforth. If you refuse to take me, that's what's
up ! And my mother said to Archelaus, " He upsets me : away
with him ! " But you did a fine thing ! You sent me gifts, great
ones, husks !! They deceived us there, on the 12th, when you sailed.
Send for me then, I beseech you. If you do not send, I won't eat,
won't drink ! There now ! I pray for your health.   Tubi 18.

(Addressed) Deliver to Theon from Theonas his son.

4. οὐ μή] In the Pauline Epp.
(1 Cor. viii 13, Gal. v 16, 1 Thess.
iv 15, v 3) this double negative
seems always to carry the full emphasis that it possesses here. For
its general use in the Gk Bible, see
Moulton's careful statement *Proleg.*
p. 187 ff.

6. ἀν]=ἐάν, a dialectic variant
which in the N.T. is confined to
the Fourth Gospel (Jo. v 19, xii 32,
xiii 20, xvi 23, xx 23 (*bis*)): see
further Moulton *Proleg.* p. 43, n. 2.

8. λυπόν]=λοιπόν, cf. 1 Cor. iv 2 *al.*
10. ἀναστατοῖ] Cf. B.G.U. 1079.
20 (=No. 15).

ἀρρον(=ἆρον) αὐτόν] Cf. Jo. xix
15 ἆρον, ἆρον, σταύρωσον αὐτόν.

12. ἀράκια] Apparently a diminutive of ἄρακος, a leguminous
plant which grows among lentils.
The irony underlying its use here
may perhaps be brought out by the
rendering 'husks': cf. Lk. xv 16
κεράτια.

πεπλάνηκαν ἡμῶ(=α)ς] This metaphorical use of the verb is common in the N.T., Mt. xxiv 4 *al.*

14, 15. οὐ μὴ φάγω κτλ.] Deissmann compares the resolution of the
Jewish zealots in Ac. xxiii 12 μήτε
φαγεῖν μήτε πεῖν.

43. LETTER OF AN ANXIOUS MOTHER

B. G. U. 380.   iii/A.D.

From the Fayûm. Edited by Krebs in *Berliner Griechische Urkunden* II, p. 40, with emendations by Viereck, p. 355. See also Preisigke, *Familienbriefe*, p. 95 f. ; Erman and Krebs, p. 212 f.

A mother has heard of an injury to her son's foot, but resolves to delay setting off to visit him, until she learns from himself how he really is. These tidings she now begs him to communicate and so relieve the anxiety of a mother.

The letter, which is in very illiterate Greek, is written on the *verso* of an official document, which had been crossed through, cut into smaller pieces, and sold for further use (cf. Intr. p. xxii f.).

'Η μήτη[ρ··]ελόχῳ τῷ υἱῶι
                    χαίρειν.
'Οψείας τῆς ὥρας ἀπελ-
τοῦσα πρὸς Σεραπίωνα
τὸν βατρανον ἐξέτασε   5
περὶ τῆς σωτηρίας σου
καὶ τῆς πεδίων σου, καὶ εἰ-
πέ μοι, ὅτι τὸν πόδαν πο-

His mother to...her son, greeting. At a late hour I went to Serapion..., and asked about your health and the health of your children. And he told me that you had a sore foot owing to a

2. ὀψείας κτλ.] Cf. Mk xi. 11 ὀψίας (ὀψὲ ℵ)...τῆς ὥρας. P. Tebt. 283. 6 f. (B.C. 93 or 60) has ὀψίτερον τῆς ὥρας.
5. βατρανον] Either = πατρῶνον

'master,' or οὐετρανόν 'veteran.'
ἐξέτασε] = ἐξήτασα. For the verb, cf. Jo. xxi 12.
6. σωτηρίας] Cf. B.G.U. 423. 13 (= No. 36), note.

νεῖς ἀπὸ σκολάπου, καὶ
ἐτολότην, ὥς σου περισό-   10
τερον νωχελευομένου.

Καὶ αἱμοῦ λαιγούσας τῷ
Σεραπίωνι, ὅτι συνε⟨ρ⟩ξέρ-
χομέ συ, ἔλεγαί μοι· Οὐδὲν
περισότε[ρ]ον ἔχι σε. Εἰ δὲ οἶ-   15
δες σατῷ, ὅτι ἔχεις ἔτι,
γράψον μοι, καὶ χαταβένω
περπατῶ μετὰ οὗ ἐὰν εὔ-
ρω. Μὴ οὖν ἀμελήσῃς, τέ-
χνον, γράψε μοι περὶ τῆς   20
                    ε
σωτηρίας [σ]ου ὥσθ ἰδὼς πό-
βον τέκνου. Ἀσπάζετέ σε
τὰ τέχνα σου. Αὐρήλιος Πτο-
λεμινο τῷ πατρεὶ χαίρι πεῖ-
σον Διονύσιον χα[ί]ρειν τέχν(ον).   25

splinter. And I was troubled because you were only able to walk
so slowly. And when I said to Serapion that I would accompany
him to (see) you, he said to me, "There is nothing so much the
matter with you." But if you yourself know that matters are still not
going well with you, write to me, and I will come down, going
with anyone I may find. Do not then forget, my child, to write
me regarding your health, for you know the anxiety (of a mother)
for a child. Your children greet you. Aurelius...greets his father.
Persuade Dionysius to greet the child.

9. σκολάπου] = σκόλοπος. This
passage shows that in the vernacular
σκόλοψ had come to mean 'splinter,'
'thorn,' rather than 'stake': cf.
Numb. xxxiii 55, Sir. xliii 19, 2 Cor.
xii 7.

10. ἐτολότην] = ἐθολώθην. Apparently an instance of the somewhat
rare verb θολόω in its metaphorical
sense, cf. Eur. *Alc.* 1067 θολοῖ δὲ
καρδίαν.

11. νωχελευομένου] The verb
occurs three times in Aquila's version
of the O.T., Prov. xviii 9, xxiv 10,
Job ii 4.

21, 22. ὥσθ' κτλ.] = ὡς εἰδὼς
φόβον.

44. LETTER OF APION

P. TEBT. 421.   iii/A.D.

Edited by Grenfell, Hunt, and Goodspeed in *Tebtunis Papyri* II, p. 298.

An urgent letter addressed to a certain Didymus informing him that his sister is ill, and bidding him come at once.

> Ἀπίων Διδύμῳ χαίρειν. πάντα
> ὑπερθέμενος ἐξαυτῆς ἅμα τῷ
> λαβεῖν σε ταῦτά μου τὰ γράμματα
> γενοῦ πρὸς ἐμὲ ἐπεὶ ἡ ἀδελφή σου
> νωθρεύεται. καὶ τὸ κιτώνιον   5
> αὐτῆς τὸ λευκὸν τὸ παρὰ σοὶ ἔνιγ-
> κον ἐρχ[ό]μενος τὸ δὲ καλλάϊνον
> μ[ὴ] ἐνίγκῃς, ἀλλὰ θέλις αὐτὸ πωλῆ-
> σα[ι] πώλησον, θέλις αὐτὸ ἀφεῖναι

Apion to Didymus greeting. Put off everything, and immediately on receipt of this letter of mine come to me, since your sister is sick. And her tunic, the white one which you have, bring when you come, but the turquoise one do not bring. But if you wish to sell it, sell it ; if you wish to let your daughter have it, let

2. ἐξαυτῆς] a late Gk word = Lat. *ilico*. It occurs six times in the N.T., e.g. Mk vi 25, Ac. x 33, Phil. ii 23.

5. νωθρεύεται] Cf. B.G.U. 449. 4 (ii/iii A.D.) ἀκούσας ὅτι νωθρεύῃ ἀγωνιοῦμεν, and for the adj. as in Heb. vi 12, cf. P. Amh. 78. 15 (ii/A.D.) ἐ]ν νωθρίᾳ μου γενομένου 'when I had shown myself sluggish or indifferent' as regards my rights.

8. μ[ὴ] ἐνίγκῃς] On the force of μή with the aor. subj. see Moulton

Proleg. p. 122.

θέλις κτλ.] In a note in the *American Journal of Theology* XII, p. 249 f. Goodspeed aptly compares the 'crisp interrogatives' used by St Paul in 1 Cor. vii 27 (cf. *v.* 18 and Jas v 3), and suggests that in both cases the writers were employing no rhetorical artifice, but simply 'the most concise conditional mechanism known to them.' Cf. also Blass *Gramm.* p. 302.

τῇ θυγατρί σ[ου] ἄφες. ἀλλὰ μὴ ἀμελή-   10
σης τι αὐτῆς [κ]αὶ μὴ σκύλης τὴν
γ[υνα]ῖκά σου ἢ τὰ παιδία, ἐρχόμε-
ν[ο]ς δὲ ἔρχου ἰς Θεογενίδα.
ἐρρῶσθαί σε εὔχομαι.

her have it. But do not neglect her in any way, and do not trouble your wife or the children. And when you come, come to Theognis. I pray for your health.

11. μὴ σκύλης] 'do not trouble.' For this weakened sense, as in Mk v 35, Lk. vii 6, viii 49, cf. further P. Oxy. 295. 5 (*c*. A.D. 35) μὴ σκ{λ}ύλλε ἐατήν, and for examples of the verb's varied usage see Moulton *Exp.* VI iii, p. 273 f.

12. ἐρχόμενος δὲ ἔρχου] a good instance of the manner in which a phrase, while suggesting Hebraistic influence, may nevertheless be true Gk, however unidiomatic: see further, Moulton *Proleg.* p. 75 f.

45. HIRE OF DANCING GIRLS

P. GRENF. II, 67.   A.D. 237.

From the Fayûm. Edited by Grenfell and Hunt in *Greek Papyri*, Series II, p. 101 ff. For the emendations that have been introduced into the following text, see Wilcken, *Archiv* III, p. 124.

An interesting glimpse into the lighter life of the Fayûm is afforded by the following document, in which the village council of Bacchias enter into a contract for the services of two dancing-girls, evidently for some approaching festival. We may compare the engagement of pantomimes and musicians in P. Flor. 74 (A.D. 181), and the accounts of the receipts and expenditure in connexion with public games at Oxyrhynchus, P. Oxy. 519 (ii/A.D.), also P. Brit. Mus. 331 (= II, p. 154) (A.D. 165) which, as Wilcken (*Archiv* I, p. 153, cf. III, p. 241) has shown, deals with a similar engagement.

[Αὐρ]ηλ(ίῳ) Θεῶνι πρωνοη(τῇ) αὐλ(ητρίδων)

[πα]ρὰ Αὐρηλίου Ἀσκλᾶ Φιλαδέλ-

[φου] ἡγουμένου συνόδου κώ-

[μη]ς Βακχιάδος. βούλομαι

[ἐ]κλαβεῖν παρὰ σοῦ Τ[.]σαῒν   5

[ὀρ]χηστρίαν σὺν ἑτέρᾳ μιᾷ [λ]ει-

[τουρ]γήσιν ἡμῖν ἐν τῇ προ[κε]ι-

[μέ]νῃ κώμῃ ἐπὶ ἡμέρας ι΄

ἀ]πὸ τῆς ιγ΄ Φαῶφι μηνὸς

[κατ]ὰ ἀρχαίους, λαβμανόντων   10

[αὐ]τῶν ὑπὲρ μισθοῦ ἡμερη-

[σί]ως (δραχμὰς) λς΄, καὶ ὑπὲρ τιμήμα-

[τος] πασῶν τῶν ἡμερῶν

To Aurelius Theon, provider of flute-girls, from Aurelius Asclas Philadelphus, president of the village council of Bacchias. I wish to hire from you T.sais the dancing-girl along with one other to perform for us in the aforesaid village for ten days from the 13th of the month Phaophi old style, they receiving by way of hire 36 drachmas daily, and by way of payment for the whole period three

1. πρω(= ο)νοη(τῇ)] For the verb cf. P. Tebt. 40. 12 (=No. 10).

αὐλ(ητρίδων)] For the conjunction with ὄρχησις, cf. Mt. xi 17 ηὐλήσαμεν ὑμῖν κ. οὐκ ὠρχήσασθε.

3. ἡγουμένου κτλ.] For the village council which was composed of the 'elders' see the note on P. Tebt. 40. 17 (=No. 10). 'Ηγ. is evidently here its 'president' or 'head,' cf. B.G.U. 270. 6 (ii/A.D.) ἡγ. κώμης, though the title is by no means limited to this signification: see Editors' note on P. Fay. 110. 26. The N.T. usage in Heb. xiii. 7 etc. may be illustrated by P. Brit. Mus. 281. 2 (=II, p. 66) (A.D. 66) where the death of a priest is notified ἡγουμένοις ἱε[ρέων].

6. [ὀρ]χηστρίαν] Cf. Mt. xiv. 6 ὠρχήσατο ἡ θυγάτηρ τ. Ἡρῳδιάδος ἐν τῷ μέσῳ.

6, 7. [λ]ει[τουρ]γήσιν]=λειτουργήσειν, a happy suggestion (Wilcken) foi the editorial δι᾽ [ὄρχ]ησιν. For the verb, cf. P. Par. 26. 2 (=No. 5).

10. [κατ]ὰ ἀρχαίους] i.e. the old Egyptian system of reckoning 365 days to the year without a leap-year, which, even after the introduction of the Augustan calendar, continued to be used in many non-official documents: see the Editors' note here and their introd. to P. Oxy. 235.

λαβμ. = λαμβανόντων.

12. δραχμὰς λς΄] In P. Flor. 74 the two pantomimes with their band receive the same money payment with a like allowance of food. According to P. Oxy. 519 an actor received as much as 496 drachmas, and an Homeric rhapsodist (ὁμηριστής) 448 drachmas, but the period of the engagement is not specified.

[πυρο]ῦ ἀρτάβας γ΄ καὶ ψωμίων
ζε[ύ]γη ιε΄, ὑπὲρ καταβάσεως   15
καὶ ἀναβάσεως ὄνους γ΄· ἐντεῦ-
θε[ν] δὲ ἐσχή(κασι) ὑπὲρ ἀραβῶνος
[τῇ τ]ιμῇ ἐλλογουμέν[ο]υ σ[ο]ι
(δραχμὰς) [·]β.
(ἔτους) γ΄΄ Αὐτοκράτορος (Καί)σαρος Γαίου Ἰουλίου   20
Οὐήρου Μαξιμίνου Εὐσεβοῦς Εὐτυχοῦς
Σεβαστοῦ Γερμανικοῦ Μεγίστου Δακικοῖ
Μεγίστου [Σα]ρματικοῦ Μεγίστου (καὶ) Γαίου
Ἰουλίου Οὐήρου Μαξίμου Γερμανικοῦ

artabas of wheat, and fifteen couples of delicacies, and for their conveyance down and back again three asses. And of this they have received   drachmas by way of earnest money to be reckoned by you in the price.

The 3rd year of the Emperor Caesar Gaius Julius Verus Maximinus Pius Felix Augustus Germanicus Maximus Dacicus Maximus Sarmaticus Maximus (and) Gaius Julius Verus Maximus

14. ψωμίων] Cf. P. Tebt. 33. 14 (= No. 11).

15. ὑπὲρ καταβάσεως κτλ.] Cf. the similar provision for conveyance on the journey 'up' and 'down' in P. Brit. Mus. 331 (= II, p. 154).

17. ἀραβῶνος] For the spelling, see Moulton *Proleg.* p. 45, Thackeray *Gramm.* I, p. 119, and for the meaning, cf. P. Par. 58. 14 (ii/B.C.) where a woman who is selling a cow receives 1000 drachmas as ἀραβῶνα. The vernacular usage (see *Lex. Notes, Exp.* VII vi, p. 280) amply confirms the N.T. sense of 'an earnest,' or a part given in advance of what will be bestowed fully afterwards, in 2 Cor. i 22, v 5, Eph. i 14.

18. [τῇ τ]ιμῇ ἐλλογ.] The Edd. read originally [τοῦ] μὴ ἐλλογ., as

if the *arrhabo* were to be supplementary to the contract price, but, as Wilcken's emendation shows, it was to be included in it.

ἐλλογουμένου] To the technical use of this word, as in Philem. 18, add such a further ex. from the papyri as P. Strass. 32. 9 f. (iii/A.D.) δότω λόγον, τί αὐτῷ ὀφείλ[ε]ται...ἵνα οὕτως αὐτῷ ἐνλογηθῇ, and for its more metaphorical sense, as in Rom. v 13, cf. the interesting rescript in which the Emperor Hadrian announces certain privileges to his soldiers: B.G.U. 140. 31 f. οὐχ ἕνεκα τοῦ δοκεῖν με αὐτοῖς ἐνλογεῖν, 'not however that I may seem thereby to be commending myself to them.'

[Μεγίστου] Δακικοῦ Μεγίστου Σαρματικ[οῦ   25
[Μεγίστου το]ῦ γενναιοτάτου (Καί)σαρος,
κυρίων [αἱ]ωνίω[ν Σε]βαστῶν Ἐπὶφ [.

Germanicus [Maximus] Dacicus Maximus Sarmaticus [Maximus],
the most noble Caesar, the aeonian lords Augusti, Epeiph...

27. [αἰ]ωνίω[ν]] a constantly re-
curring epithet of the Imperial power
at any rate from the time of Hadrian
(B.G.U. 176. 12 τοῦ αἰωνίου κόσμου
τοῦ κι[ρί]ου Καίσαρος), and always
apparently in the sense of the Lat.

perpetuus. In the vernacular therefore the word does not do more
than depict that of which the horizon
is not in view. Cf. Deissmann *BS.*
p. 363, and the exx. in *Exp.* VI
viii, p. 424 f., and VII v, p. 174.

46. MAGICAL FORMULA

P. OXY. 886.   iii/A.D.

Edited by Grenfell and Hunt in *Oxyrhynchus Papyri* VI, p. 200 f.

A formula for obtaining an omen, purporting to be derived
from a sacred book.

Μεγάλη Ἶσις ἡ κυρία.
ἀντίγραφον ἱερᾶς βί-
βλου τῆς εὑρετίσης ἐν

Great is the Lady Isis.   Copy of a sacred book found in the

1. Μεγάλη Ἶσις κτλ.] an invocation to the goddess, which lends
additional confirmation to Ramsay's
view (*Church in the Roman Empire*
p. 135 ff.) that in Ac. xix. 28 Μεγάλη
ἡ (om. ἡ D¹) Ἄρτεμις Ἐφεσίων we
have 'a stock phrase of Artemis-
worship,' which rose at once to the
lips of the excited mob, rather than
an argument directed against St

Paul's doctrine.
2—4. ἱερ. βίβλου τ. εὑρετίσης
(= εὑρεθείσης) κτλ.] A striking
parallel (suggested by Cumont to
the Editors) is found in *Catal. codd.
Astr. Graec.* vii, p. 62 Βίβλος
εὑρεθεῖσα ἐν Ἡλιουπόλει τῆς Αἰγύπτου
ἐν τῷ ἱερῷ ἐν ἀδύτοις ἐγγεγραμμένη
ἐν ἱεροῖς γράμμασι κτλ.

τοῖς τοῦ Ἑρμοῦ ταμίοις.
ὁ δὲ τρόπος ἐστὶν τὰ περ[ὶ]   5
τὰ γράμματα κθ'
δι' ὧν ὁ Ἑρμῆς κὲ ἡ Ἶσις
ζητοῦσα ἑαυτῆς τὸν ἀ-
δελφὸν κὲ ἄνδρα Ὄ-
σιρειν. ἐπικαλοῦ μὲ[ν (?)   10
τὸν (ἥλιον) κὲ τοὺς ἐν βυ-
θῷ θεοὺς πάντας πε-
ρὶ ὧν θέλις κληδονισ-
θῆναι. λαβὼν φύνι-
κος ἄρσενος φύλλα κθ'   15
ἐπίγρ(αψον) ἐν ἑκάστῳ τῶν
φύλλων τὰ τῶν θεῶν
ὀνόματα κὲ ἐπευξά-
μενος ἔρε κατὰ δύο

archives of Hermes. The method is concerned with the 29 letters,
which were used by Hermes and by Isis, when she was seeking for
her brother and husband Osiris. Call upon the sun and all the
gods in the deep concerning those things about which you wish to
receive an omen. Take 29 leaves of a male palm, and write upon
each of the leaves the names of the gods, and having prayed lift

6. τὰ γράμματα κθ'] The letters
of the alphabet played a large part
in magical divination (cf. Reitzenstein *Poimandres* pp. 260, 288 ff.),
though no reason has as yet been
suggested why their number here
should be 29 instead of 24. For a
corresponding use of the vowels
cf. P. Brit. Mus. 121. 705 ff. (= I,
p. 107), partly to be explained by
the fact that 'they form an amplifi-
cation of the name ιαω or ιαεω
which represented the Hebrew name
of the Deity' (Kenyon).
10. ἐπικαλοῦ] With the frequent
occurrence of this word in magical
formulae (e.g. l. 350 of the Brit.
Mus. papyrus cited above) cf.
such passages from the Gk Bible as

Sir. xlvii 5 ἐπεκαλέσατο γὰρ Κύριον
τὸν ὕψιστον, Ac. vii 59 Στέφανον
ἐπικαλούμενον καὶ λέγοντα Κύριε
Ἰησοῦ κτλ.
13. κληδονισθῆναι] a LXX word,
e.g. Deut. xviii 10 οὐχ εὑρεθήσεται...
κληδονιζόμενος.
16. ἐπίγρ(αψον) ἐν] Cf. Ac. xvii 23
βωμὸν ἐν ᾧ ἐπεγέγραπτο ΑΓΝΩΣΤΩ
ΘΕΩ.
19, 20. ἔρε (= αἷρε) κατὰ δύο
δύο] For the mixed distributives,
cf. Lk. x 1 ἀνὰ δύο δύο BK, and for
evidence that we need no longer
find a 'Hebraism' in δύο δύο and
similar combinations, see Moulton
Proleg. p. 97, Thackeray *Gramm.*
I, p. 54.

δύο, τὸ δὲ ὑπολιπό[μ]ε-   20
νον ἔσχατον ἀνάγνω-
τι κὲ εὑρήσις σου τὴν κλη-
δόνα ἐν οἷς μέτεστειν
καὶ χρημαθισθήσῃ τη-
λαυγῶς.   25

them up two by two, and read that which is left at the last, and you
will find in what things your omen consists, and you will receive a
clear answer.

24. χρημαθ(=τ)ισθήσῃ] Cf. P.
Par. 46. 2 ff. (B.C. 153) τὰ παρὰ τῶν
θεῶν κατὰ λόγον σοι χρηματίζεται,
and for a similar use of the pass. in
the N.T., see Mt. ii 12, 22, Lk. ii
26, Ac. x 22, Heb. viii 5, xi 7.

τηλαυγῶς] Cf. Μκ viii 25 ἐνέ-
βλεπεν τηλαυγῶς ἅπαντα. The corresponding adj. and substantives are
found in the LXX, e.g. Pss. xviii. 8,
xvii. 12, Lev. xiii. 23.

47. MAGICAL INCANTATION

P. PAR. 574.   iii/A.D.

Edited by Wessely in *Denkschriften der philosophisch-historischen
Classe der Kaiserlichen Akademie der Wissenschaften zu Wien*, XXXVI
(1888), p. 75. See also the same writer's *Monuments du Christianisme*,
p. 183 ff., and his article *On the Spread of Jewish-Christian Religious
Ideas among the Egyptians* in *Exp.* III iv, p. 194 ff.

The following extract from the great Paris magical papyrus
contains the Greek text of an ancient Coptic spell, which
probably goes back as far as the second century. It will be
noticed that the native Egyptian terms are simply transcribed
into Greek characters. Apart from its other features, the
papyrus is of special interest to Biblical students as showing
how widely Jewish-Christian names and ideas had spread
among the Egyptians at this early date. Wessely indeed
claims this spell as 'one of the most ancient traces of the
propagation of Christianity in Egypt' (*Monuments du Christianisme*, p. 185).

πρᾶξις γενναία ἐκβάλλουσα δαίμονας.   1227
λόγος λεγόμενος ἐπὶ τῆς κεφαλῆς αὐτοῦ.
βάλε ἔμπροσθεν αὐτοῦ κλῶνας ἐλαίας
καὶ ὄπισθεν αὐτοῦ σταθεὶς λέγεις·   1230
χαῖρε φνουθι ν 'Αβραάμ· χαῖρε πνου
τε ν 'Ἰσάκ· χαῖρε πνουτε ν 'Ἰακώβ·
'Ἰησοῦς πι Χρηστὸς πι ἅγιος ν πνεῦμα
ψιηρινφιωθ εθσαρηϊ ν Ισασφε
εθσαχουν ν Ισασφι· ενα Ιαω Σα   1235
βαωθ μαρετετενσομ σωβι σα
βολ ἀπὸ τοῦ δ(ε)ἶ(να) σατετεννουθ παϊ
π ἀκάθαρτος ν δαίμων πι σαδαιᾶς
εθιηϊωθφ ἐξορκίζω σε δαῖμον,
ὅστις ποτ' οὖν εἶ, κατὰ τούτου   1240
τοῦ θεοῦ σαβαρβαρβαθιωθ σαβαρ

A notable spell for driving out demons. Invocation to be uttered over the head (of the possessed one). Place before him branches of olive, and standing behind him say: Hail, spirit of Abraham; hail, spirit of Isaac; hail, spirit of Jacob; Jesus the Christ, the holy one, the spirit...drive forth the devil from this man, until this unclean demon of Satan shall flee before thee. I adjure thee, O demon, whoever thou art, by the God Sabarbarbathiôth

1227. πρᾶξις] Cf. Ac. xix 18, where the word is similarly used of magical spells, and the apocryphal *Gospel of Nicodemus* i, where the Jews bring the charge against Jesus that δαιμονιζομένους ἐθεράπευσεν ἐν σαββάτῳ ἀπὸ κακῶν πράξεων.

ἐκβάλλουσα] Cf. Mt. vii 22 τῷ σῷ ὀνόματι δαιμόνια ἐξεβάλομεν.

1231, 2. 'Αβραάμ κτλ.] The appeal to *the God of Abraham*, of *Isaac and of Jacob* is very common in the magical papyri. Deissmann (*BS.* p. 282) quotes Origen *c. Cels.* v 45 to the effect that these names had to be left untranslated in the adjurations if the *power* of the incantation was not to be lost.

1233. 'Ἰησοῦς κτλ.] Another exorcism in the same papyrus begins l. 3019 f., ὁρκίζω σε κατὰ τοῦ θ(εο)ῦ τῶν 'Εβραίων 'Ἰησοῦ, where, as Deissmann (*LO.*[2] p. 192 n. 14) points out, the name Jesus can only have been inserted by a heathen: neither a Jew nor a Christian would have described Him as 'the god of the Hebrews.'

1239. ἐξορκίζω] Cf. the quotation in the previous note, and P. Leid. v 431 (iii/A.D.) ἐξορκίζω σε τὴν δύναμίν σου: see also Mt. xxvi 63, Ac. xix 13, and ἐνορκίζω 1 Thess. v 27 (note).

1240, 1. κατὰ τούτου τοῦ θεοῦ] Cf. P. Petr. iii p. 20 (= P. Par. 63,

βαρβαθιουθ· σαβαρβαρβαθιωνηθ
σαβαρβαρβαφαï· ἔξελθε, δαῖμον,
ὅστις ποτ' οὖν εἶ, καὶ ἀπόστηθι ἀπὸ τοῦ δ(ε)ῖ(να)
ἄρτι ἄρτι ἤδη. ἔξελθε δαῖμον,   1245
ἐπεί σε δεσμεύω δεσμοῖς ἀδαμαντίνοις
ἀλύτοις, καὶ παραδίδωμί σε εἰς τὸ μέ-
λαν χάος ἐν ταῖς ἀπωλίαις.

Sabarbarbathiuth Sabarbarbathionêth Sabarbarbaphai. Come forth, O demon, whoever thou art, and depart from so and so at once, at once, now. Come forth, O demon, for I chain thee with adamantine chains not to be loosed, and I give you over to black chaos in utter destruction.

38 ff.) ὅ]ρκους παρ' ὑμῶν λαβεῖν μὴ μόνον ἐπὶ τῶ[ν] θεῶν ἀλλὰ καὶ κατὰ τῶν βασιλέων γραπτούς, 'to exact oaths from you not only by the gods, but also by the kings in the forms specially written.' (Edd.)

1243. ἔξελθε] Cf. Mk i 25, v 8, ix 25.

1245. ἄρτι κτλ.] a common magical formula, cf. e.g. P. Brit. Mus. 121. 373 (=I, p. 96) (iii/A.D.) ἐν [τ]ῇ ἄρτι ὥρᾳ ἤδη ἤδη ταχύ ταχύ, and for the strictly *present* time

implied in ἄρτι see 1 Thess. iii 6 (note).

1247. παραδίδωμι] Cf. P. Brit. Mus. 46. 334 ff. (iv/A.D.) νεκυδαίμων ...παραδίδωμί σοι τὸν δ(εῖνα) ὅπως κτλ., and see the similar formula in 1 Cor. v 5 παραδοῦναι τὸν τοιοῦτον τῷ Σατανᾷ εἰς ὄλεθρον τῆς σαρκός.

1248. χάος. The word is found twice in the LXX, Mic. i 6, Zech. xiv 4.

ἀπωλί(=εἰ)αις] Cf. 2 Thess. ii 3, (note).

48. CERTIFICATE OF PAGAN SACRIFICE

B. G. U. 287.   A.D. 250.

From the Fayûm. Edited by Krebs in *Berliner Griechische Urkunden* I, p. 282; cf. *Sitzungsb. Berl. Akad.* 1893, p. 1007 ff. For various emendations and restorations see also Harnack, *Theol. Literaturz.* 1894, p. 162, and Wessely, *Monuments du Christianisme*, p. 115 ff.

The well-known account by Cyprian of the Christians who, during the Decian persecution, obtained false certificates from the magistrates to the effect that they had sacrificed in the heathen manner ('qui se ipsos infideles inlicita nefariorum libellorum professione prodiderant' *Ep.* 30 (3), cf. 55 (2)) has been strikingly illustrated by the publication of five of these *libelli*, which can be conveniently studied in Wessely's collection cited above: cf. also *Oxyrhynchus Pap.* IV, p. 49 f. A sixth *libellus* is included among the Rylands Papyri, edited by Dr A. S. Hunt, see vol. I p. 20 f.

The different documents resemble one another very closely in phraseology, showing that there was a stereotyped formula employed, which doubtless followed the language of the original edict, ordering the sacrifices to be offered. In view of the fact that all five fall within the narrow limits of 13—25 June A.D. 250, it has been conjectured that at that time the whole population, pagan as well as Christian, furnished themselves with *libelli*, which for the time being took the place of the usual census-returns (Wessely, *op. cit.* p. 123 f.). As further pointing in the same direction, it may be noted that one of the certificates, now at Vienna, is on behalf of a priestess of Petesuchus, who is hardly likely to have been accused of being a Christian (*ibid.* p. 119 f., and *Anzeiger d. phil.-hist. Klasse*, xxv (1907) of the Vienna Academy).

> Τοῖς ἐπὶ [τ]ῶν θυσιῶν ᾑρη-
> μένοις κώμ(ης) Ἀλεξ(άνδρου) Νήσου
> παρὰ Αὐρηλ(ίου) Διογένου Σατα-
> βοῦτος ἀπὸ κώμ(ης) Ἀλεξάνδ(ρου)
> Νήσου ὡς (ἐτῶν) οβ′ οὐλ(ὴ)   5
> ὀφρύι δεξ(ιᾷ·) καὶ ἀεὶ
> θύων τοῖς θεοῖς διετέ-
> λεσα καὶ νῦν ἐπὶ πα-
> ρούσιν ὑμεῖν κατὰ

To those chosen to superintend the sacrifices at the village of Alexander-Island, from Aurelius Diogenes, the son of Satabus, of the village of Alexander-Island, being about 72 years old, a scar on the right eyebrow. It has always been my custom to sacrifice to the gods, and now in your presence in accordance with the

τὰ προστε[τ]ατα[γ]μ[έ-   10
να ἔθυσα [κα]ὶ ἔσ[πεισα]
[κ]αὶ τῶν ἱ[ε]ρείων [ἐγευ·]
σάμην καὶ ἀξι[ῶ] ὑμ[ᾶς]
ὑποσημιώσασθαι,
          Διευτυχεῖται.   15
Αὐρήλ(ιος) [Δι]ογένης ἐπιδ[έ(δωκα)].

(2nd hand) Αὐρή[λ(ιος)] Σύρος Δι[ογένη]
θύοντα ἅμα ἡ[μῖν?]
κοινωνὸς σεσ-[ημείωμαι).

(1st hand) [(ἔτους)] α΄ Αὐτοκράτορο[ς] Καί[σαρος]   20
[Γα]ίου Μεσσίου Κ[ο]ίν[του]
[Τρ]αια[νοῦ Δε]κίου Εὐσ[εβοῦς]
[Ε]ὐτ[υχοῦς] Σε[β]α[σ]τοῦ
'Επ[εὶφ] β΄.

decrees I have sacrificed and poured libations and tasted the offerings, and I request you to counter-sign my statement. May good fortune attend you. I, Aurelius Diogenes, have made this request. (2nd hand) I, Aurelius Syrus, as a participant have certified Diogenes as sacrificing along with us. (1st hand.) The first year of the Emperor Caesar Gaius Messius Quintus Trajanus Decius Pius Felix Augustus, Epeiph 2.

10. τὰ προστε[τ]ατα[γ]μ[έ]να] = τὰ προστεταγμένα, the imperial edict, or the magisterial decrees by which it was enforced. For the verb, cf. Ac. xvii 26 ὁρίσας προστεταγμένους καιρούς.

11. ἔθυσα κτλ.] Cf. the striking figurative use made by St Paul of these familiar acts of worship, Phil. ii 17 ἀλλὰ εἰ καὶ σπένδομαι ἐπὶ τῇ θυσίᾳ καὶ λειτουργίᾳ τῆς πίστεως ὑμῶν; see also 2 Tim. iv 6.

12, 13. [ἐγευ]σάμην] c. gen.; as always in the N.T. except Jo. ii 9, Heb. vi 5 (note the significant change of construction from v. 4). In the LXX the acc. is fairly frequent. See further Abbott Joh. Gramm. p. 76 ff.

49. LETTER OF PSENOSIRIS

P. GRENF. II, 73.   LATE iii/A.D.

From the Great Oasis. Edited by Grenfell and Hunt in *Greek Papyri*, Series II, p. 115 f., and the subject of a special study by Deissmann, *The Epistle of Psenosiris* (Lond. 1902 and 1907). See also the same writer's *Licht vom Osten²*, pp. 24 f., 149 ff. (E. Tr. pp. 37 f., 201 ff.), and Wessely, *Monuments du Christianisme*, p. 125 ff., where the literature to which the letter has given rise is fully detailed.

The situation of this letter has been reconstructed with great ingenuity and probability by Deissmann. A Christian woman, by name Politike, has been banished to the Great Oasis during the Diocletian persecution. At Kysis, in the south of the Oasis, she finds a protector in the Christian presbyter Apollon, who, to secure her greater safety, sends her under the care of a party of grave-diggers to a Christian community in the interior, presided over by Psenosiris. The journey is accomplished safely, and in the following letter Psenosiris reports the arrival of Politike to Apollon, and promises that her son Neilus, who is on his way to rejoin his mother, will shortly send further particulars.

> Ψενοσίρι πρεσβ[υτέ]ρῳ ᾿Απόλλωνι
> πρεσβυτέρῳ ἀγαπητῷ ἀδελφῷ
> ἐν Κ(υρί)ῳ χαίρειν.
> πρὸ τῶν ὅλων πολλά σε ἀσπά-

Psenosiris the presbyter to Apollo the presbyter, his beloved brother in the Lord, greeting! Before all else I salute you much

2. πρεσβ[υτέ]ρῳ] For the religious sense of this word see Deissmann *BS.* pp. 154 ff., 233 ff., and cf. P. Tebt. 40. 17 (=No. 10), B.G.U. 22. 11 (=No. 29), and 16. 6 (=No. 33), notes.

2, 3. ἀδελφῷ ἐν Κ(υρί)ῳ] Cf. Phil. i 14, and for the use of ἀδελφός to denote a member of the same religious community see 1 Thess. i 4 (note).

ζομαι καὶ τοὺς παρὰ σοὶ πάντας　　5
ἀδελφοὺς ἐν Θ(ε)ῷ. γινώσκειν
σε θέλω, ἀδελφέ, ὅτι οἱ νεκρο-
τάφοι ἐνηνόχασιν ἐνθάδε
εἰς τὸ ἔγω τὴν Πολιτικὴν τὴν
πεμφθεῖσαν εἰς Ὄασιν ὑπὸ τῆς　　10
ἡγεμονίας. καὶ [τ]αύτην πα-
ραδέδωκα τοῖς καλοῖς καὶ πι-
στοῖς ἐξ αὐτῶν τῶν νεκροτά-
φων εἰς τήρησιν, ἔστ᾽ ἂν ἔλθῃ ὁ υἱὸς αὐτῆς Νεῖλος. καὶ　　15
ὅταν ἔλθῃ σὺν Θεῷ, μαρτυρή-
σι σοι περὶ ὧν αὐτὴν πεποι-

and all the brethren who are with you in God. I would have you know, brother, that the grave-diggers have brought here into the interior Politike, who was sent into the Oasis by the Government. And her I have handed over to the good and true men among the grave-diggers themselves that they may take care of her, until her son Nilus arrives. And when he arrives by the help of God, he will bear you witness of what they have done to her.

8. ἐνηνόχασιν] For this 'strong perfect,' see Moulton *Proleg.* p. 154.

9. εἰς τὸ ἔγω] According to Wilcken ἔγω must be read, but it is evidently a mistake for ἔσω. For similar decrees of banishment to the mines in the interior of Egypt, see P. Flor. 3 (A.D. 301), and the Rainer papyrus published by Wessely, *Monuments du Christianisme*, p. 132 f.

Πολιτικήν] The interpretation of this word as a proper name rather than as an opprobrious designation = πόρνη (cf. Theophanes Continuatus, vi 44 (p. 430, Bekker)), as the first Editors imagined, first suggested to Deissmann the view of the papyrus

indicated above. It should be noted, however, that a certain support has recently been given to the original view by the discovery of P. Oxy. 903. 37 (iv/A.D.) μετὰ μῆναν λαμβάνω πολιτικὴν ἐμαυτῷ, 'a month hence I will take a mistress' (Edd.).

10. πεμφθεῖσαν] 'banished.' Instead of this somewhat 'colourless' word, perhaps chosen intentionally on that account by Psenosiris (Deissmann), the Rainer and Florentine papyri (see the note on l. 9) use for this purpose ἀποστέλλω and προαποστέλλω.

11. ἡγεμονίας] Cf. Lk. iii 1.

12, 13. καλοῖς κ. πιστοῖς] Cf. Mt. xxv 21, 23 ἀγαθὲ κ. πιστέ.

ἥκασιν. δ[ή]λω[σ]ον [δέ] μοι
κ[αὶ σὺ] περὶ ὧν θέλεις ἐνταῦ-
θα ἡδέως ποιοῦντι.   20
ἐρρῶσθαί σε εὔχομαι
ἐν Κ(υρί)ῳ Θ(ε)ῷ.

On the *verso*

'Απόλλωνι × παρὰ Ψενοσίριο[ς]
πρεσβυτέρῳ × πρεσβυτέρου ἐν Κ(υρί)ῳ.

Do you also on your part tell me what you wish done here—I will do it gladly. I pray for your health in the Lord God.

(Addressed)   To Apollo the presbyter from Psenosiris the presbyter in the Lord.

18. δ[ή]λω[σ]ον κτλ.] a common   e.g. P. Fay. 122. 14 (*c.* A.D. 100).
epistolary phrase in the papyri,

50. LETTER REGARDING FUNERAL EXPENSES

P. GRENF. II, 77.   iii/iv A.D.

From the Great Oasis. Edited by Grenfell and Hunt in *Greek Papyri*, Series II, p. 121 ff. See also Wessely *Monuments du Christianisme* p. 129 ff.

Melas writes to Sarapion and Silvanus stating that he had dispatched to them the body of their brother Phibion, and asking for repayment of various expenses to which he had been put in connexion with the latter's illness and death.   The naïve way in which he expresses surprise that the brothers had contented themselves with carrying off Phibion's effects, while leaving his body, is very delightful.   The letter concludes with a request for the proper entertainment of the man who was conveying the body.

[Μέλας . . . . .] Σαραπίωνι καὶ Σιλβανῷ
[. . . . . . χ]αίρειν.   ἀπέστιλα ὑμῖν
[διὰ τοῦ ν]εκροτάφου τὸ σῶμα τοῦ
[ἀδελφοῦ] Φιβίωνος, καὶ ἐπλήρωσα
[αὐ]τὸν [το]ὺς μισθοὺς τῆς παρακομι-   5
δῆς τοῦ σώματος ὄντας ἐν δραχμαῖς
τριακοσίαις τεσσαράκοντα παλαιοῦ
νομίσματος, καὶ θαυμάζω πάνυ
[ὅτι] ἀλόγως ἀπέστητε μὴ ἄραντες
[τὸ σ]ῶμα τοῦ ἀδελφοῦ ὑμῶν, ἀλλὰ   10
σ[υ]νλέξαντες ὅσα εἶχεν καὶ οὕτως
ἀπέστητε. καὶ ἐκ τούτου ἔμαθον
ὅτι οὐ χάριν τοῦ νεκροῦ ἀνήλθατε
ἀλλὰ χάριν τῶν σκευῶν αὐτοῦ.

(Melas...) to Sarapion and Silvanus...greeting. I dispatched to you through the gravedigger the body of your brother Phibion, and I paid him the costs of the carriage of the body amounting to three hundred and forty drachmas in the old coinage. I wonder exceedingly that you went off so cruelly, without taking the body of your brother, but that having collected all that he had you then went off. From this I learned that it was not on account of the dead man you came here, but on account of his goods. See to it

1. Σιλβανῷ] the regular form in the papyri (but see No. 55. 4) for the N.T. Σιλουανός, e.g. 1 Thess. i 1 (Σιλβανός DG).

4. ἐπλήρωσα] 'paid,' 'discharged in full,' cf. B.G.U. 1055. 23 f. (i/B.C.) μέχρει τοῦ πληρωθῆναι τὸ δάνηον.

6. ἐν] For ἐν = 'amounting to,' cf. P. Oxy. 724. 7 (A.D. 155) ἔσχες τὴν πρώτην δόσιν ἐν δραχμαῖς τεσσαράκοντα, and the parallel usage in Ac. vii 14 (LXX) ἐν ψυχαῖς ἐβδομήκοντα πέντε.

7. παλαιοῦ] i.e. prior to the new coinage of Diocletian.

9. ἀλόγως] Cf. the curious a-crostic P. Tebt. 278. 30 f. (early i/A.D.) in which the loss of a garment is told in laconic sentences, beginning with the successive letters of the alphabet

ζητῶι καὶ οὐχ εὑρίσκωι.
ἤρτε ἀλόγως.

Additional exx. of the word are given in *Lex. Notes, Exp.* VII v, p. 179 f.

11. σ[υ]νλέξαντες] Cf. Mt. xiii 41, Lk. vi 44.

13. χάριν] Cf. P. Par. 47. 17 (= No. 7), note.

φροντίσατε οὖν τὰ ἀναλωθέντα ἑτοι- 15
μάσαι.   ἔστι δὲ τὰ ἀναλώματα
τιμ(ὴ) φαρμάκου παλ(αιαὶ) (δραχμαὶ) ξ′,
  τιμ(ὴ) οἴνου τῇ πρώτῃ
ἡμέρα χό(ες) β′ παλ(αιαὶ) (δραχμαὶ) λβ′,
[ὑπ(ὲρ)] δαπάνης ἐν ψω- 20
μίοις καὶ προσφαγίοις (δραχμαὶ) ιϛ′,
[τ]ῷ νεκροτάφῳ εἰς τὸ ὄρος
με[τ]ὰ τὸν γεγραμμένον
μισθόν, χο(ῦν) ἕνα (δραχμαὶ) κ′,
ἐλαίου χό(ες) β′ (δραχμαὶ) ιβ′, 25
κρ[ι]θῆς (ἀρτάβη) α′ (δραχμαὶ) κ′,
τιμ[ὴ] σινδόνος (δραχμαὶ) κ′,
καὶ μισθοῦ ὡς πρόκ(ειται) (δραχμαὶ) τμ′,
(γίνεται) ἐπὶ τοῦ λ[όγο]υ τῆς
ὅλης δα[πά]νης παλαιοῦ 30

therefore that you furnish the sums expended. The expenses are—
the price of medicine 60 old drachmas, the price of wine on the
first day, two *choi* 32 old drachmas, for outlay in delicacies and
foods 16 drachmas, to the undertaker (for conveying the body) to
the desert, in addition to the payment agreed upon, one *chous*
(of wine) 20 drachmas, two *choi* of olive-oil 12 drachmas, one artaba
of barley 20 drachmas, the price of a linen-cloth 20 drachmas,
and of cost (for the transport of the body) as is detailed above
340 drachmas. Total of the account for the whole outlay five

15. τὰ ἀναλωθέντα] Cf. P. Hib.
54. 7 f. (*c.* B.C. 245) ἐάν τι δέῃι
ἀνηλῶσαι δός, 'if any expense is
necessary, pay it' (Edd.).
  20, 21. ψωμίοις καὶ προσφαγίοις]
For ψωμίον see P. Tebt. 33. 14
(=No. 11), note, and for evidence
that προσφάγιον is to be regarded
as a staple article of food, probably
of the genus fish (cf. Jo. xxi 5),

cf. B.G.U. 916 (i/A.D.) where it
forms part of a hireling's *wages*.
  27. σινδόνος] for burial, as Mt.
xxvii 59 and parallels. In Egypt
the word is specially associated
with the cult of Isis, e.g. Dieterich
Abraxas, p. 79 σινδόνα καθαρὰν περι-
βεβλημένος Ἰσιακῷ σχήματι: see
further Dittenberger *Syll.* 754. 4,
note.

νομίσματος δραχμαὶ
πεντακόσιαι εἴκοσι,
   γί(νεται) (δραχμαὶ) φκ'.
[π]ᾶν οὖν ποιήσετε ὑπηρετῆσαι τὸν
μέλλοντα ἐνεγκ[εῖ]ν τὸ σῶμα   35
ἐν ψωμίοις καὶ [οἰ]ναρίῳ καὶ ἐλαίῳ
καὶ ὅσα δυνατὸν ὑ[μῖ]ν ἐστιν ἵνα μαρ-
τυρήσῃ μοι. μη[δ]ὲν δὲ δράσητε

At right angles along the left edge of the papyrus are three much mutilated lines.

On the *verso*

Σαρ]απίωνι καὶ
Σι]λβανῷ ἀδελφοῖς ✕ Μέλας χι( ).
Φιβίωνος

hundred and twenty drachmas of the old coinage. Total 520 drachmas.

You will take every care therefore to entertain the man who is about to convey the body with delicacies and a little wine and olive-oil and whatever is in your power, that he may report to me. But do nothing...

(Addressed) To Sarapion and Silvanus brothers of Phibion Melas....

38. δράσητε] so Wilcken (*Ar-*   δωλῆτε (= δηλῶτε).
chiv III, p. 125) for the Editors'

51. A LETTER TO ABINNAEUS

P. BRIT. MUS. 417.   *c.* A.D. 346.

Edited by Kenyon in *British Museum Papyri* II, p. 299 f. See
also Deissmann, *Licht vom Osten*[2], p. 153 ff. (E. Tr. p. 205 ff.).

Of the correspondence of Abinnaeus, who occupied the
position of *praefectus alae* and *praefectus castrorum* at Dionysias
to the south of Lake Moeris, about the middle of the fourth
century A.D., nearly sixty documents have been recovered. Of
these the larger number have been published with an important
introduction by Kenyon in *British Museum Papyri* II, p. 266 ff.,
and the remainder by Nicole in *Les Papyrus de Genève* p. 60 ff.
Many of these documents consist of petitions addressed to
Abinnaeus in his official character, while others are concerned
with military matters.   But there are also a few private letters,
of which the following possesses the most general interest.

It is a request by the village priest of Hermopolis to pardon
'just this once' a certain deserter named Paulus, who had
apparently taken refuge with him, and whom he is now
sending back to his duties.   The letter is extremely illiterate,
due perhaps to the fact that Greek was not the writer's native
tongue (cf. l. 8 note), but it is written with evident sincerity of
feeling, and may consequently not unfittingly be compared with
S. Paul's letter to Philemon, with whose circumstances it has
so much in common.

Τῷ δεσπότῃ μο^υ καὶ ἀγαπητῷ
ἀδελφῷ ᾿Αβιννέῳ πραι(ποσίτῳ)

To my master and beloved brother Abinnaeus the Praepositus,

Κάορ πάπας Ἑρμουπόλεως χαίρειν.

ἀσπάζομαι τὰ πεδία σου πολλά.

γινώσκιν σε θέλω, κύριε,   5

π[ερὶ] Παύλω τοῦ στρατιότη

περὶ τῆς φυγῆς,/συνχωρῆσε

αὐτοῦ τούτω τὸ ἄβαξ,

ἐπειδὴ ἀσχολῶ ἐλθῖν πρὸ[ς]

σὲν αὐτεημερέ,/ καὶ πάλειν,   10

ἀμ μὴ παύσεται, ἔρχεται

εἰς τὰς χεῖράς σο⁰ ἄλλω ἄβαξ.

    Ἐρρῶσθαί σε εὔχο-

    μαι πολλοῖς χρό-

    νοις, κύριε μο⁰   15

    ἀδελφέ.

Kaor, Papa of Hermopolis, sends greeting. I salute your children much. I wish you to know, lord, with regard to the soldier Paulus, with regard to his flight, pardon him just this once, since I am not at leisure to come to you this very day. And again, if he does not desist, he will come into your hands still another time. I pray for your health for many years, my lord brother.

3. πάπας Ἑρμ.] not the bishop of either Hermopolis Magna or Parva, as Kenyon at first conjectured, but the priest of a small village of the same name in the S.W. of the Fayûm (Wilcken, Deissmann). We have thus here an early instance of the more popular use of a word (cf. No. 2. 9), which was raised to such distinction as an ecclesiastical title.

7, 8. συνχωρῆσε αὐτοῦ] = συνχωρῆσαι αὐτῷ 'pardon him,' a late use of συνχωρέω, cf. P. Tebt. 381. 6 (= No. 30), common in ecclesiastical writers.

8. τούτω τὸ ἄβαξ] = τοῦτο τὸ ἅπαξ, a substantival use of ἅπαξ, which has been traced to Coptic influence (cf. *O.G.I.S.* 201, n. 7

and 10). If this can be maintained, we may perhaps conjecture, with Deissmann, that Coptic was the writer's mother-tongue, and in this way explain his astonishingly bad Greek.

10. αὐτεημερέ] = αὐθημερόν. Cf. P. Petr. III 56 (*b*) 12 (iii/B.C.) αὔθ < ἒ > μερόν.

11. ἀμ μὴ παύσεται] = ἐὰν μὴ παύσηται, a reading now adopted by Kenyon (after GH., Wilcken) in place of his original πεύδεται (= ψεύδηται).

14. χρόνοις] = 'years,' as in modern Gk; cf. P. Gen. 1 22, another of the Abinnaeus letters, where ἐτεσειν (= ιν) takes its place in the same formula. For dat., as in Rom. xvi 25, see Moulton, *Proleg.* p. 75.

52. AN EARLY CHRISTIAN LETTER

P. HEID. 6.   iv/A.D.

Edited by Deissmann in *Veröffentlichungen aus der Heidelberger Papyrus-Sammlung* I, p. 94 ff. ; *Licht vom Osten*², p. 151 ff. (E. Tr. p. 203 ff.).

Among the original Christian documents that have been discovered in Egypt the following letter possesses various features of interest. An unknown Justinus addresses himself to a Christian 'brother' Papnuthius in terms of deep reverence, asking to be remembered in his prayers in view, it would appear, of some sin which was pressing on his conscience. Then, after a brief reference to a small gift which is being forwarded by the same hand, the writer sends a general greeting to the 'brethren,' and concludes with a special prayer on Papnuthius' behalf. The preservation of the address on the *verso* permits the restoration of the opening greeting: see Deissmann *ut supra*, to whom the whole of the following commentary is much indebted.

[Τῷ κυρίῳ μου καὶ ἀγαπητῷ
[ἀδελφῷ Παπνουθίῳ Χρηστο-]
[φόρου Ἰουστῖνος χαίρειν.]
.[· · · · · · · · · · · · · · · · · ·]
ἥ[ν ἔδει γρα]φῆν[α]ι π[ρὸς τὴν]   5
σὴν χρ[ηστότ]ητα, κύριε μου
ἀγαπιτέ. πιστεύομεν γὰρ

[To my lord and dear brother Papnuthius, the son of Chrestophorus, Justinus sends greeting.......] which it was necessary to be written to your clemency, my dear lord. We believe that your

6. χρ[ηστότ]ηταν] a mode of address, much like our 'your Grace'; cf. B.G.U. 984. 2 f. (iv/A.D.) ἔγρα[ψα ...τ]ῇ χρηστ[ότ]ητί σου.

7. πιστεύομεν] for 1st sing. in

accordance with a not uncommon practice. See further *Thess.* p. 131 f., where the bearing of this on Pauline usage is discussed.

τὴν πολιτία[ν σ]ου ἐνν οὐρανῷ.
ἐγῖθεν θεορούμέν σε τὸν
δεσπότην καὶ κενὸν (π)ά[τ]ρω[να].   10
ἵνα οὖν μὴ πολλὰ γράφω καὶ
φλυαρήσω, ἐν γὰρ [πο]λλῇ
λαλιᾷ οὐκ ἐκφεύξοντ[αι]
(τ ἠ(ν) ἁμαρτίη, παρακαλῶ [ο]ὖν,
δέσποτα, ἵνα μνημον[ε]ύῃς   15
μοι εἰς τὰς ἁγίας σου εὐχάς, ἵ-
να δυνηθῶμεν μέρος τῶν (ἁμ-)
αρτιῶν καθαρίσεως. εἰς γάρ
ἱμει τὸν ἁμαρτουλὸν. παρακα-

citizenship is in heaven. Wherefore we regard you as master and
new patron. In order that I may not by much writing prove
myself an idle babbler, for 'in the multitude of words they
shall not escape sin,' I beseech you, master, to remember me in
your holy prayers, in order that I may be able (to receive) my part
in the cleansing of sins. For I am one of the sinners. I pray you,

8. πολιτία[ν]] For the corresponding verb in a religious sense,
as in Phil. iii 20, cf. P. Par. 63,
col. viii 13 f. (ii/B.C.) πρὸς οὓs (sc.
θεοὺs) ὁσίωs καὶ δικ...δικαίωs [πολι]-
τευσάμενος.
9. ἐγῖθεν] l. ἐκεῖθεν, the word
being used here apparently in a
causal sense, 'wherefore,' 'hence'
(Deissmann).
10. (π)ά[τ]ρω[να]] The restoration is by no means clear, but
πάτρωνα suits the sense, and is
favoured by a similar conjunction
with δεσπότηs in the Abinnaeus
correspondence, e.g. P. Brit. Mus.
411. 1 f. (=II, p. 281) (c. A.D. 346).
11. ἵνα οὖν κτλ.] Cf. 2 Jo. 12,
3 Jo. 13.
12. φλυαρήσω] misspelt for
φλυαρήσω: cf. 3 Jo. 10 λόγοιs πονη-
ροῖs φλυαρῶν ἡμᾶs, and for the corresponding adj. see 4 Macc. v 10 οὐκ
ἐξυπνώσειs ἀπὸ τῆs φλυάρου φιλοσοφ-

ίαs ὑμῶν;
12, 13. ἐν γὰρ πολλῇ λαλιᾷ κτλ.]
a loose citation from Prov. x 19.
14, 15. παρακαλῶ...ἵνα] Cf.
1 Thess. iv 1 (note).
15, 16. μνημον[ε]ύῃς μοι] The
more regular gen. construction is
found in Gal. ii 10, Col. iv 18.
16. εἰs...εὐχάs] For this encroachment of εἰs on ἐν in N.T.
narrative, see P. Oxy. 294. 6 (=No.
13).
17. δυνηθῶμεν] sc. λαβεῖν.
18. καθαρίσεωs] a form that does
not seem to occur outside the LXX.
Lev. xii 4, BᵃˑᵇF, and Aquila
ad l. 'Did Justinus derive it from
his Bible?' (Deissmann).
19. τὸν ἁμαρτουλὸν] l. τῶν ἁμαρ-
τωλῶν. For the religious use of ἁ.
even in 'profane' Gk cf. O.G I.S.
55. 31 f. (iii/B.C.) ἁμαρτωλοὶ ἔστωσαν
[θεῶ]ν πάντων, and see Deissmann
LO.² p. 89 f.

λῶ καταξίωσον δέξεσθαι   20
τὸ μικρὸν ἐλέου διὰ τοῦ ἀδελ-
φοῦ ἡμῶν Μαγαρίου. πολλὰ
προσαγωρεύ(ω) πάντες τοὺς ἀ-
δελφοὺς ἡμῶν ἐν κ̄ω̄. ἐρρω-
        μένον σε ἡ θί-   25
    α πρόνοια φυλάξα[ι]
    ἐπὶ μέγιστον χρό-
    νον ἐν κ̄ω̄ Χ̄ω̄,
    κύριε ἀγαπητ[έ].

On the *verso*

[τῷ κυρίῳ] μου καὶ ἀγαπητῷ ἀδελφῷ Παπνουθίῳ   30
                    Χρηστοφόρ[ου]
                    παρ' Ἰουστίνου.

be pleased to accept the little gift of oil at the hands of our brother
Magarius. I add many greetings to all our brethren in the Lord.
May the divine providence preserve you in good health for very
many years in the Lord Christ, dear lord.

(Addressed) To my lord and dear brother Papnuthius, the son
of Chrestophorus, from Justinus.

20. δέξεσθαι κτλ.] The practice
of sending gifts along with letters
was very common: cf. e.g. the
delightful letter of a daughter to her
mother, P. Fay. 1·7 (ii/iii A.D.),
announcing the dispatch of various
articles including μικ⟨κ⟩ὸν ποτήριν
Θεονᾶτι τῷ μικ⟨κ⟩ῷ, 'a little cup for
little Theonas.'

23. προσαγω(=ο)ρεύ(ω)] frequent

in the salutations of papyrus letters,
e.g. P. Oxy. 928. 13 f. (ii/iii A.D.) τὰ
παιδία παρ' ἐμοῦ...προσαγόρε[υ]ε. In
the N.T. the verb is confined to
Heb. v 10.

24, 26. ἐρρωμένον σε κτλ.] Cf.
B.G.U. 984. 26 f. (iv/A.D.) ἐρρωμένον σε...ἡ θεία πρόνοια διαφυλάξ(ε)ιεν
κτλ. (Deissmann).

53. LETTER TO FLAVIANUS

P. OXY. 939.   iv/A.D.

Discovered at Oxyrhynchus, and edited by Grenfell and Hunt in *Oxyrhynchus Papyri* VI, p. 307 f.

Apart from its contents this Christian letter, evidently written by a servant to his master regarding the illness of his mistress, is interesting from its numerous echoes of N. T. language. The style is more literary than we are accustomed to in the letters of this period.

[Τῷ κυρίῳ] μου   Φλαβιανῶι
[Δημήτ]ριος   χαίρειν
[ὡς ἐν ἄλ]λοις πλείστοις νῦν ἔτι μᾶλλον ἢ πρὸς σὲ
[τοῦ δεσπό]του θεοῦ γνῶσις ἀνεφάνη ἄπασιν ἡμῖν
[ὥστε τὴν] κυρίαν ἀνασφῆλαι ἐκ τῆς καταλαβούσης   5
[αὐτὴν νόσ]ου, καὶ εἴη διὰ παντὸς ἡμᾶς χάριτας ὁμο-
[λογοῦντα]ς διατελεῖν ὅτι ἡμῖν ἵλεως ἐγένετο
[καὶ ταῖς εὐ]χαῖς ἡμῶν ἐπένευσεν διασώσας ἡμῖν
[τὴν ἡμῶν] κυρίαν· ἐν γὰρ αὐτῇ πάντες τὰς ἐλπίδας

To my lord Flavianus Demetrius sends greeting. As on many other occasions so now still more plainly the favour of the Lord God towards you has been revealed to all of us, in that my mistress has recovered from the illness that struck her down, and may it be granted to us evermore to continue acknowledging thanks to Him, because He was gracious to us, and paid heed to our prayer in preserving our mistress : for in her we all of us centre our hopes.

4. ἀνεφάνη] Cf. Lk. xix 11 παραχρῆμα μέλλει ἡ βασιλεία τοῦ θεοῦ ἀναφαίνεσθαι.
7. ἵλεως ἐγένετο] Par. 51. 24 (=No. 6).
8. ἐπένευσεν] A good vernacular instance of this verb, which in the N.T. is confined to Ac. xviii 20, is

afforded by P. Petr. II, 32 (1) 28 f. κωίδια ἃ ἐπένευσεν ὁ Φίλιππος πᾶσιν ἡμῖν ἐργάζεσθαι ἐξενήνοχεν, 'the skins which Philip permitted all of us to prepare, he carried off'—a complaint to the epimeletes by a tanner.
διασώσας] Cf. Mt. xiv 36, Lk. vii 3.

[ἔχομεν.] συνγνώμην δέ, κύριέ μου, σχοίης μοι   10
[καὶ εὔνους] ἀποδέξει με εἰ καὶ ἐς τηλικαύτην σε
[ἀγωνία]ν ἄκων ἐνέβαλον γράψας περὶ αὐτῆς ὅσα
[ἐκομίσω.] τὰ μὲν γὰρ πρῶτα ἐν θλίψει αὐτῆς
[πολλῇ οὔ]σης οὐκ ὢν ἐν ἐμαυτῷ ἀπέστειλα
[σπουδάζων] εἴ πως ἐκ παντὸς τρόπου δυνηθείης   15
[πρὸς ἡμᾶς] ἀφικέσθαι, τοῦτο τοῦ καθήκοντος
ἀπ[α]ι̣[τοῦντ]ος· ὡ[ς δὲ ἐπὶ τ]ὸ ῥᾷον ἔδοξεν τετράφθαι
ἕτερά σε γράμματα ἐπικαταλαβεῖν ἐσπούδασα διὰ
Εὐφροσύνου ἵνα σε εὐθυμότερον καταστήσω.
νὴ γὰρ τὴν σὴν σωτηρίαν, κύριέ μου, ἧς μάλιστά   20
μοι μέλει, εἰ μὴ ἐπινόσως ἐσχήκει τὸ σωμάτιον
τότε ὁ υἱὸς Ἀθανάσιος, αὐτὸν ἂν ἀπέστειλα πρός σε

But pray, my lord, do you pardon me and receive me kindly,
although unwillingly I cast you into such distress by writing
regarding her the messages which you received. For my first
messages I despatched when she was in great affliction, not being
master of myself, and being anxious that by every means in your
power you might succeed in coming to us, this being what duty
demanded. But when she seemed to have taken a turn for the
better, I was anxious that other letters should reach you by the
hands of Euphrosynus, in order that I might make you more
cheerful. For by your own safety, my lord, which chiefly concerns
me, unless my son Athanasius had then been in a sickly state of
body, I would have sent him to you along with Plutarchus, at the

11. [εὔνους]] The Editors suggest
alternatively the restoration ἵλεως
(as l. 7), and recall the Sophoclean
ἵλεως δέξασθαι, *Aj.* 1009, *Tr.* 763.
For the subst. εὔνοια, as in Eph.
vi 7, cf. P. Oxy. 494. 6 (A.D. 156)
where a testator sets free certain
slaves κατ᾽ εὔνοιαν καὶ φιλοστοργίαν
(cf. Rom. xii 10), 'for their goodwill and affection' towards him.
13. θλίψει] Cf. 1 Thess. i 6 (note).
14. οὐκ ὢν κτλ.] Cf. Lk. xv 17.
19. εὐθυμότερον] Cf. 2 Macc. xi

26, Ac. xxvii 36.
20. νὴ γὰρ κτλ.] For this common form of Attic adjuration cf.
P. Brit. Mus. 897. 11 f. (= III,
p. 207) (A.D. 84) κέκρικα γὰρ νὴ τοὺς
θεοὺς ἐν Ἀλεξανδρείᾳ ἐπιμένειν, and
its solitary occurrence in the N.T.,
1 Cor. xv 31. In P. Oxy. 33. iv
13 ff. (late ii/A.D.) νὴ τὴν σὴν τύχην
οὔτε μαίνομαι οὔτε ἀπονενόημαι (cf.
Ac. xxvi 25), the particle is used
with negatives in place of the
obsolete μά.

M

ἅμα Πλουτάρχῳ ἡνίκα ἐβαρεῖτο τῇ νόσῳ. νῦν δὲ
πῶς πλίονα γράψω περὶ αὐτῆς ἀπορῶ, ἔδοξεν
μὲν γὰρ ὡς προεῖπον ἀνεκτότερον ἐσχηκέναι ἀνακα-
θεςθεῖ-   25
σα, νοσηλότερον δὲ ὅμως τὸ σωμάτιον ἔχει. παρα-
μυθούμ[ε]θα δὲ αὐτὴν ἑκάστης ὥρας ἐκδεχόμε-
νοι τὴν [σ]ὴν ἄφιξιν.· ἐρρῶσθαί σε, κύριέ μου,
                    διὰ παντὸς τῷ τῶν ὅλων
                    δεσπότῃ εὔχομαι.   30
          Φαρμοῦθι ϛ′.

On the *verso*

Φλαβιανῶι
Δημήτριος.

time when she was oppressed by the sickness. But now I am at a
loss how to write more regarding her, for she seems, as I said
before, to be in a more tolerable state, in that she has sat up, but
nevertheless she is still in a somewhat sickly state of body. But
we are comforting her by hourly expecting your arrival. That you
may be in continued health, my lord, is my prayer to the Master
of all.

Pharmouthi 6.

(Addressed) To Flavianus from Demetrius.

23. ἐβαρεῖτο τῇ νόσῳ] Cf. P.
Tebt. 327. 24 ff. (late ii/A.D.) γ]υνὴ
οὖσα ἀβοήθητος πο[λλο]ῖς ἔτεσι βε-
βαρημένη, and from the N.T. Lk ix
32 βεβαρημένοι ὕπνῳ. The metaph.
usage, as in 2 Cor. i 8, v 4, may be
illustrated from P. Oxy. 525. 3 f.
(early ii/A.D.) where, with reference
to a voyage he has undertaken, the
writer complains, βαροῦμαι δι' αὐτὸν
καὶ λείαν τῷ πράγματι καταξύομαι,
'I am burdened on account of it,
and I am extremely worn out with
the matter' (Edd.): cf. Exod. vii

14, 2 Macc. xiii 9, the only two
passages in the LXX where βαρέω
is found (elsewhere βαρύνω).

25. ἀνεκτότερον] Cf. Mt. x 15, &c.

ἀνακαθεσθεῖσα] This word, common in medical writings, is twice
used by the physician Luke, Lk. vii
15, Ac. ix 40.

26. σωμάτιον] Cf. l. 21. The
word is frequently used by Marcus
Aurelius (i 17, iv 39, 50 &c.).

28. ἄφιξιν] 'arrival.' Cf. 3 Macc.
vii 18, and contrast Ac. xx 29 (with
Knowling's note).

54. A CHRISTIAN PRAYER

P. OXY. 925.   v/vi A.D.

Discovered at Oxyrhynchus, and edited by Grenfell and Hunt in
Oxyrhynchus Papyri VI, p. 291.

The following prayer offers an interesting Christian counterpart to the pagan inquiry in P. Fay. 137 (= No. 25). According
to the Editors, it was probably intended to be deposited in
some church, just as the similar pagan documents were left in
the temples.

+ Ὁ θ(εὸ)ς ὁ παντοκράτωρ ὁ ἅγιος
ὁ ἀληθινὸς φιλάνθρωπος καὶ
δημιουργὸς ὁ π(ατ)ὴρ τοῦ κ(υρίο)υ (καὶ) σω(τῆ)ρ(ο)ς
ἡμῶν Ἰ(ησο)ῦ Χ(ριστο)ῦ φανέρωσόν μοι τὴν
παρὰ σοὶ ἀλήθιαν εἰ βούλη με ἀπελθεῖν   5
εἰς Χιοὺτ ἢ εὑρίσκω σε σὺν ἐμοὶ
πράττοντα (καὶ) εὐμενῆν. γένοιτο, qθ.

O God, the all ruling, the holy, the true One, merciful and
creative, the Father of our Lord and Saviour Jesus Christ, reveal
to me Thy truth, whether Thou wishest me to go to Chiout, or
whether I shall find Thee aiding me and gracious. So let it be;
Amen.

1. παντοκράτωρ] frequent in the
LXX, but in the N.T. confined to
2 Cor. vi 18, and nine occurrences
in Rev. (i 8, &c.). For a pagan
instance of this same attribute
Cumont (*Les Religions Orientales*,
p. 267) quotes a dedicatory inscription from Delos, Διὶ τῷ πάντων
κρατοῦντι καὶ Μητρὶ μεγάλῃ τῇ πάντων κρατούσῃ (*B.C.H.* 1882, p. 502,
No. 25).

2. ἀληθινός] For an early in-

stance of this rare word cf. P. Petr.
II, 19 (1 a) 5 f. (iii/B.C.), where a
prisoner asserts 'in the name of God
and of fair play' (οὕνεκα τοῦ θεοῦ καὶ
τοῦ καλῶς ἔχοντος) that he has said
nothing ἄτοπον, ὅπερ καὶ ἀληθινόν
ἐστι, and the other exx. in *Lex.
Notes, Exp.* VIII, v, p. 178.

7. qθ] 'the common symbol for
ἀμήν, 99 being the sum of the
numerical equivalents of the letters'
(Edd.).

55. A CHRISTIAN AMULET

Edited by Wilcken in *Archiv* I, p. 431 ff., and assigned by him approximately to vi/A.D.

The following interesting text was discovered by Wilcken in the course of the excavations at Heracleopolis Magna in 1899. It evidently formed one of those amulets which, as we know, the early Christians were in the habit of carrying in counterpart to the old heathen practice (cf. No. 54 Intr.), and the fact that the papyrus-roll had been closely pressed together for ease in wearing round the neck made its decipherment a work of the greatest difficulty. Thanks however to the discoverer's skill and patience the text can now be reproduced in an intelligible form.

Apart from its general character, the principal significance of the text for us lies in the use made of the Lord's Prayer, which here takes the place of the meaningless words in the old magical charms (cf. the similar occurrence of the Prayer on an ostracon from Megara, as interpreted by R. Knopf in *Z.N.T.W.* II (1901), p. 228 ff.).

+ Δέσποτα θε(ὲ) παντοκράτωρ
ὁ πατὴ[ρ] τοῦ κ(υρίο)υ καὶ σ(ωτῆρ)ο(ς ἡ)μῶν
['Ι(ησο)ῦ Χ(ριστο)ῦ κ]αὶ (?) ἅγιε Σέρηνε,
εὐχαριστῶ ἐγὼ Σιλουανὸς υἱὸς

O lord God all ruling, the Father of our Lord and Saviour Jesus Christ, and thou, O holy Serenus. I Silvanus, the son of

---

3. Σέρηνε] the local patron-saint.
4. εὐχαριστῶ] In Hellenistic Gk εὐχ. generally = 'give thanks' (cf. I Thess. i 2, note), but Wilcken understands it here rather = 'pray,' a sense which the word seems to

have in at least two passages of the Abinnaeus correspondence, P. Brit. Mus. 413. 3 (=II, p. 301), 418 (=II, p. 303), both as amended by GH. (III, p. 387).

Σαραπίωνος καὶ κλίνω τὴν   5
κεφαλήν [μο]υ κα⟨τ⟩ενώπιόν σου
αἰτῶν καὶ παρακαλῶν, ὅπως διώ-
ξῃς ἀπ' ἐμοῦ τοῦ δούλου σου τὸν
δαίμονα προβασκανίας καὶ
τὸν κ····ε·πας καὶ τὸν τῆς   10
ἀηδίας κα[ὶ] (?) πᾶσαν δὲ νόσον
καὶ πᾶσαν μαλακίαν ἄφελε
ἀπ' ἐμοῦ, ὅπως ὑγιανῶ καὶ··[·]
λ···· εἰπεῖν τὴν εὐαγγελικὴν
εὐχὴν [οὕτως? Πάτερ ἡμῶν ὁ ἐν τοῖς]   15
οὐ(ρα)ν[οῖς, ἁγιασθήτω] τὸ ὄνομά σου· ἐλθ[ά]-
τω ἡ βα[σιλεία σ]ου, γενηθήτω τὸ θ[έ]-
λη[μ]ά [σου, ὡς] ἐν οὐ(ρα)νῷ καὶ ἐπὶ γῆ[ς· τὸν]
ἄρτον ἡ[μῶν τὸ]ν ἐπιούσιον δὸς ἡ[μῖν]
σήμερον καὶ ἄφες ἡμῖν τὰ ὀφειλ[ή]-   20

Sarapion, pray and bow my head before Thee, begging and
beseeching that Thou mayst drive from me thy servant the demon
of witchcraft...and of pain. Take away from me all manner of
disease and all manner of sickness that I may be in health...to say
the prayer of the Gospel (thus): Our Father who art in heaven
hallowed be Thy name, Thy kingdom come, Thy will be done, as
in heaven so on earth. Give us to-day our daily bread, and forgive

6. κα⟨τ⟩ενώπιον] as in Eph. i 4, Col. i 22, Jude 24. The word was hitherto believed to be confined wholly to the Bibl. writings.

9. προβασκανίας] This fem. form is not found in the Lexicons, but is evidently used here in the sense of the simple βασκανία (as in Sap. iv 12).

11. ἀηδίας] Cf. P. Brit. Mus. 42. 14 (= No. 4), note.
πᾶσαν δὲ νόσον κτλ.] Cf. Mt. iv 23 θεραπεύων πᾶσαν νόσον καὶ πᾶσαν μαλακίαν.

14. τ. εὐαγγ. εὐχήν] Wilcken

notes that at first Serenus wrote τὴν ἀγγελικὴν εὐχήν, afterwards by adding ευ above the line correcting this into τὴν εὐαγγελικὴν εὐχήν. On the history of εὐαγγελικός and its cognates, see *Thess.* p. 141 ff.

15 ff. Πάτερ ἡμῶν κτλ.] The text follows Mt. vi 9 ff., but with certain interesting variations, of which the most important are l. 21 ἀφεί⟨ο⟩-[μεν] (cf. Lk. xi 4) for ἀφήκαμεν, l. 22 ἄγε for εἰσενέγκῃς, l. 24 τῆς πο[ν]ηρ[ίας] for τοῦ πονηροῦ, and the addition of the (shortened) doxology in l. 24 f.

ματα ἡμῶν [κα]θὰ καὶ ἡμεῖς ἀφεί⟨ο⟩[μεν]
τοῖς ὀφει[λέταις ἡμῶν] καὶ [μὴ] ἄγε
ἡμᾶς εἰς πειρασμόν, κ(ύρι)ε, ἀ[λλὰ] ῥῦ[σαι ἡ]-
μᾶς ἀπὸ τῆς πο[ν]ηρ[ίας. Σοῦ γάρ ἐστιν] ἡ δόξ[α εἰς]
τοὺς αἰῶν[ας·······] καὶ ἡ τῶν [···   25
ἐν ἀρχῇ εισυ [········]ς βίβλος κε
·τ[······]·ο·[······]
ὁ φῶς ἐκ φωτός, θ(εὸ)ς ἀληθινὸς χάρισον
ἐμὲ τὸν δοῦλόν σου τὸ φῶς. Ἅγιε Σέρηνε,
πρόσπεσε ὑπὲρ ἐμοῦ, ἵνα τελείως ὑγιανῶ.   30

us our debts, even as we also forgive our debtors. And lead us not
into temptation, O Lord, but deliver us from evil. For Thine is
the glory for ever....O Light of light, true God, graciously give Thy
servant light. O holy Serenus, supplicate on my behalf, that I may
be in perfect health.

24. τ. πο[ν]ηρ[ίας]] a passage
which some may be tempted to
quote in support of the A.V.
rendering of Mt. vi 13.
28. ὁ φῶς κτλ.] as in the Nicene
Creed. For this use of ἐκ, as in
Phil. iii 5, cf. also the description
of Ptolemy Epiphanes, *O.G.I.S.* 90.
10 (Rosetta stone—ii/B.C.) ὑπάρχων
θεὸς ἐκ θεοῦ καὶ θεᾶς, and see
Moulton *Proleg.* p. 102.
χάρισον] l. χάρισαι, c. acc. as in
late Gk, see Hatzidakis *Einl.* pp.

198, 222. A striking use of the
verb is found in P. Flor. 61. 59 ff.
(A.D. 85) where the Prefect, after
pronouncing with reference to a
certain Phibion—ἄξιος μ[ὲ]ν ἦν
μαστιγωθῆναι (Jo. xix 1), adds
χαρίζομαι δέ σε τοῖς ὄχλοις (Mk
xv 15): see Vitelli *ad l.* and cf.
Deissmann *LO.⁶* p. 200 f.
30. τελείως ὑγιανῶ] Cf. 1 Pet.
i 13 νήφοντες τελείως (with Hort's
note).

INDEXES

"Nec praetermittendum est, Papyros puram putamque dialectum referre, quae per ora vulgi volitabat....Maior difficultas oritur a potestate verborum, quae quandoque Graecis prorsus inaudita, propria erat Aegyptiorum. Quare consului affines scriptores, praesertim LXX Interpretes, Scriptores Novi Testamenti, Polybium atque Aristeam."

A PEYRON in 1826.

I. INDEX OF GREEK WORDS

The references are to documents and lines. The word note in brackets following a reference means that the word referred to is to be found not in the document itself, but in the accompanying commentary.

διατελέω **4.** 4, **43.** 8
διατροφή 20. 19
διαφωνέω 22. 31
διδασκαλεῖον 6. 9
διδασκαλική 20. 34
δίδυμος 5. 2, 6. 8
διευλυτόω 30. 18
διευτυχέω 43. 15
διΐημι 9. 2
δίκη 1. 12
διμισσωρία 41. 13
δισσός 34. 19
διώκω 24. 20, 55. 7
δοκιμάζω 1. 8
δουλαγωγία 19. 10
δραπέτης 7. 15
δράσσω 50. 38
δραχμή 30. 15, 45. 12
δύναμις 14. 5
δύο δύο 46. 19
δυσωπέω 37. 8

ἐὰν for ἄν 21. 5, 30. 18
ἑαυτοῦ 20. 7, 38. 11, 46. 8
ἐγβατηρία 11. 9
ἔγγαιος 1. 13
ἐγγυάω 34. 18
ἔγγυος 19. 6, 34. 18 (note)
ἐγκαλέω 1. 7, 16. 18 f., 29. 35
ἐγχαράσσω 26. 11
ἐγχειρίζω 18. i. 8, 23, 19. 3
ἔδνον 16. 15 (note)
ἐθισμός 10. 20, 26
εἰδέναι 20. 43
εἶδος 33. 8, 34. 6
εἰκόνιον 36. 21
εἰκών 36. 21 (note)
εἶ μήν 17. 15
εἰς 6. 2, for ἐν 13. 6, 52. 16
εἰσπηδάω 18. i. 16
ἐκ 10. 11, 24. 16, 55. 28
ἐκβάλλω 12. 10, 47. 1227
ἐκδέχομαι 11. 7, 53. 27
ἐκδίδωμι 20. 6
ἔκδοτος 34. 5
ἐκειδεν 52. 9
ἔκθεμα 27. 1
ἐκκενόω 41. 7
ἔκτισις 34. 18
ἐλαία 47. 1229
ἔλαιον 50. 36, 52. 21
ἐλαιών 24. 21
ἐλεέω 6. 24, 15. 23

ἐλεύθερος 1. 3
ἐλλογέω 45. 18
ἐλπίζω 37. 6
ἐμβάλλω 7. 8
ἐμβλέπω 4. 21
ἐμμένω 19. 16
ἐμποδίζω 33. 8 (note)
ἐμφανίζω 5. 18
ἐν 39. 3, 50. 6, for εἰς 13. 4, 29. 13
ἐναλείφω 13. 15
ἐναντίον 1. 7
ἐνδομενία 30. 13
ἐνδόξως 11. 6 (note)
ἐνθυμέομαι 4. 20
ἐνιαυτός 20. 9
ἐνίστημι 18. i. 11, 20. 10, 32. 10
ἐνορκίζω 47. 1239 (note)
ἔνοχος 20. 32
ἐντάγιον 40. 43
ἐντέλλομαι 24. 11
ἔντευξις 5. 5, 32. 12 (note)
ἐντρέπομαι 7. 4
ἐνύπνιον 7. 30
ἐξαίφνης 6. 7
ἐξαυτῆς 44. 2
ἐξέρχομαι 47. 1243
ἐξετάζω 43. 5
ἐξέτασις 33. 8
ἑξῆς, τὸ 5. 48
ἐξορκίζω 47. 1239
ἑορτή 23. 7
ἐπακούω 6. 24
ἔπαρχος 28. 18
ἐπείγω 5. 8
ἐπεισάγω 1. 8
'Επείφ p. xviii, 4. 33, 41. 6, 45. 27, 48. 24
ἐπεκφέρω 1. 14 ff.
ἐπέξοδος 29. 37
ἐπέρχομαι 29. 13
ἐπερωτάω 34. 20
ἐπεύχομαι 6. 12, 46. 18
ἐπηρεάζω 27. 10
ἐπιβάλλω 10. 12
ἐπιγένησις 32. 12
ἐπιγίνομαι 4. 23
ἐπιγράφω 46. 16
ἐπιδείκνυμι 1. 7, 10
ἐπιδέομαι 4. 22
ἐπιδημέω 5. 4
ἐπιδίδωμι 17. 16, 32. 11, 35. 10, 48. 16
ἐπικαλέω 46. 10

II. INDEX OF BIBLICAL REFERENCES

The texts followed are for the Septuagint, the Cambridge edition edited by Prof. Swete, and for the New Testament, the Greek Text of Westcott and Hort.

M.

III. INDEX OF SUBJECTS

The following index is not intended in any way to be exhaustive, but simply to facilitate reference to some of the subjects mentioned in the introductions and notes. The references are to pages.

For EU product safety concerns, contact us at Calle de José Abascal, 56–1°,
28003 Madrid, Spain or eugpsr@cambridge.org.

www.ingramcontent.com/pod-product-compliance
Ingram Content Group UK Ltd.
Pitfield, Milton Keynes, MK11 3LW, UK
UKHW020315140625
459647UK00018B/1891